Praise for *DuckDB: Up and Running*

The book is a must read for anyone interested in learning DuckDB. The author's clear explanations and practical examples make this complex topic accessible to both beginners and experienced developers. This book is particularly insightful about the growing trend of data-intensive applications, offering valuable guidance on how to optimize performance and scale efficiently.

—*Karen Zhang, data engineer*

This book is a comprehensive and insightful guide, offering both newcomers and seasoned data engineers an exceptional roadmap to mastering DuckDB.

—*Balachandar Paulraj, tech lead, data engineering, PlayStation*

This book is a great reference for using DuckDB in an enterprise environment. Database administrators, engineers, and architects should refer to this book to realize the full potential of DuckDB across on premise and cloud platforms.

—*Akhil Behl, Red Hat*

A good beginner-friendly book for those starting out to explore data analytics with SQL and Python using DuckDB.

—*Vivek Vaddina, freelance data scientist*

DuckDB: Up and Running
Fast Data Analytics and Reporting

Wei-Meng Lee

DuckDB: Up and Running

by Wei-Meng Lee

Published by O'Reilly Media, Inc., 1005 Gravenstein Highway North, Sebastopol, CA 95472.

O'Reilly books may be purchased for educational, business, or sales promotional use. Online editions are also available for most titles (*http://oreilly.com*). For more information, contact our corporate/institutional sales department: 800-998-9938 or *corporate@oreilly.com*.

Acquisition Editor: Andy Kwan	**Indexer:** nSight, Inc.
Development Editor: Melissa Potter	**Interior Designer:** David Futato
Production Editor: Clare Laylock	**Cover Designer:** Karen Montgomery
Copyeditor: Penelope Perkins	**Illustrator:** Kate Dullea
Proofreader: Helena Stirling	

December 2024:   First Edition

Revision History for the First Edition

2024-12-05:   First Release

See *http://oreilly.com/catalog/errata.csp?isbn=9781098159696* for release details.

978-1-098-15969-6

[LSI]

Table of Contents

Preface

In an era where data reigns supreme, the ability to efficiently analyze and derive insights from vast datasets is more crucial than ever. Organizations, researchers, and data enthusiasts are constantly seeking tools that not only streamline their analytical processes but also deliver high performance without the overhead often associated with traditional database systems. DuckDB emerges as a beacon in this landscape—a powerful, in-memory database management system designed specifically for analytical workloads. It stands out for its simplicity, efficiency, and versatility, making it an ideal choice for users ranging from individual data scientists to large-scale enterprises.

This book serves as a comprehensive guide to understanding and mastering DuckDB, providing readers with the knowledge and tools to harness its full potential in diverse applications. From the initial installation to advanced querying techniques, each chapter guides you through a well-structured learning path. The intent is to equip both beginners and experienced users with the skills necessary to leverage DuckDB effectively, whether for personal projects or within larger organizational frameworks.

Chapter 1, "Getting Started with DuckDB", begins with an introduction to DuckDB, exploring its unique features and advantages over other database solutions. We will dive into why DuckDB is a preferred choice for high-performance analytical queries and will showcase its ability to integrate seamlessly with multiple programming languages and environments. This chapter sets the stage for a deeper exploration of the functionalities that make DuckDB a compelling option for data analysis.

Chapter 2, "Importing Data into DuckDB", delves into the practical aspects of importing data into DuckDB. You will learn how to create databases, load data from various sources such as CSV, Parquet, and Excel files, and utilize different methods for loading data, including SQL queries and registration methods. This foundational knowledge is crucial for efficiently working with data in DuckDB.

In Chapter 3, "A Primer on SQL", we'll provide a primer on SQL tailored specifically for DuckDB users. Understanding SQL is essential for any data analyst or engineer, and this chapter will cover everything from basic commands to complex joins and aggregations. The hands-on examples will help you become proficient in querying and manipulating data and will make you more comfortable with DuckDB's SQL syntax.

Building on the SQL knowledge from Chapter 3, Chapter 4, "Using DuckDB with Polars", introduces Polars, an exciting DataFrame library that synergizes perfectly with DuckDB. This chapter will guide you through creating, manipulating, and querying Polars DataFrames using DuckDB, while emphasizing the benefits of lazy evaluation and efficient memory usage. Polars and DuckDB together can significantly enhance your data analysis workflows, and this chapter will showcase how to harness their combined power.

Chapter 5, "Performing EDA with DuckDB", shifts the focus to exploratory data analysis (EDA), utilizing the 2015 Flight Delays and Cancellations dataset as a practical case study. Here, you will learn how to conduct various analyses, from basic descriptive statistics to advanced geospatial analysis using DuckDB's spatial extension. This chapter provides insights into real-world data challenges and demonstrates how DuckDB can be used to uncover meaningful patterns and trends in data.

Chapter 6, "Using DuckDB with JSON Files", explores the intricacies of working with JSON files, a common data format in today's web applications. You will learn how to load, query, and export JSON data within DuckDB, including handling complex nested structures and arrays. Understanding how to work with JSON effectively expands your capabilities in data manipulation and analysis.

In Chapter 7, "Using DuckDB with JupySQL", we explore JupySQL, a powerful tool that integrates SQL capabilities directly into Jupyter Notebooks. This chapter will cover installation, usage, and best practices for combining DuckDB with Jupyter, allowing for interactive and visual data analysis. You will also discover how to create compelling visualizations to represent your data insights effectively.

As we progress, Chapter 8, "Accessing Remote Data Using DuckDB", focuses on accessing remote data using DuckDB's httpfs extension. This chapter will teach you how to query remote CSV and Parquet files hosted on platforms like GitHub and Hugging Face, enabling you to work with datasets from anywhere. The ability to access and analyse remote data opens new avenues for data exploration and collaboration.

Chapter 9, "Using DuckDB in the Cloud with MotherDuck", concludes the book with a deep dive into using DuckDB in the cloud through MotherDuck. You will learn how to sign up for MotherDuck, create and manage databases, and perform hybrid queries that combine local and cloud datasets. This chapter highlights the future of data analytics in a cloud-centric world, providing you with the tools to adapt to emerging trends in data management.

This book is designed for a diverse audience, including data analysts, data scientists, software developers, and decision-makers who are looking for efficient solutions to their data challenges. Whether you are new to DuckDB or have some experience with it, you will find valuable insights, practical examples, and best practices that will enhance your understanding and application of this powerful database system.

I invite you to embark on this journey through DuckDB, exploring its capabilities and applications across various domains. May this book serve as a valuable resource in your quest for data-driven insights, enabling you to unlock the full potential of your datasets.

Conventions Used in This Book

The following typographical conventions are used in this book:

Italic
> Indicates new terms, URLs, email addresses, filenames, and file extensions.

`Constant width`
> Used for program listings, as well as within paragraphs to refer to program elements such as variable or function names, databases, data types, environment variables, statements, and keywords.

`Constant width bold`
> Shows commands or other text that should be typed literally by the user. In some cases, **`constant width bold`** is used to highlight the code currently under discussion.

`Constant width italic`
> Shows text that should be replaced with user-supplied values or by values determined by context.

 This element signifies a tip or suggestion.

 This element signifies a general note.

 This element indicates a warning or caution.

Using Code Examples

Supplemental material (code examples, exercises, etc.) is available for download at *https://oreil.ly/supp-DuckDB*.

If you have a technical question or a problem using the code examples, please send an email to *support@oreilly.com*.

This book is here to help you get your job done. In general, if example code is offered with this book, you may use it in your programs and documentation. You do not need to contact us for permission unless you're reproducing a significant portion of the code. For example, writing a program that uses several chunks of code from this book does not require permission. Selling or distributing examples from O'Reilly books does require permission. Answering a question by citing this book and quoting example code does not require permission. Incorporating a significant amount of example code from this book into your product's documentation does require permission.

We appreciate, but generally do not require, attribution. An attribution usually includes the title, author, publisher, and ISBN. For example: "*DuckDB: Up and Running* by Wei-Meng Lee (O'Reilly). Copyright 2025 Wei-Meng Lee, 978-1-098-15969-6."

If you feel your use of code examples falls outside fair use or the permission given above, feel free to contact us at *permissions@oreilly.com*.

O'Reilly Online Learning

 For more than 40 years, *O'Reilly Media* has provided technology and business training, knowledge, and insight to help companies succeed.

Our unique network of experts and innovators share their knowledge and expertise through books, articles, and our online learning platform. O'Reilly's online learning platform gives you on-demand access to live training courses, in-depth learning paths, interactive coding environments, and a vast collection of text and video from O'Reilly and 200+ other publishers. For more information, visit *https://oreilly.com*.

How to Contact Us

Please address comments and questions concerning this book to the publisher:

O'Reilly Media, Inc.
1005 Gravenstein Highway North
Sebastopol, CA 95472
800-889-8969 (in the United States or Canada)
707-827-7019 (international or local)
707-829-0104 (fax)
support@oreilly.com
https://oreilly.com/about/contact.html

We have a web page for this book, where we list errata, examples, and any additional information. You can access this page at *https://oreil.ly/duckDB_upAndRunning*.

For news and information about our books and courses, visit *https://oreilly.com*.

Find us on LinkedIn: *https://linkedin.com/company/oreilly-media*.

Watch us on YouTube: *https://youtube.com/oreillymedia*.

Acknowledgements

I would like to extend my heartfelt gratitude to everyone who contributed to the realization of this book.

First and foremost, I would like to thank my family for their unwavering support and encouragement throughout this journey. Their patience and understanding have been invaluable.

I am deeply appreciative of my technical reviewers—Balachandar Paulraj, Vivek Vaddina, Karen Zhang, and Akhil Behl. Your expertise and insightful feedback greatly enhanced the quality of this book. Your contributions have helped ensure that the content is accurate, relevant, and beneficial to readers.

I would also like to express my gratitude to Melissa Potter, my content development editor. Your guidance and keen eye for detail have been instrumental in shaping the structure and flow of the chapters, making the material more accessible to readers.

A special thank you to Andy Kwan, my acquisitions editor, for believing in this project and providing the support needed to bring it to fruition. Your vision and encouragement were key motivators in the development of this book.

I would also like to express my gratitude to my copy editor, Penelope Perkins, and my production editor, Clare Laylock, for enhancing the readability and enjoyment of this book!

To all of you, thank you for your invaluable contributions. This book would not have been possible without your support and expertise.

## CHAPTER 1

Getting Started with DuckDB

When it comes to data analytics, pandas is often the go-to library for many developers. Recently, Polars has emerged as a faster and more efficient alternative for handling DataFrames. However, despite the popularity of these libraries, SQL (Structured Query Language) remains the most widely recognized and used language among developers. If your data is stored in a database that supports SQL, using SQL to query and manipulate that data is often the most intuitive and effective approach.

While Python has become the dominant language in data science—particularly for working with data in tabular formats through DataFrame objects—SQL continues to be the universal language of data. Given that most developers are already comfortable with SQL, wouldn't it be more efficient to use SQL directly for data manipulation?

This is where DuckDB shines. DuckDB was initially conceptualized in 2018 as an OLAP (online analytical processing) database optimized for fast analytical queries. Its aim was to bridge the gap between fully-fledged database systems and the simplicity of embedded DBs like SQLite, but with a focus on analytical rather than transactional workloads. The first stable release of DuckDB was in 2019, and its ease of integration with Python and R made it a very popular choice among the data science and analytics communities. While DuckDB is open source, DuckDB Labs was founded in 2021 to provide commercial support and further development. To bring DuckDB to the cloud, MotherDuck was built around DuckDB, enabling users to access it as a SaaS (software as a service). With MotherDuck, developers can now use DuckDB in a distributed and managed environment, making it much easier to scale for larger datasets and collaborative use cases (more on this in Chapter 9).

In this chapter, we'll dive into what DuckDB is, why it's a powerful tool for data analytics, and how you can harness its capabilities to streamline your data analysis tasks. DuckDB offers the performance and flexibility of SQL right within your Python environment, making it an invaluable tool for any data scientist or analyst.

Introduction to DuckDB

DuckDB is a relational database management system (RDBMS) that supports SQL and is specifically engineered for OLAP, making it ideal for data analytics tasks.

Unlike traditional database systems that require a separate installation process, DuckDB operates entirely in-process, so you don't need to worry about installation or setup. One of the most compelling features of DuckDB is its ability to run SQL queries directly on pandas data without the need for importing or duplicating the data. This seamless integration with pandas makes DuckDB an exceptionally powerful tool for data scientists and analysts who are already familiar with the pandas ecosystem.

Moreover, DuckDB is built with vectorized data processing, significantly boosting its efficiency by processing data in CPU-friendly chunks within a single machine. This contrasts with big data frameworks like Spark or Flink, which distribute data and computation across multiple nodes to achieve scalability through parallelism in large clusters.

Additionally, instead of using the traditional row-based storage format found in databases like MySQL and SQLite, DuckDB employs a columnar storage format. This columnar structure is key to its high performance—particularly for large-scale analytical queries—enabling DuckDB to excel in scenarios where speed and efficiency are critical.

Why Use DuckDB?

Today, your datasets typically come from one or more of the following sources:

- CSV (comma-separated values) files
- Excel spreadsheets
- XML files
- JSON files
- Parquet files
- Databases

If you want to use SQL in an ELT (extract, load, transform) process, you'd typically first load the dataset (such as a CSV file) into a database server. From there, you would load the data into a pandas DataFrame through an application (such as written in Python) using SQL (see Figure 1-1).

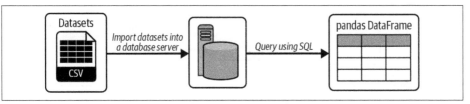

Figure 1-1. You typically have to load your dataset into a database server before you can process it

ELT is a data integration process used in data pipelines to move and prepare data for analysis. Its three main steps are:

- Extract data from multiple sources such as databases, APIs, or flat files.
- Load the extracted data directly into a target system, such as a data warehouse or data lake.
- Transform the data, such as by filtering, aggregating, cleaning, etc.

DuckDB eliminates the need to load the dataset into a database server, allowing you to directly manipulate the dataset using SQL. This streamlined process simplifies data manipulation and analysis, enabling you to work more efficiently with your data (see Figure 1-2).

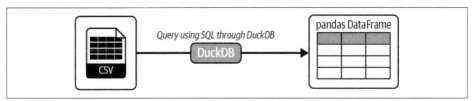

Figure 1-2. With DuckDB, you can directly query your datasets without needing to load them into database servers

Once the pandas DataFrame is loaded, you can use DuckDB and SQL to further slice and dice the data. This allows for powerful and flexible data manipulation directly within your Python environment, leveraging the strengths of SQL without the overhead of a separate database server (see Figure 1-3).

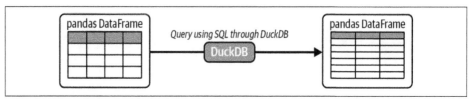

Figure 1-3. You can use DuckDB to work directly with pandas DataFrames

In the following sections, you will learn about the various features of DuckDB and what makes it so powerful.

High-Performance Analytical Queries

One of DuckDB's strengths lies in its ability to execute fast analytical queries, making it a powerful tool for data-intensive tasks. This performance is driven by several key design features:

Columnar storage format
> Unlike traditional databases and file systems that store data in a row-based format (in which all fields of a row are stored together), DuckDB uses a *columnar storage format*. In a columnar format, data is stored column by column, rather than row by row. This design is particularly beneficial for analytical workloads, where queries often require reading and analyzing a small subset of columns over many rows (e.g., summing or filtering one or two columns across a large dataset).

> By reading only the necessary columns from disk, DuckDB significantly reduces the amount of data that needs to be transferred into memory, speeding up query execution. For example, if a query needs data from only two columns out of ten, DuckDB can ignore the rest, whereas a row-based database would need to load all columns of every row.

Vectorized execution engine
> DuckDB processes data in vectors, operating with chunks of rows rather than processing one row at a time. This technique, known as *vectorized execution*, allows for more efficient use of the CPU. By working on multiple rows in one go, DuckDB minimizes the overhead that comes with handling data row-by-row, such as memory access and instruction dispatch, which can slow down processing.

> Additionally, vectorized execution makes better use of the CPU cache, reducing the frequency of cache misses (when the CPU has to access slower memory). This design optimizes the use of modern hardware, leading to faster execution times, especially for complex analytical queries.

Efficient memory usage

DuckDB is designed to work directly on in-memory data structures, meaning that it doesn't need to create unnecessary copies of data that could potentially slow down operations. This allows DuckDB to handle large datasets without requiring excessive amounts of memory, and it manages memory intelligently to prevent bottlenecks during query execution.

DuckDB's ability to process data in chunks also plays a role here, as it can operate on data that's too large to fit into memory all at once by processing it piece-by-piece, further optimizing resource usage.

Parallel execution

Modern CPUs typically have multiple cores, allowing them to perform multiple operations at the same time. DuckDB takes full advantage of this by running queries in parallel across different CPU cores. This *parallel execution* allows it to process large datasets more quickly, as parts of the query can be run simultaneously on different portions of the data.

For example, if you are performing an aggregation or a join across a large dataset, DuckDB can break this task into smaller chunks and process them concurrently, leveraging all available processing power to complete the task more quickly.

Late materialization

DuckDB uses a technique called *late materialization*, where data is only fetched or processed when absolutely necessary. In traditional databases, *materializing data* (i.e., fetching and loading full rows into memory) is done early in query execution, even if only a subset of columns is needed for the final result. DuckDB, however, postpones this materialization step as much as possible, working with metadata (e.g., column indices) rather than actual row data until it needs to materialize only the specific columns required for the query result.

This approach minimizes unnecessary data movement and processing, leading to substantial performance improvements, especially for complex queries that involve filtering or joining large datasets.

Optimized query planner

DuckDB features an *optimized query planner* that analyzes and restructures queries before they are executed. The query planner's job is to find the most efficient way to execute a query, especially for operations that are typically resource-intensive, such as joins, aggregations, and filtering operations.

By reorganizing the query plan and applying advanced optimization techniques like *predicate pushdown* (pushing filters as close as possible to the data source) and *join reordering* (choosing the most efficient order in which to join tables), DuckDB reduces the computational load, making query execution faster and more efficient.

Portability

One of DuckDB's standout features is its portability. Unlike many traditional database systems that require complex server setups or external dependencies, DuckDB is an *in-process database*, meaning it runs directly within the application without needing a separate server. This makes it highly portable, as it can be embedded into a wide range of environments, from local applications to data science notebooks, without any special configuration.

DuckDB's portability is particularly beneficial for data scientists and developers who want to analyze data on their own machines without relying on heavy infrastructure. It can be embedded in Python, R, or even inside other applications with minimal effort. Additionally, DuckDB's small footprint and ability to work seamlessly with various file formats like CSV and Parquet mean it can be used across different platforms (Windows, Linux, macOS) with ease, allowing users to take their analytical workflows anywhere.

The powerful performance features of DuckDB are complemented by its versatility and ease of use across multiple programming environments, which you will learn in the next section.

Versatile Integration and Ease of Use Across Multiple Programming Languages

DuckDB offers full support for standard SQL syntax, including SELECT, INSERT, UPDATE, and DELETE statements. It integrates smoothly with various data formats, such as CSV, Parquet, JSON, and pandas DataFrames. By running directly within the same process as your application—whether it's a Jupyter Notebook or a Python script—DuckDB eliminates the need for complex setups or network communications.

Its ease of handling basic operations makes DuckDB an excellent choice for both beginners and experienced users. Whether you're executing simple queries, loading data, or performing quick transformations, DuckDB provides a fast, efficient, and user-friendly experience that enhances productivity and supports a broad range of data processing tasks.

DuckDB is also designed to work seamlessly with several programming languages, making it a versatile option for data analysis and processing in various environments. Here are some of the languages that DuckDB supports:

- Python
- R
- C/C++
- Julia

- Java
- Go
- Node.js
- Rust

In addition to its broad language support, DuckDB is open source, which greatly enhances its appeal.

Open Source

DuckDB is open source, making it freely accessible to anyone who wants to use, modify, or contribute to its development. As an open source project, DuckDB's source code is available to the public, allowing developers and data professionals to inspect, enhance, and tailor the software to their specific needs. This brings several key advantages:

Transparency
Users can view exactly how DuckDB is implemented, fostering trust and confidence among developers through its open and transparent design.

Rapid iteration and updates
The open source nature of DuckDB enables quick iteration and the continuous addition of new features. The community can propose, test, and implement improvements swiftly, ensuring the software stays at the forefront of technological advancements.

Cost-effective
DuckDB is completely free, with no licensing fees, allowing users to deploy it in any environment without concerns about cost.

Strong ecosystem
The open source model nurtures the growth of a vibrant ecosystem of tools, libraries, and extensions that enhance DuckDB's functionality. Users gain access to a wealth of community-contributed resources, including documentation, tutorials, and plug-ins.

Now that you have seen the features that make DuckDB so useful and powerful, it is time to dive in and see how it works.

A Quick Look at DuckDB

In the following sections, we will walk through a few examples of how to use DuckDB to:

- Create a database
- Create a table
- Insert records into the table
- Retrieve records from the table
- Perform aggregation on the records

- Perform joins on multiple tables
- Load data directly from pandas DataFrames

 For this book, we'll be using Jupyter Notebook for coding, unless stated otherwise. You can use the Jupyter Notebook for Windows, macOS, or Linux.

To use DuckDB, you first need to install the duckdb package. You can do so via the pip command in Jupyter Notebook:

```
!pip install duckdb
```

To create a DuckDB database, you can use the connect() function of the duckdb package:

```
import duckdb

# create a connection to a new DuckDB database file
conn = duckdb.connect('my_duckdb_database.db')
```

This creates a *persistent* database file named *my_duckdb_database.db* in the current directory where you launched your Jupyter Notebook.

Alternatively, you can create an *in-memory* copy of the database by passing the :memory: argument to the connect() function:

```
# alternatively, to create an in-memory database:
conn = duckdb.connect(':memory:')
```

 Whatever changes you made to the in-memory database will be lost when you shut down the database. To retain data between sessions, you should use a persistent DuckDB database file instead of an in-memory database.

In the next section, you will learn how to create a table within the database that you have just created.

Loading Data into DuckDB

Once you have created the database, you can create a table by passing the CREATE TABLE SQL statement to the connection's execute() method:

```
# create a table
conn.execute('''
  CREATE TABLE employees (
    id INTEGER PRIMARY KEY,
    name VARCHAR,
```

```
    age INTEGER,
    department VARCHAR
  )
''')
```

To verify that the table is created correctly, use the SHOW TABLES statement:

```
conn.execute('SHOW TABLES').df()
```

Because the execute() method runs the SQL query and returns a DuckDB result set, you need to convert it to a DataFrame so that you can view the result.

Figure 1-4 shows the table name returned as a DataFrame.

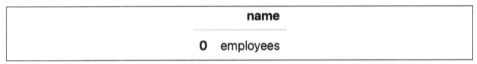

Figure 1-4. The DuckDB database contains a table named employees

Now that the table is created, it is time to insert a few records into the table. The next section shows you how.

Inserting a Record

Now let's insert a few rows into the table using the INSERT INTO statement:

```
# insert data into the table
conn.execute('''
  INSERT INTO employees VALUES
    (1, 'Alice', 30, 'HR'),
    (2, 'Bob', 35, 'Engineering'),
    (3, 'Charlie', 28, 'Marketing'),
    (4, 'David', 40, 'Engineering')
''')
```

In this statement, I added three rows to the *employees* table. To verify that the records are correctly inserted into the table, we'll perform a query, which you will see demonstrated in the next section.

Querying a Table

Now that the records are inserted into the table, we can retrieve them by using the SELECT statement:

```
conn.execute('''
  SELECT * FROM employees
''').df()
```

Figure 1-5 shows the result.

	id	name	age	department
0	1	Alice	30	HR
1	2	Bob	35	Engineering
2	3	Charlie	28	Marketing
3	4	David	40	Engineering

Figure 1-5. The result of querying the employees *table*

Performing Aggregation

A common operation performed on a table is *aggregation*, which involves summarizing data by grouping it based on one or more columns and then applying functions such as COUNT, SUM, AVERAGE, MIN, and MAX. Aggregation is essential for extracting insights, as it condenses large datasets into meaningful summaries, enabling more straightforward analysis.

Let's perform some aggregation on the records in our table. First, let's count the number of employees in each department using the COUNT function and the GROUP BY statement in SQL:

```
conn.execute('''
  SELECT
    department,
    COUNT(*) AS employee_count
  FROM
    employees
  GROUP BY
    department
''').df()
```

Figure 1-6 shows the result returned as a DataFrame.

	department	employee_count
0	Engineering	2
1	Marketing	1
2	HR	1

Figure 1-6. The number of employees in each department

You can calculate the average age of employees in the company using the AVG function:

```
conn.execute('''
  SELECT
```

```
    AVG(age) AS average_age
  FROM
    employees
''').df()
```

Figure 1-7 shows the result as a DataFrame.

	average_age
0	33.25

Figure 1-7. The average age of employees in the company

If you want to find the oldest employee in each department, use the MAX function in SQL:

```
conn.execute('''
  SELECT
    department,
    MAX(age) AS oldest_age
  FROM
    employees
  GROUP BY
    department
''').df()
```

Figure 1-8 shows the result as a DataFrame.

	department	oldest_age
0	HR	30
1	Engineering	40
2	Marketing	28

Figure 1-8. The oldest employee in each department

Finally, you can find the average age of employees in each department:

```
conn.execute('''
  SELECT
    department,
    AVG(age) AS average_age
  FROM
    employees
  GROUP BY
    department
''').df()
```

Figure 1-9 shows the result.

	department	average_age
0	Engineering	37.5
1	HR	30.0
2	Marketing	28.0

Figure 1-9. The average age of employees in each department

Now that you have seen how to perform aggregation on your table, let's see in the next section how to perform *joins*, another common operation involving multiple tables in a database.

Joining Tables

In addition to working with single tables, DuckDB enables you to perform joins on multiple tables. Let's illustrate this by creating two tables in the existing database and then populating them with some records:

```
# create an in-memory copy of the database
conn = duckdb.connect()

# create first table - orders
conn.execute('''
  CREATE TABLE orders (
    order_id INTEGER,
    customer_id INTEGER,
    amount FLOAT)
  ''')

# add some records to the orders table
conn.execute('''
  INSERT INTO orders
  VALUES (1, 1, 100.0),
         (2, 2, 200.0),
         (3, 1, 150.0)
  ''')

# create second table - customers
conn.execute('''
  CREATE TABLE customers (
    customer_id INTEGER,
    name VARCHAR)
  ''')

conn.execute('''
  INSERT INTO customers
  VALUES (1, 'Alice'),
         (2, 'Bob')
  ''')
```

Let's display the contents of the two tables we just created:

```
display(conn.execute('''
  SELECT * FROM orders
''').df()
)
display(conn.execute('''
  SELECT * FROM customers
''').df()
)
```

Figure 1-10 shows the contents of the two tables.

	order_id	customer_id	amount
0	1	1	100.0
1	2	2	200.0
2	3	1	150.0

	customer_id	name
0	1	Alice
1	2	Bob

Figure 1-10. The contents of the orders *and* customers *tables*

Suppose you want a list of amounts spent by each customer. You can achieve this by joining the *orders* and *customers* tables based on the customer_id field in each table:

```
# join the two tables
conn.execute('''
  SELECT
    customers.customer_id,
    customers.name,
    orders.amount,
  FROM
    orders
  JOIN
    customers
  ON
    orders.customer_id = customers.customer_id
  ORDER by
    customers.customer_id
''').df()
```

The result is shown as a DataFrame (see Figure 1-11).

	customer_id	name	amount
0	1	Alice	100.0
1	1	Alice	150.0
2	2	Bob	200.0

Figure 1-11. The result of joining the two tables

Suppose you now want to know the total amount spent by each customer. You can achieve this by aggregating the amount spent using the SUM function in SQL. In addition, you need to use the GROUP BY statement for aggregating the total amount spent:

```
# join the two tables
conn.execute('''
  SELECT
    customers.customer_id,
    customers.name,
    SUM(orders.amount) as total_spent
  FROM
    orders
  JOIN
    customers
  ON
    orders.customer_id = customers.customer_id
  GROUP BY
    customers.customer_id,
    customers.name
  ORDER by
    customers.customer_id
''').df()
```

The result is shown as a DataFrame (see Figure 1-12).

	customer_id	name	total_spent
0	1	Alice	250.0
1	2	Bob	200.0

Figure 1-12. The result of joining the two tables and aggregating the total amount spent for each customer

The next section will show how to use DuckDB to directly manipulate pandas Data-Frames.

Reading Data from pandas

All the examples up to this point have involved creating the database directly in DuckDB. What if your data is already in a pandas DataFrame? Well, DuckDB can work directly with the pandas DataFrames that you already have in memory.

Suppose you have the following DataFrames:

```
import pandas as pd

# Employee DataFrame
employees = pd.DataFrame({
    'employee_id': [1, 2, 3, 4],
    'name': ['Alice', 'Bob', 'Charlie', 'David'],
    'age': [30, 35, 28, 40],
    'department': ['HR', 'Engineering', 'Marketing', 'Engineering']
})
```

```
# Sales DataFrame
sales = pd.DataFrame({
    'sale_id': [101, 102, 103, 104, 105],
    'employee_id': [1, 2, 1, 3, 4],
    'sale_amount': [200, 500, 150, 300, 700],
    'sale_date': ['2023-01-01', '2023-01-03', '2023-01-04',
            '2023-01-05', '2023-01-07']
})

display(employees)
display(sales)
```

Figure 1-13 shows the contents of the `employees` and the `sales` DataFrames.

	employee_id	name	age	department
0	1	Alice	30	HR
1	2	Bob	35	Engineering
2	3	Charlie	28	Marketing
3	4	David	40	Engineering

	sale_id	employee_id	sale_amount	sale_date
0	101	1	200	2023-01-01
1	102	2	500	2023-01-03
2	103	1	150	2023-01-04
3	104	3	300	2023-01-05
4	105	4	700	2023-01-07

Figure 1-13. The contents of the employees and sales DataFrames

Suppose you want to find the total sales for each department, as well as find out the average sales per employee for each department. To do this, you'll need to join the two DataFrames and perform some aggregations. Most importantly, in DuckDB you simply refer to the DataFrames by their names, as this code snippet shows:

```
# create an in-memory copy of the database using DuckDB
conn = duckdb.connect()

# join the DataFrames, group by department, and perform aggregations
query = '''
    SELECT
        e.department,
        SUM(s.sale_amount) AS total_sales,
        AVG(s.sale_amount) AS average_sale_per_employee,
        COUNT(DISTINCT e.employee_id) AS number_of_employees
    FROM
        employees e
```

```
    LEFT JOIN
        sales s ON e.employee_id = s.employee_id
    GROUP BY
        e.department
'''

conn.execute(query).df()
```

The result is shown in Figure 1-14.

	department	total_sales	average_sale_per_employee	number_of_employees
0	HR	350.0	175.0	1
1	Marketing	300.0	300.0	1
2	Engineering	1200.0	600.0	2

Figure 1-14. Finding the average sales per employee for each department

How about finding the top performers in the company and listing their departments? The following code snippet shows how this is done:

```
query = '''
    SELECT
        e.department,
        e.name AS top_employee,
        MAX(s.sale_amount) AS top_sale_amount
    FROM
        employees e
    LEFT JOIN
        sales s ON e.employee_id = s.employee_id
    GROUP BY
        e.department,
        e.name
    ORDER BY
        top_sale_amount DESC
'''

conn.execute(query).df()
```

Figure 1-15 shows the result of the query.

	department	top_employee	top_sale_amount
0	Engineering	David	700
1	Engineering	Bob	500
2	Marketing	Charlie	300
3	HR	Alice	200

Figure 1-15. Getting the top performers in the company

As demonstrated, DuckDB enables direct reference to pandas DataFrames within SQL statements.

Why DuckDB Is More Efficient

Earlier in this chapter, we mentioned that DuckDB is both efficient and high-performing. When working with CSV files, for example, it does not need to load the entire CSV file into memory before it can process it. Rather, DuckDB can read and process data from the file on the fly. To see this in action, let's use the 2015 Flight Delays and Cancellations dataset.

> We'll use this dataset more in Chapter 2, where you learn how to download the various CSV files in the dataset.

For this example, we will use the *flights.csv* file in the dataset, which contains the details of all the flights in the US for 2015. This file is a good candidate for evaluating the efficiency of DuckDB, as it is relatively large (nearly 600 MB) and has more than 5.8 million rows of data. It has the following fields: YEAR, MONTH, DAY, DAY_OF_WEEK, AIRLINE, FLIGHT_NUMBER, TAIL_NUMBER, ORIGIN_AIRPORT, DESTINATION_AIRPORT, SCHEDULED_DEPARTURE, DEPARTURE_TIME, DEPARTURE_DELAY, TAXI_OUT, WHEELS_OFF, SCHEDULED_TIME, ELAPSED_TIME, AIR_TIME, DISTANCE, WHEELS_ON, TAXI_IN, SCHEDULED_ARRIVAL, ARRIVAL_TIME, ARRIVAL_DELAY, DIVERTED, CANCELLED, CANCELLATION_REASON, AIR_SYSTEM_DELAY, SECURITY_DELAY, AIRLINE_DELAY, LATE_AIRCRAFT_DELAY, WEATHER_DELAY.

There are two aspects that we will examine in this example:

- The speed of execution of DuckDB
- The memory usage of DuckDB

Execution Speed

Let's examine the traditional approach of manipulating the CSV file using pandas. First, you need to load the CSV file into a pandas DataFrame:

```
import pandas as pd

# load the CSV file and time it
%timeit df = pd.read_csv('flights.csv')
```

This code uses the %timeit magic command in Jupyter Notebook to measure the time it takes to load the CSV file into a DataFrame. On my machine, it took about 7.5 seconds to load the 5.8 millions rows of data:

```
7.46 s ± 568 ms per loop (mean ± std. dev. of 7 runs, 1 loop each)
```

 The percent symbol (%), when used in Jupyter Notebook, is a prefix to denote a *magic command*. Magic commands are special commands that provide various functionalities and utilities for working within the Jupyter environment.

Next, we will perform a simple aggregation on the data by calculating the mean arrival delay time for each airline:

```
df = pd.read_csv('flights.csv')
%timeit df.groupby('AIRLINE')['ARRIVAL_DELAY'].mean().reset_index()
```

Running the aggregation without the %timeit magic command should yield the result shown in Figure 1-16:

```
df.groupby('AIRLINE')['ARRIVAL_DELAY'].mean().reset_index()
```

	AIRLINE	ARRIVAL_DELAY
0	AA	3.451372
1	AS	-0.976563
2	B6	6.677861
3	DL	0.186754
4	EV	6.585379
5	F9	12.504706
6	HA	2.023093
7	MQ	6.457873
8	NK	14.471800
9	OO	5.845652
10	UA	5.431594
11	US	3.706209
12	VX	4.737706
13	WN	4.374964

Figure 1-16. Calculating the mean arrival delay for each airline

On average, it took pandas about 186 milliseconds to perform the aggregation:

```
186 ms ± 8.74 ms per loop (mean ± std. dev. of 7 runs, 1 loop each)
```

In total, using the pandas approach took about 7.5 seconds.

Let's now try the aggregation using DuckDB. DuckDB has a function named `read_csv_auto()` to read the CSV file:

```
import duckdb

conn = duckdb.connect()
query = '''
    SELECT
        AIRLINE,
        AVG(ARRIVAL_DELAY) AS MEAN_ARRIVAL_DELAY
    FROM
        read_csv_auto('flights.csv')
    GROUP BY
        AIRLINE
    ORDER BY
        AIRLINE;
'''
%timeit df = conn.execute(query).df()
```

The `read_csv_auto()` function does not need to load the CSV file into memory; rather, it processes the data on the fly, allowing for efficient querying without the overhead of memory consumption associated with loading the entire dataset. This enables DuckDB to handle larger datasets seamlessly, leveraging disk I/O for analytical operations while maintaining low memory usage. At the same time, the above statements also perform the data aggregation.

These statements took about half a second to complete:

```
496 ms ± 29.1 ms per loop (mean ± std. dev. of 7 runs, 1 loop each)
```

From this simple example, you can draw the following observations:

- Using DuckDB dramatically shortens the time needed to perform analytics on your data. This is because DuckDB doesn't need to spend extra time loading the CSV into memory before it starts to perform the data aggregation. This is useful if you usually perform one-off operations on your CSV file.

- If you need to perform multiple operations on your data, it might be more efficient to load your data into a pandas DataFrame if you have enough memory on your system to store the data.

- Overall, DuckDB works efficiently on large datasets.

Now that we have examined the performance aspect of DuckDB, let's examine its memory usage.

Memory Usage

To examine the memory usage of DuckDB, let's first create a function to calculate the memory used by a process using the psutil package:

```
import psutil

def memory_usage():
    process = psutil.Process()
    return process.memory_info().rss / (1024 ** 2)  # convert bytes to MB
```

Let's measure the memory used by the current process before and after loading the CSV file into a DataFrame:

```
import pandas as pd

# measure memory before query execution
memory_before = memory_usage()
print(f"Memory used before query: {memory_before:.2f} MB")

# load the CSV file
df = pd.read_csv('flights.csv')

# measure memory after query execution
memory_after = memory_usage()
print(f"Memory used after query: {memory_after:.2f} MB")
```

You'll see something like the following:

```
Memory used before query: 130.64 MB
Memory used after query: 4362.61 MB
```

> Be sure to restart the kernel in your Jupyter Notebook to get a more accurate view of the memory used by the DataFrame.

The memory used is a whopping 4.2 GB! All of this memory was used just to load the CSV file into a DataFrame in memory. Let's now compare it with DuckDB, where we don't have to load the entire CSV file into memory before we can perform processing:

```
import duckdb

conn = duckdb.connect()
query = '''
    SELECT
        AIRLINE,
        AVG(ARRIVAL_DELAY) AS MEAN_ARRIVAL_DELAY
    FROM
        read_csv_auto('flights.csv')
    GROUP BY
        AIRLINE
    ORDER BY
        AIRLINE;
'''
```

```
# measure memory before query execution
memory_before = memory_usage()
print(f"Memory used before query: {memory_before:.2f} MB")

# run the query
df = conn.execute(query).df()

# measure memory after query execution
memory_after = memory_usage()
print(f"Memory used after query: {memory_after:.2f} MB")
```

The result looks like the following:

```
Memory used before query: 72.19 MB
Memory used after query: 348.48 MB
```

As you can see, DuckDB used only about 280 MB of memory, compared to the 4.2 GB used by pandas.

Summary

In this chapter, I have introduced some of the key features of DuckDB and provided a quick overview of its capabilities and features. I began by introducing what DuckDB is and why it stands out in the realm of data management and analytics. Its high-performance analytical queries—combined with versatile integration across multiple programming languages—make DuckDB a powerful tool for various data processing tasks.

I also highlighted DuckDB's open source nature, which not only makes it cost-effective but also fosters a robust, community-driven ecosystem that continuously enhances its functionality.

Through a quick look at DuckDB, we covered essential operations including loading data, inserting records, querying tables, performing aggregations, and joining tables. We also demonstrated how to seamlessly read data from pandas, showcasing DuckDB's compatibility with popular data science tools.

Overall, DuckDB offers a unique blend of performance, flexibility, and ease of use, making it an excellent choice for both simple and complex data processing needs. Whether you're a beginner looking for a straightforward solution or an experienced user seeking a high-performance analytics tool, DuckDB provides a versatile and powerful platform to support your data-driven projects.

In the next chapter, you'll learn how to use DuckDB to work with various data formats—CSV, Parquet, Excel, and MySQL databases.

## CHAPTER 2

Importing Data into DuckDB

In Chapter 1, you saw how you can create a simple DuckDB database and load tables into it. In the real world, your data often comes from different data sources and file formats—such as CSV, Excel, Parquet, or database servers. In this chapter, you'll first learn the different ways to create your DuckDB databases, and then learn how to load them using various data sources. By the end of this chapter, you'll have a clear idea of how to work with each data source, as well as tips and tricks for dealing with them.

Creating DuckDB Databases

In this section, we will dive into the different ways you can create DuckDB databases and provide suggestions on which methods may suit your purposes.

The simplest way to create a DuckDB database is to use the `connect()` function in the duckdb module:

```
import duckdb

conn = duckdb.connect()
```

The `connect()` function returns a `DuckDBPyConnection` object. By default, this statement opens a modifiable in-memory database, as seen here:

```
conn = duckdb.connect(':memory:')
```

If you wish to create a DuckDB database that is persisted on storage, set the `database` argument to the name of a database, for example, *mydb.duckdb* (you can use any extension you wish for the filename):

```
conn = duckdb.connect(database = 'mydb.duckdb', read_only = False)
```

The first time you run this statement, the *mydb.duckdb* database file will be created in the same folder as your code (such as Jupyter Notebook). You can set the `read_only` argument to `True` only if the database file already exists. Opening the file in read-only mode is required if multiple Python processes need to access the same database file at the same time.

After you run this statement, you'll see the *mydb.duckdb* file in your current directory.

If you create an in-memory DuckDB database and set the `read_only` argument to `True`, the database becomes immutable (read-only), and you will not be able to attach any tables to it. Hence, for in-memory databases, be sure to set the `read_only` argument to `False` (or simply omit it, as `False` is the default).

Now that the DuckDB database has been created, in the next section you'll learn how to load it with data from different data sources and formats.

Loading Data from Different Data Sources and Formats

DuckDB supports different types of data sources and file formats. In this section, you'll learn how to load data from:

- CSV files
- Parquet files
- Excel files
- MySQL databases

Working with CSV Files

One of the most common data source file formats is the CSV file, a common and straightforward way to store and exchange tabular data. CSV files are:

Lightweight
    CSV files don't have complex metadata or formatting. This makes them very suitable for data exchange between devices and platforms.

Simple
    CSV files consist of plain text data organized into rows and columns. Each line represents a row and the values in each column are separated by a delimiter.

Flexible

   CSV files can store different types of data, such as numbers, strings, dates, and more.

For this chapter, you'll be using the 2015 Flight Delays and Cancellations dataset from Kaggle (*https://oreil.ly/5WXfY*) (Licensing: CC0: Public Domain). This dataset contains three CSV files:

airlines.csv

   A list of American airlines

airports.csv

   A list of airports in the US

flights.csv

   A list of flight details for the various airlines in 2015

Once you've downloaded the dataset, unzip the individual files and put them into the same folder as your Jupyter Notebook.

In this section, you'll learn two ways to load CSV files into a DuckDB database (the SQL query method and the register method) as well as explore exporting data from DuckDB to CSV.

Loading using the SQL query method

The first method we will use to load a CSV file into a DuckDB database is the SQL query method. We'll use the CREATE TABLE statement, together with the SELECT FROM SQL statement, to load the CSV file via the execute() method of the connection object:

```
import duckdb

conn = duckdb.connect()

conn.execute('''
    CREATE TABLE flights
    as
    SELECT
        *
    FROM read_csv_auto('flights.csv')
''')
```

The read_csv_auto() function is the simplest method of loading CSV files. It tries to figure out the correct configuration of the CSV header and automatically deduces the data types of the columns in the CSV file. If the CSV file has a header, it will use the names found in that header to name the columns. If not, the columns will be named with the default names column0, column1, column2, etc.

You can specify the location of a file using its relative path or absolute path. If you specify just the filename, the path is assumed to be in the same location as your Jupyter Notebook.

The execute() method returns a DuckDBPyConnection object. To examine the result of what has been loaded, you can call the df() method on the DuckDBPyConnection object to return a pandas DataFrame:

```
import duckdb

conn = duckdb.connect()

conn.execute('''
    CREATE TABLE flights
    as
    SELECT
        *
    FROM read_csv_auto('flights.csv')
''').df()
```

In this code snippet, DuckDB is configured to use in-memory storage and the *flights* table is created in memory. Even though we loaded the CSV file into DuckDB, DuckDB does not fully load everything into memory until you later query or manipulate it. It optimizes memory usage by only bringing data into memory when needed (*lazy loading*), even though the table itself is stored in memory rather than on disk. When you call the df() method, DuckDB will then load the content of the table into a pandas DataFrame. In practice, you should only use the df() method when you want to examine the final result of your query.

Figure 2-1 shows the DataFrame containing the number of rows loaded from the CSV file. Observe that the *flights.csv* file has more than 5.8 million rows. This explains why it takes a bit of time for these statements to execute.

Count
0 5819079

Figure 2-1. The number of rows loaded into the DuckDB database table

The SELECT clause is optional, as is the read_csv_auto() function. To retrieve all columns from the CSV file, you can simply rewrite your SQL statement without them:

```
conn.execute('''
    CREATE TABLE flights
    as
    FROM 'flights.csv'
''').df()
```

If you attempt to create a table in DuckDB that already exists, an error will occur. To avoid this, you can drop the existing table before creating a new one:

```
conn.execute('''
    DROP TABLE IF EXISTS flights;
    CREATE TABLE flights
    as
    FROM 'flights.csv'
''').df()
```

Alternatively, you can use the CREATE OR REPLACE statement:

```
conn.execute('''
    CREATE OR REPLACE TABLE flights
    as
    FROM 'flights.csv'
''').df()
```

If your CSV file is large—as this one is—you may want to load only a portion of it. For example, you can use the LIMIT clause to load only the first 1,000 rows:

```
conn.execute('''
    DROP TABLE IF EXISTS flights;
    CREATE TABLE flights
    as
    FROM read_csv_auto('flights.csv')
    LIMIT 1000
''').df()
```

To verify the tables created in the DuckDB database, use the SHOW TABLES query:

```
display(conn.execute('SHOW TABLES').df())
```

Figure 2-2 shows that the DuckDB database contains a single table named *flights*.

name
0   flights

Figure 2-2. The DuckDB database contains a single table

To view the content of the *flights* table, use the SELECT statement with the execute() method:

```
display(conn.execute('SELECT * FROM flights').df())
```

Figure 2-3 shows the content of the *flights* table.

	YEAR	MONTH	DAY	DAY_OF_WEEK	AIRLINE	FLIGHT_NUMBER	TAIL_NUMBER	ORIGIN_AIRPORT	DESTINATION_AIRPORT	SCHEDUL
0	2015	1	1	4	AS	98	N407AS	ANC	SEA	
1	2015	1	1	4	AA	2336	N3KUAA	LAX	PBI	
2	2015	1	1	4	US	840	N171US	SFO	CLT	
3	2015	1	1	4	AA	258	N3HYAA	LAX	MIA	
4	2015	1	1	4	AS	135	N527AS	SEA	ANC	
...	...	...	...	...	...	...	...	...	...	
5819074	2015	12	31	4	B6	688	N657JB	LAX	BOS	
5819075	2015	12	31	4	B6	745	N828JB	JFK	PSE	
5819076	2015	12	31	4	B6	1503	N913JB	JFK	SJU	
5819077	2015	12	31	4	B6	333	N527JB	MCO	SJU	
5819078	2015	12	31	4	B6	839	N534JB	JFK	BQN	

5819079 rows × 31 columns

Figure 2-3. The content of the flights *table in the database*

Another way to load a CSV file is by manually creating a table and then using the COPY statement to load the data into the table:

```
conn.execute('''
    CREATE TABLE airports(
        IATA_CODE VARCHAR, AIRPORT VARCHAR, CITY VARCHAR,
        STATE VARCHAR, COUNTRY VARCHAR, LATITUDE VARCHAR,
        LONGITUDE VARCHAR);
    COPY airports FROM 'airports.csv' (AUTO_DETECT TRUE);
''')

display(conn.execute('SELECT * FROM airports').df())
```

When you use this method, the total number of columns in the CSV file must match the total number of columns in the table. In addition, the contents of the columns must be convertible to the column types specified in the table. If they are not, an error will be thrown.

This approach is often used when you want to have more control over the data loading process. For example, you might want to define specific data types or constraints for each column in the table. Another advantage of using this method to load your CSV file is that you have the flexibility to define the column headers of the table. Additionally, the COPY command yields the best performance for large datasets.

An alternative is to set the names of the columns in the `names` parameter of the `read_csv()` function:

```
conn.execute('''
    DROP TABLE IF EXISTS airports;
    CREATE TABLE airports
    AS
    FROM
    read_csv('airports.csv',
        names=['IATA_CODE', 'AIRPORT', 'CITY',
        'STATE', 'COUNTRY', 'LATITUDE',
        'LONGITUDE'
])
''')
```

If you want to check the total number of columns created for a table, you can use the `information_schema.columns` table that contains metadata about columns in all tables:

```
result = conn.execute('''
    SELECT COUNT(*) AS column_count
    FROM information_schema.columns
    WHERE table_name = 'airports';
''').fetchall()
```

Figure 2-4 shows the content of the *airports* table.

	IATA_CODE	AIRPORT	CITY	STATE	COUNTRY	LATITUDE	LONGITUDE
0	ABE	Lehigh Valley International Airport	Allentown	PA	USA	40.65236	-75.4404
1	ABI	Abilene Regional Airport	Abilene	TX	USA	32.41132	-99.6819
2	ABQ	Albuquerque International Sunport	Albuquerque	NM	USA	35.04022	-106.60919
3	ABR	Aberdeen Regional Airport	Aberdeen	SD	USA	45.44906	-98.42183
4	ABY	Southwest Georgia Regional Airport	Albany	GA	USA	31.53552	-84.19447
...	...	...	...	...	...	...	...
317	WRG	Wrangell Airport	Wrangell	AK	USA	56.48433	-132.36982
318	WYS	Westerly State Airport	West Yellowstone	MT	USA	44.6884	-111.11764
319	XNA	Northwest Arkansas Regional Airport	Fayetteville/Springdale/Rogers	AR	USA	36.28187	-94.30681
320	YAK	Yakutat Airport	Yakutat	AK	USA	59.50336	-139.66023
321	YUM	Yuma International Airport	Yuma	AZ	USA	32.65658	-114.60597

322 rows × 7 columns

Figure 2-4. The content of the airports *table in the database*

Note that if you want to treat all the columns in your CSV file as string types (regardless of the actual data type in the file), you can specify the `all_varchar` parameter in the `read_csv()` function and set it to `true`:

```
conn.execute('''
    DROP TABLE IF EXISTS airports;
    CREATE TABLE airports
    AS
    FROM read_csv('airports.csv', all_varchar=true)
''')
```

There are now two tables in the database (see Figure 2-5):

```
display(conn.execute('SHOW TABLES').df())
```

	name
0	airports
1	flights

Figure 2-5. The two tables in the DuckDB database

Loading using the register() method

Another way to load a CSV file into DuckDB is to use the `register()` method of the connection object. The `register()` method enables you to load a CSV file or other external data sources as an in-memory virtual table without needing to explicitly create or copy data into a DuckDB table. This method is useful in scenarios where flexibility and temporary access to external data are desired. Let's see how it's done.

The following code snippet shows how you can use a `SELECT` statement together with the `read_csv()` function to load the contents of the file *airlines.csv* and return it as a pandas DataFrame:

```
airlines = conn.execute('''
    SELECT
        *
    FROM read_csv('airlines.csv',
                  Header = True,
                  Columns = {'IATA_CODE': 'VARCHAR', 'AIRLINE': 'VARCHAR'})
''').df()
airlines
```

The `airlines` DataFrame is shown in Figure 2-6.

	IATA_CODE	AIRLINE
0	UA	United Air Lines Inc.
1	AA	American Airlines Inc.
2	US	US Airways Inc.
3	F9	Frontier Airlines Inc.
4	B6	JetBlue Airways
5	OO	Skywest Airlines Inc.
6	AS	Alaska Airlines Inc.
7	NK	Spirit Air Lines
8	WN	Southwest Airlines Co.
9	DL	Delta Air Lines Inc.
10	EV	Atlantic Southeast Airlines
11	HA	Hawaiian Airlines Inc.
12	MQ	American Eagle Airlines Inc.
13	VX	Virgin America

Figure 2-6. The content of the `airlines` DataFrame

read_csv_auto() versus read_csv()]

Observe that for this example, instead of `read_csv_auto()`, we used `read_csv()` along with the `Header` argument to indicate that the first row in the CSV file is the header. We then used the `Columns` argument to specify the column names and their associated types. This is sometimes required because the CSV file might not be properly formatted, or the header in the CSV file may contain values that resemble data entries.

If you use the `read_csv_auto()` function instead, you will soon realize that the first row of the CSV file was not recognized as the header (see Figure 2-7):

```
airlines = conn.execute('''
    SELECT
        *
    FROM read_csv_auto('airlines.csv')
''').df()

airlines
```

	column0	column1
0	IATA_CODE	AIRLINE
1	UA	United Air Lines Inc.
2	AA	American Airlines Inc.
3	US	US Airways Inc.

Figure 2-7. The first row in the CSV file is not recognized as the header of the table

Note that this behavior might change in a future release of DuckDB, so you should always experiment with both functions and see if they worked correctly.

Once the `airlines` DataFrame is loaded, you need to use the `register()` method to associate the table with the DuckDB database:

```
conn.register("airlines", airlines)
```

You can now verify that the *airlines* table is in the database using the SHOW TABLES query:

```
display(conn.execute('SHOW TABLES').df())
```

Figure 2-8 shows the three tables currently in the DuckDB database.

	name
0	airlines
1	airports
2	flights

Figure 2-8. The three tables in the DuckDB database

To verify that the *airlines* table is loaded correctly, use the SELECT statement:

```
display(conn.execute('SELECT * FROM airlines').df())
```

The output should be the same as Figure 2-6.

If you don't want to use the connection object to load the CSV file, you can optionally use the more traditional method of loading the CSV file with the pandas `read_csv()` function and then use the `register()` method:

```
import pandas as pd

# load the CSV using pandas
df_airlines = pd.read_csv("airlines.csv")
```

```
# associate the DataFrame with the DuckDB database
conn.register("airlines", df_airlines)
```

Exporting a table to CSV

So far we have discussed loading CSV files into DuckDB databases. What about exporting data from DuckDB databases to CSV files? To do that, you can use the COPY statement:

```
conn.execute('''
    COPY
        (SELECT IATA_CODE, LATITUDE, LONGITUDE FROM airports)
    TO
    'airports_location.csv' WITH (HEADER 1, DELIMITER ',');
''')
```

The HEADER 1 argument indicates that the CSV file should include a header row (column name). This code snippet creates a CSV file named *airports_location.csv* with three columns:

```
IATA_CODE,LATITUDE,LONGITUDE
ABE,40.65236,-75.4404
ABI,32.41132,-99.6819
ABQ,35.04022,-106.60919
ABR,45.44906,-98.42183
ABY,31.53552,-84.19447
...
```

If you want to copy part of a file to another file without loading any data into DuckDB, you can read the data directly from a file and specify the number of rows to copy:

```
conn.execute('''
    COPY
        (SELECT
            IATA_CODE, LATITUDE, LONGITUDE
        FROM 'airports.csv'
        LIMIT 10)
    TO
    'airports_location.csv' WITH (HEADER 1, DELIMITER ',');
''')
```

These statements copy three columns from the first 10 rows of the *airports.csv* file into a file named *airports_location.csv*.

When you are done with your connection, remember to close it:

```
conn.close()
```

Now that you have seen how to work with CSV files using DuckDB, let's move to the next file format—Parquet.

Working with Parquet Files

Another file format that is gaining popularity among data scientists is Parquet. Parquet, or Apache Parquet, is a file format designed to support fast data processing for complex data. It is an open source format under the Apache Hadoop license and is compatible with most Hadoop processing frameworks. Parquet is self-describing—metadata, including the schema and structure, is embedded within each file. More importantly, Parquet stores your data in columns, rather than rows.

Consider the DataFrame shown in Figure 2-9 with three columns.

Name	Age	Salary
Alice	28	55000.50
Bob	35	75000.25
Charlie	22	45000.75

Figure 2-9. A sample DataFrame with three columns

When you save the DataFrame as a CSV file, it uses row-based storage. When a CSV file is loaded into a DataFrame, each row is loaded one at a time, and each row contains three different data types (see Figure 2-10).

Alice	28	55000.50
Bob	35	75000.25
Charlie	22	45000.75

Figure 2-10. Using row-based storage to store a DataFrame

Parquet, however, stores your data using column-based storage. Each column of data is organized as a column of a specific data type (see Figure 2-11).

Name	Age	Salary
Alice	28	55000.50
Bob	35	75000.25
Charlie	22	45000.75

Figure 2-11. Using column-based storage to store a DataFrame

In short, when you store your data in column-based storage, your file will be more lightweight, since all similar data types are grouped together and you can apply compressions to each column. More importantly, using column-based storage makes it really efficient to extract specific columns, something you often need to do in data analytics projects—especially in OLAP workloads, which DuckDB was designed to deal with. Because of this, Parquet is one of the most popular file formats for data analysts.

Loading Parquet files

Now that you have a better idea of how Parquet organizes its data, let's see how we can work with Parquet using DuckDB.

For the example in this section, since we don't have a Parquet file we'll create one using the CSV file that we have: you'll load the *airlines.csv* file into a pandas DataFrame and then save it in Parquet format using the *fastparquet* engine. Fastparquet is an open source Python library that provides a fast and efficient engine for reading and writing Parquet files. To use fastparquet, you need to install it using the `pip` command:

```
$ pip install fastparquet
```

You can now read the CSV file as a pandas DataFrame and then save it as a Parquet file:

```
import pandas as pd

df_airports = pd.read_csv("airports.csv")
df_airports.to_parquet('airports.parquet', engine='fastparquet')
```

If you want to view a Parquet file, you can download Tad (*https://www.tadviewer.com*), a viewer for CSV, Parquet, SQLite, and DuckDB databases.

Figure 2-12 shows Tad displaying the *airports.parquet* file.

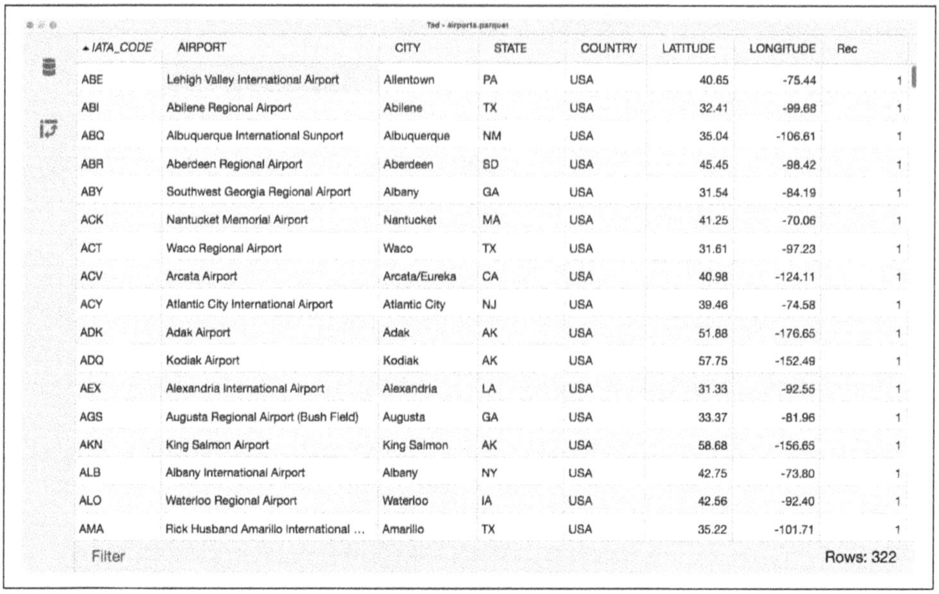

▲ IATA_CODE	AIRPORT	CITY	STATE	COUNTRY	LATITUDE	LONGITUDE	Rec
ABE	Lehigh Valley International Airport	Allentown	PA	USA	40.65	-75.44	1
ABI	Abilene Regional Airport	Abilene	TX	USA	32.41	-99.68	1
ABQ	Albuquerque International Sunport	Albuquerque	NM	USA	35.04	-106.61	1
ABR	Aberdeen Regional Airport	Aberdeen	SD	USA	45.45	-98.42	1
ABY	Southwest Georgia Regional Airport	Albany	GA	USA	31.54	-84.19	1
ACK	Nantucket Memorial Airport	Nantucket	MA	USA	41.25	-70.06	1
ACT	Waco Regional Airport	Waco	TX	USA	31.61	-97.23	1
ACV	Arcata Airport	Arcata/Eureka	CA	USA	40.98	-124.11	1
ACY	Atlantic City International Airport	Atlantic City	NJ	USA	39.46	-74.58	1
ADK	Adak Airport	Adak	AK	USA	51.88	-176.65	1
ADQ	Kodiak Airport	Kodiak	AK	USA	57.75	-152.49	1
AEX	Alexandria International Airport	Alexandria	LA	USA	31.33	-92.55	1
AGS	Augusta Regional Airport (Bush Field)	Augusta	GA	USA	33.37	-81.96	1
AKN	King Salmon Airport	King Salmon	AK	USA	58.68	-156.65	1
ALB	Albany International Airport	Albany	NY	USA	42.75	-73.80	1
ALO	Waterloo Regional Airport	Waterloo	IA	USA	42.56	-92.40	1
AMA	Rick Husband Amarillo International ...	Amarillo	TX	USA	35.22	-101.71	1

Filter   Rows: 322

Figure 2-12. Viewing a Parquet file using the Tad application

To load a Parquet file into a DuckDB database, use the `read_parquet()` function:

```
import duckdb

conn = duckdb.connect()
conn.execute('''
    CREATE TABLE airports
    as
    SELECT * FROM read_parquet('airports.parquet')
    LIMIT 100
''')
```

In this code snippet, we loaded the first 100 rows of the Parquet file into a table named *airports* in the DuckDB database. Once the table is loaded, you can view its content:

```
display(conn.execute('SELECT * FROM airports').df())
```

Figure 2-13 shows the content of the *airports* table.

	IATA_CODE	AIRPORT	CITY	STATE	COUNTRY	LATITUDE	LONGITUDE
0	ABE	Lehigh Valley International Airport	Allentown	PA	USA	40.65236	-75.44040
1	ABI	Abilene Regional Airport	Abilene	TX	USA	32.41132	-99.68190
2	ABQ	Albuquerque International Sunport	Albuquerque	NM	USA	35.04022	-106.60919
3	ABR	Aberdeen Regional Airport	Aberdeen	SD	USA	45.44906	-98.42183
4	ABY	Southwest Georgia Regional Airport	Albany	GA	USA	31.53552	-84.19447
...	...	...	...	...	...	...	...
95	EAU	Chippewa Valley Regional Airport	Eau Claire	WI	USA	44.86526	-91.48507
96	ECP	Northwest Florida Beaches International Airport	Panama City	FL	USA	NaN	NaN
97	EGE	Eagle County Regional Airport	Eagle	CO	USA	39.64257	-106.91770
98	EKO	Elko Regional Airport	Elko	NV	USA	40.82493	-115.79170
99	ELM	Elmira/Corning Regional Airport	Elmira	NY	USA	42.15991	-76.89144

100 rows × 7 columns

Figure 2-13. The content of the airports *table in the database*

If you want to load the last 100 rows, you can use the `ORDER BY 1 DESC` statement to sort the rows by the first column in descending order and then load the first 100 rows. This effectively retrieves the last 100 rows in the Parquet file:

```
conn.execute('''
    INSERT INTO airports
    SELECT * FROM read_parquet('airports.parquet')
    ORDER BY 1 DESC
    LIMIT 100
''')

display(conn.execute('SELECT * FROM airports').df())
```

Figure 2-14 shows that the *airports* table now has the first 100 and last 100 rows from the Parquet file.

	IATA_CODE	AIRPORT	CITY	STATE	COUNTRY	LATITUDE	LONGITUDE
0	ABE	Lehigh Valley International Airport	Allentown	PA	USA	40.65236	-75.44040
1	ABI	Abilene Regional Airport	Abilene	TX	USA	32.41132	-99.68190
2	ABQ	Albuquerque International Sunport	Albuquerque	NM	USA	35.04022	-106.60919
3	ABR	Aberdeen Regional Airport	Aberdeen	SD	USA	45.44906	-98.42183
4	ABY	Southwest Georgia Regional Airport	Albany	GA	USA	31.53552	-84.19447
...	...	...	...	...	...	...	...
195	OME	Nome Airport	Nome	AK	USA	64.51220	-165.44525
196	OMA	Eppley Airfield	Omaha	NE	USA	41.30252	-95.89417
197	OKC	Will Rogers World Airport	Oklahoma City	OK	USA	35.39309	-97.60073
198	OGG	Kahului Airport	Kahului	HI	USA	20.89865	-156.43046
199	OAK	Oakland International Airport	Oakland	CA	USA	37.72129	-122.22072

200 rows × 7 columns

Figure 2-14. The table now has the first 100 and last 100 rows from the Parquet file

To load a Parquet file into an existing table in a DuckDB database, use the COPY FROM statement:

```
conn.execute('''
    COPY airports
    FROM 'airports.parquet' (FORMAT PARQUET);
''')
```

Exporting Parquet files

To export a table in DuckDB to a Parquet file, use the following query:

```
conn.execute('''
    COPY airports
    TO
    'airports_all.parquet' (FORMAT PARQUET);
''')
```

This exports all the rows in the *airports* table and saves them into a file named *airports_all.parquet*.

If you want to export only some rows, you can use LIMIT:

```
conn.execute('''
    COPY
        (SELECT * FROM airports LIMIT 100)
    TO
    'airports_100.parquet' (FORMAT PARQUET);
''')
```

This exports the first 100 rows from the airports table and saves them into a file named *airports_100.parquet*.

Exporting data to Parquet from DuckDB is useful in scenarios where efficient storage, fast querying, and interoperability with big data tools are required. Because of its optimized structure for columnar data and support for compression, Parquet is a go-to format for cloud storage, data lakes, analytical workloads, and machine learning pipelines.

Now that you have learned how to work with Parquet files in DuckDB, it's time to move to the most popular data file format of all time—Excel files.

Working with Excel Files

Excel is a versatile spreadsheet application that is widely used across all industries and multiple professions. Whether you are a programmer or not, chances are you have used Excel in one way or another. In this section, you'll learn how to work with Excel files in DuckDB.

For the demos in this section, we'll use an Excel file that has two worksheets: *airports* and *airlines* (see Figure 2-15). The content of the *airports* worksheet is from the *airports.csv* file, while the content for the *airlines* worksheet is from *airlines.csv*.

Figure 2-15. The contents of the Excel spreadsheet

Observe that the *airlines* worksheet has no header. This is done on purpose so that we can learn how to specify the header manually when loading the worksheet into a table in DuckDB.

Loading Excel files

To load data from an Excel spreadsheet, you need to use the `spatial` extension, which provides support for geospatial data processing in DuckDB.

 DuckDB supports a number of extensions:

- `httpfs` enables reading and writing files over HTTP or cloud storage.

- `icu` provides advanced string processing and internationalization features via the ICU (International Components for Unicode) library.

- `sqlite` provides the ability to read and query SQLite database files.

- `inet` adds support for working with IP addresses and network data.

To install these extensions, you use the `INSTALL` keyword, a SQL command used to download and install extensions.

First, let's load an Excel worksheet into a DuckDB database. The following code snippet loads the *airports* worksheet into a DuckDB table named *airports*:

```
import duckdb

conn = duckdb.connect()

conn.execute('INSTALL spatial')
conn.execute('LOAD spatial')
conn.execute('''
    CREATE TABLE airports
    as
    SELECT * FROM st_read('airports_and_airlines.xlsx', layer='airports');
''')
display(conn.execute('SELECT * FROM airports').df())
```

There are a few points worth explaining:

- The `spatial` extension must be installed and loaded before importing the Excel data. This needs to be done only once—the extension will be remembered until DuckDB is uninstalled.

- The st_read() function reads from the Excel spreadsheet. The worksheet to load is specified through the layer argument. DuckDB doesn't currently support reading a password-protected Excel spreadsheet. If your file is password-protected, you'll need to decrypt it first.

The output is shown in Figure 2-16.

	IATA_CODE	AIRPORT	CITY	STATE	COUNTRY	LATITUDE	LONGITUDE
0	ABE	Lehigh Valley International Airport	Allentown	PA	USA	40.65236	-75.44040
1	ABI	Abilene Regional Airport	Abilene	TX	USA	32.41132	-99.68190
2	ABQ	Albuquerque International Sunport	Albuquerque	NM	USA	35.04022	-106.60919
3	ABR	Aberdeen Regional Airport	Aberdeen	SD	USA	45.44906	-98.42183
4	ABY	Southwest Georgia Regional Airport	Albany	GA	USA	31.53552	-84.19447
...	...	...	...	...	...	...	...
317	WRG	Wrangell Airport	Wrangell	AK	USA	56.48433	-132.36982
318	WYS	Westerly State Airport	West Yellowstone	MT	USA	44.68840	-111.11764
319	XNA	Northwest Arkansas Regional Airport	Fayetteville/Springdale/Rogers	AR	USA	36.28187	-94.30681
320	YAK	Yakutat Airport	Yakutat	AK	USA	59.50336	-139.66023
321	YUM	Yuma International Airport	Yuma	AZ	USA	32.65658	-114.60597

322 rows × 7 columns

Figure 2-16. The content of the airports table loaded from the Excel spreadsheet

As you can see, the values in the first row of the worksheet are automatically detected and used as the column names for the table. However, this behavior can be controlled through the use of the environment variable OGR_XLSX_HEADERS, which is part of the GDAL/OGR library (*https://oreil.ly/SgTDo*), which DuckDB uses to read Excel files.

If you don't want to use the fields in the first row as the column names for your table, set the OGR_XLSX_HEADERS environment variable to DISABLE:

```
import os

os.environ['OGR_XLSX_HEADERS'] = 'DISABLE'
```

Once you do this, the default column names will be Field1, Field2, and so on.

However, if you want to force the fields in the first row to be used as the column names for your table, set the environment variable to FORCE:

```
os.environ['OGR_XLSX_HEADERS'] = 'FORCE'
```

The default value for the environment variable is AUTO, which means that the behavior is automatic, allowing the OGR driver for Excel files to decide whether or not to treat the first row as column headers based on its content:

```
os.environ['OGR_XLSX_HEADERS'] = 'AUTO'
```

Let's now try loading the *airlines* worksheet into DuckDB:

```
conn.execute('''
    CREATE TABLE airlines
    AS
    SELECT * FROM st_read('airports_and_airlines.xlsx', layer='airlines');
''')
display(conn.execute('SELECT * FROM airlines').df())
```

This time, observe that the st_read() function has detected that there are no field names that can be used as column names for your table. Hence, the default column names are Field1 and Field2 (see Figure 2-17).

	Field1	Field2
0	UA	United Air Lines Inc.
1	AA	American Airlines Inc.
2	US	US Airways Inc.
3	F9	Frontier Airlines Inc.
4	B6	JetBlue Airways
5	OO	Skywest Airlines Inc.
6	AS	Alaska Airlines Inc.
7	NK	Spirit Air Lines
8	WN	Southwest Airlines Co.
9	DL	Delta Air Lines Inc.
10	EV	Atlantic Southeast Airlines
11	HA	Hawaiian Airlines Inc.
12	MQ	American Eagle Airlines Inc.
13	VX	Virgin America

Figure 2-17. The column names are set to defaults

To ensure that your table has custom column names, you can first create a table with the desired column names and data types, and then use the INSERT statement to load the data from the Excel spreadsheet:

```
conn = duckdb.connect()

conn.execute('INSTALL spatial')
conn.execute('LOAD spatial')
conn.execute('''
    CREATE TABLE airlines (
        IATA_CODE STRING,
        AIRLINES STRING
```

```
    );
    INSERT INTO airlines
    SELECT * FROM st_read('airports_and_airlines.xlsx', layer='airlines');
    ''')
display(conn.execute('SELECT * FROM airlines').df())
```

 Beware of the performance implications of using the INSERT statement (*https://oreil.ly/45GqV*) in DuckDB. In general, try to avoid
using INSERT to insert rows individually, especially if your dataset is
large. Also, note that the COPY statement in DuckDB doesn't work
with Excel files.

Figure 2-18 shows the table with the column names applied.

	IATA_CODE	AIRLINES
0	UA	United Air Lines Inc.
1	AA	American Airlines Inc.
2	US	US Airways Inc.
3	F9	Frontier Airlines Inc.
4	B6	JetBlue Airways
5	OO	Skywest Airlines Inc.
6	AS	Alaska Airlines Inc.
7	NK	Spirit Air Lines
8	WN	Southwest Airlines Co.
9	DL	Delta Air Lines Inc.
10	EV	Atlantic Southeast Airlines
11	HA	Hawaiian Airlines Inc.
12	MQ	American Eagle Airlines Inc.
13	VX	Virgin America

Figure 2-18. The table with the correct column names

Another environment variable that you can use when loading Excel data is
OGR_XLSX_FIELD_TYPES. By default, when parsing Excel spreadsheets, DuckDB will
automatically detect the data types in the file. If you want to force all the data types to
string, set this environment variable to STRING:

```
os.environ['OGR_XLSX_FIELD_TYPES'] = 'STRING'   # default is AUTO
```

Exporting tables to Excel

Just like with the other file formats, you can export a DuckDB table to Excel format:

```
conn.execute('''
    COPY airlines
    TO 'airlines.xlsx' WITH (FORMAT GDAL, DRIVER 'xlsx');
''')
```

In this code snippet, the *airlines* table is saved to the *airlines.xlsx* file. The FORMAT GDAL option enables you to export data to a file format that is supported by GDAL (Geospatial Data Abstraction Library).

 If the destination file already exists, an error will be thrown. Also, dates and timestamps are not supported by the *xlsx* writer driver. If your table contains columns of these types, be sure to cast them to VARCHAR prior to creating the *xlsx* file.

With all the popular file formats covered, it's time to move to the last section in this chapter and learn how to use DuckDB to load your data from a database server. For this example, we'll be using MySQL server.

Working with MySQL

The last file format that we will discuss in this chapter is MySQL. Very often, your source data might be stored in a database server, such as MySQL. Hence, it would be useful to be able to load your data stored in MySQL into DuckDB.

For the example in this section, we'll assume the following:

- You have an instance of MySQL server running on your computer
- You have a database named *My_DB*, containing a single table named *airlines*. The content of the *airlines* table is shown in Figure 2-19.
- You have an account on the MySQL server named *user1*, with a password of "*password*". This account has privileges to access the *My_DB* database and its tables.

IATA_CODE	AIRLINES
AA	American Airlines Inc.
AS	Alaska Airlines Inc.
B6	JetBlue Airways
DL	Delta Air Lines Inc.
EV	Atlantic Southeast Airlines
F9	Frontier Airlines Inc.
HA	Hawaiian Airlines Inc.
MQ	American Eagle Airlines Inc.
NK	Spirit Air Lines
OO	Skywest Airlines Inc.
UA	United Air Lines Inc.
US	US Airways Inc.
VX	Virgin America
WN	Southwest Airlines Co.
NULL	NULL

Figure 2-19. The content of the airlines *table in the* My_DB *database on the MySQL database server*

To load a table from MySQL into DuckDB, here are the steps you need to take:

1. Create a DuckDB connection.
2. Create a MySQL connection.
3. Retrieve the data from the MySQL server.
4. Create a table in the DuckDB database with the same schema as that of the table in MySQL.
5. Iterate through each row obtained from MySQL and insert it into the DuckDB table.
6. Close the connections to MySQL and DuckDB.

To connect to a MySQL database using Python, you need to install the *mysql-connector-python* library using:

```
!pip install mysql-connector-python
```

The following code snippet implements these steps:

```python
import mysql.connector
import duckdb

# MySQL connection information
mysql_host     = 'localhost'
mysql_user     = 'user1'
mysql_password = 'password'
mysql_database = 'My_DB'
mysql_table    = 'airlines'

# create a DuckDB connection
duckdb_conn = duckdb.connect()

# connect to MySQL
mysql_conn = mysql.connector.connect(
    host = mysql_host,
    user = mysql_user,
    password = mysql_password,
    database = mysql_database
)

# create a cursor for MySQL
mysql_cursor = mysql_conn.cursor()

# query data from MySQL
mysql_query = f'SELECT * FROM {mysql_table}'
mysql_cursor.execute(mysql_query)

# create a DuckDB table with the same schema as MySQL
duckdb_create_table_query = \
    f'CREATE TABLE airlines (IATA_CODE VARCHAR(2), AIRLINES VARCHAR)'
duckdb_conn.execute(duckdb_create_table_query)

# get column names from MySQL result
mysql_columns = [column[0] for column in mysql_cursor.description]

# fetch data from MySQL and insert into DuckDB table
duckdb_insert_query = \
    f'INSERT INTO airlines VALUES ({", ".join(["?" for _ in mysql_columns])})'
for row in mysql_cursor.fetchall():
    duckdb_conn.execute(duckdb_insert_query, row)

# query the data in DuckDB
display(duckdb_conn.execute('SELECT * FROM airlines').df())

# close the MySQL and DuckDB connections
mysql_cursor.close()
mysql_conn.close()
duckdb_conn.close()
```

Figure 2-20 shows the results of the *airlines* table stored in DuckDB.

	IATA_CODE	AIRLINES
0	AA	American Airlines Inc.
1	AS	Alaska Airlines Inc.
2	B6	JetBlue Airways
3	DL	Delta Air Lines Inc.
4	EV	Atlantic Southeast Airlines
5	F9	Frontier Airlines Inc.
6	HA	Hawaiian Airlines Inc.
7	MQ	American Eagle Airlines Inc.
8	NK	Spirit Air Lines
9	OO	Skywest Airlines Inc.
10	UA	United Air Lines Inc.
11	US	US Airways Inc.
12	VX	Virgin America
13	WN	Southwest Airlines Co.

Figure 2-20. The content of the airlines *table loaded from MySQL*

Alternatively, you can use the mysql extension and load the table from the database in MySQL directly using DuckDB:

```
import duckdb

# create a DuckDB connection
conn = duckdb.connect()

# install and load the MySQL extension
conn.execute('INSTALL mysql')
conn.execute('LOAD mysql')

# define MySQL connection parameters
mysql_host     = 'localhost'
mysql_user     = 'user1'
mysql_password = 'password'
mysql_database = 'My_DB'
mysql_table    = 'airlines'
mysql_port     = 3306

# create a MySQL connection
mysql_connection = \
    f'mysql://{mysql_user}:{mysql_password}@{mysql_host}/{mysql_database}'
```

```
# attach the MySQL database with authentication
attach_command = f'''
    ATTACH 'host={mysql_host}
    user={mysql_user}
    password={mysql_password}
    port={mysql_port}
    database={mysql_database}'
    AS mysqldb (TYPE MYSQL);
'''

conn.execute(attach_command)
conn.execute('USE mysqldb;')

display(conn.execute(f'''
    SELECT * FROM {mysql_table}
''').df())

display(conn.execute(f'''
    show tables
''').df())

# close the DuckDB connection
conn.close()
```

The output is the same as Figure 2-20.

So which method is better? Here's a general rule of thumb:

- If you need simplicity, better performance, and direct access to MySQL data with minimal setup, the `mysql` extension is the better choice.
- If you need greater flexibility in controlling the schema, performing transformations, or dealing with environments where the extension cannot be used, the manual method is more appropriate.

For most use cases involving frequent data access and analysis, the `mysql` extension will likely be the better option due to its efficiency and ease of use.

Summary

In this chapter, you learned techniques to load different types of data into your DuckDB database:

CSV files
> For large datasets, consider using the COPY command for optimal performance.

Parquet files
> Parquet is an efficient file format, and importing data from it into DuckDB can be efficient too.

Excel files

DuckDB doesn't have direct support for Excel files, but you can either use the `special` extension to load Excel data into DuckDB databases or convert your Excel files into CSV before loading into DuckDB.

MySQL databases

You can create a DuckDB table with the same schema as your MySQL table and the load the data into DuckDB. Alternatively, you can use the `mysql` extension supported by DuckDB.

With this knowledge, you are now ready to learn the various ways to manipulate the data in your DuckDB databases using SQL, which is the focus of the next chapter. See you in the next chapter!

## CHAPTER 3

A Primer on SQL

In Chapter 2, you learned how to import various data sources (CSV, Parquet, Excel, and databases) into DuckDB through the Python programming language. With that knowledge, the next step for you to work on is manipulating the data loaded into DuckDB using SQL. After all, using SQL in DuckDB is one of the main features of DuckDB. And so in this chapter, our focus is on using SQL in DuckDB. Specifically, this chapter will focus on two areas:

- Using the DuckDB CLI (command line interface) to work with DuckDB databases without the need to use a programming language such as Python.

- Using SQL with DuckDB databases. Rather than providing an exhaustive exploration of SQL, our focus will be on learning through practical examples.

With that, let's dive right in!

Using the DuckDB CLI

The DuckDB CLI is a tool that allows users to interact with DuckDB directly from the command line. In Chapter 2, you saw how to interact with DuckDB using Python. However, there are times where you simply want to work with the databases directly—such as when creating new tables, importing data from different data sources, and performing database-related tasks. In such instances, it is much more efficient to use the DuckDB CLI directly.

The DuckDB CLI has been precompiled for the various platforms: Windows, macOS, and Linux. See the installation page (*https://oreil.ly/mJjZn*) for instructions on installing the DuckDB CLI for your platform (see Figure 3-1).

Figure 3-1. Downloading the DuckDB CLI

For example, for macOS, you can install (no admin privileges required) the DuckDB CLI using a package manager such as brew:

```
$ brew install duckdb
```

Homebrew, often referred to as "brew," is a popular package manager for macOS and Linux. It simplifies the process of installing, updating, and managing software packages and dependencies on these operating systems. You can install brew on your machine using the following command (one single line):

```
/bin/bash -c "$(curl -fsSL https://raw.githubusercontent.com
/Homebrew/install/HEAD/install.sh)"
```

For Windows, you can download the DuckDB CLI using the Windows Package Manager at a command prompt:

```
winget install DuckDB.cli
```

Once the DuckDB CLI is downloaded, you can use it with the following syntax:

```
$ duckdb [OPTIONS] [FILENAME]
```

You can get the full list of command-line argument options from the DuckDB website (*https://oreil.ly/G2PjO*). Alternatively, you can use the -help option to display a list of options:

```
$ duckdb -help
Usage: duckdb [OPTIONS] FILENAME [SQL]
FILENAME is the name of an DuckDB database. A new database is created
if the file does not previously exist.
OPTIONS include:
   -append               append the database to the end of the file
   -ascii                set output mode to 'ascii'
   -bail                 stop after hitting an error
   -batch                force batch I/O
   -box                  set output mode to 'box'
   -column               set output mode to 'column'
   -cmd COMMAND          run "COMMAND" before reading stdin
   -c COMMAND            run "COMMAND" and exit
   -csv                  set output mode to 'csv'
   -echo                 print commands before execution
   -init FILENAME        read/process named file
   -[no]header           turn headers on or off
   -help                 show this message
   -html                 set output mode to HTML
   -interactive          force interactive I/O
   -json                 set output mode to 'json'
   -line                 set output mode to 'line'
   -list                 set output mode to 'list'
   -markdown             set output mode to 'markdown'
   -newline SEP          set output row separator. Default: '\n'
   -nofollow             refuse to open symbolic links to database files
   -no-stdin             exit after processing options instead of reading stdin
   -nullvalue TEXT       set text string for NULL values. Default ''
   -quote                set output mode to 'quote'
   -readonly             open the database read-only
   -s COMMAND            run "COMMAND" and exit
   -separator SEP        set output column separator. Default: '|'
   -stats                print memory stats before each finalize
   -table                set output mode to 'table'
   -unredacted           allow printing unredacted secrets
   -unsigned             allow loading of unsigned extensions
   -version              show DuckDB version
```

If you don't supply a FILENAME argument, the DuckDB CLI will open a temporary in-memory database and display the version number, information on the connection, and a prompt starting with a D:

```
$ duckdb
v0.10.1 4a89d97db8
Enter ".help" for usage hints.
```

```
Connected to a transient in-memory database.
Use ".open FILENAME" to reopen on a persistent database.
D
```

When you create an in-memory database, everything is lost when you exit the DuckDB CLI. So this option is only useful if you want to experiment with how DuckDB works.

To exit the DuckDB CLI, press Ctrl+C twice on macOS and Linux, or press Ctrl+C once on Windows.

A more common use of the DuckDB CLI is with a persistent database. This ensures data is saved across sessions, allowing for long-term use and reuse without needing to reload or reprocess data every time.

The following example shows how you can use the DuckDB CLI together with a persistent database (named *mydb.duckdb*):

```
$ duckdb mydb.duckdb
v0.10.1 4a89d97db8
Enter ".help" for usage hints.
D
```

Now that the database has been created, you can learn how to import data into it.

Importing Data into DuckDB

When you are in the DuckDB CLI, you can import data into your database by first creating a table and then importing data from a CSV file.

The following statement assumes that there is currently a file named *airlines.csv* in the same directory from which you launched the DuckDB CLI:

```
D CREATE TABLE airlines as FROM airlines.csv;
```

Chapter 2 discussed the various functions that you can use to load files from data sources into DuckDB. For this chapter, the focus is on manipulating tables using SQL. So for simplicity, we will directly read a CSV file into DuckDB.

Please ensure that your command ends with a semicolon (;). Omitting it will prompt the DuckDB CLI to await further statements upon pressing Enter. Execution will only occur once the semicolon is added.

If you run the above on a persistent database (e.g., *mydb.duckdb*), the persistent database will be created in the file system.

This statement creates a table named *airlines* in the database, and then reads the *airlines.csv* file and imports it into the *airlines* table. To confirm the existence of the *airlines* table, you can use the show tables statement:

```
D show tables;
```

To verify that the CSV file has indeed been loaded into the *airlines* table, use the
SELECT statement:

```
D SELECT * FROM airlines;
┌───────────┬─────────────────────────────┐
│ IATA_CODE │           AIRLINE           │
│  varchar  │           varchar           │
├───────────┼─────────────────────────────┤
│ UA        │ United Air Lines Inc.       │
│ AA        │ American Airlines Inc.      │
│ US        │ US Airways Inc.             │
│ F9        │ Frontier Airlines Inc.      │
│ B6        │ JetBlue Airways             │
│ OO        │ Skywest Airlines Inc.       │
│ AS        │ Alaska Airlines Inc.        │
│ NK        │ Spirit Air Lines            │
│ WN        │ Southwest Airlines Co.      │
│ DL        │ Delta Air Lines Inc.        │
│ EV        │ Atlantic Southeast Airlines │
│ HA        │ Hawaiian Airlines Inc.      │
│ MQ        │ American Eagle Airlines Inc.│
│ VX        │ Virgin America              │
├───────────┴─────────────────────────────┤
│ 14 rows                        2 columns │
└──────────────────────────────────────────┘
```

The DuckDB CLI provides a set of commands to perform administrative tasks,
known as the *dot commands*. In the next section, you will see how you can use some
of them to administer your database.

Dot Commands

Within the DuckDB CLI, you can execute commands that are specific to the DuckDB
CLI environment using the dot (.) command. For example, if you want to view the list
of dot commands available within the DuckDB CLI, use the .help command:

```
D .help
.bail on|off           Stop after hitting an error.  Default OFF
.binary on|off         Turn binary output on or off.  Default OFF
.cd DIRECTORY          Change the working directory to DIRECTORY
.changes on|off        Show number of rows changed by SQL
.check GLOB            Fail if output since .testcase does not match
.columns               Column-wise rendering of query results
.constant ?COLOR?      Sets the syntax highlighting color used for
                       constant values
.constantcode ?CODE?   Sets the syntax highlighting terminal code
                       used for constant values
.databases             List names and files of attached databases
.dump ?TABLE?          Render database content as SQL
```

```
.echo on|off              Turn command echo on or off
.excel                    Display the output of next command in spreadsheet
.exit ?CODE?              Exit this program with return-code CODE
.explain ?on|off|auto?    Change the EXPLAIN formatting mode.  Default: auto
.fullschema ?--indent?    Show schema and the content of sqlite_stat tables
.headers on|off           Turn display of headers on or off
.help ?-all? ?PATTERN?    Show help text for PATTERN
.highlight [on|off]       Toggle syntax highlighting in the shell on/off
.import FILE TABLE         Import data from FILE into TABLE
.indexes ?TABLE?          Show names of indexes
.keyword ?COLOR?          Sets the syntax highlighting color used for keywords
.keywordcode ?CODE?       Sets the syntax highlighting terminal code used
                          for keywords
.lint OPTIONS             Report potential schema issues.
.log FILE|off             Turn logging on or off.  FILE can be stderr/stdout
.maxrows COUNT            Sets the maximum number of rows for display
                          (default: 40). Only for duckbox mode.
.maxwidth COUNT          Sets the maximum width in characters. 0 defaults
                          to terminal width. Only for duckbox mode.
.mode MODE ?TABLE?        Set output mode
.nullvalue STRING         Use STRING in place of NULL values
.once ?OPTIONS? ?FILE?    Output for the next SQL command only to FILE
.open ?OPTIONS? ?FILE?    Close existing database and reopen FILE
.output ?FILE?            Send output to FILE or stdout if FILE is omitted
.parameter CMD ...        Manage SQL parameter bindings
.print STRING...          Print literal STRING
.prompt MAIN CONTINUE     Replace the standard prompts
.quit                     Exit this program
.read FILE                Read input from FILE
.rows                     Row-wise rendering of query results (default)
.schema ?PATTERN?         Show the CREATE statements matching PATTERN
.separator COL ?ROW?      Change the column and row separators
.sha3sum ...              Compute a SHA3 hash of database content
.shell CMD ARGS...        Run CMD ARGS... in a system shell
.show                     Show the current values for various settings
.system CMD ARGS...       Run CMD ARGS... in a system shell
.tables ?TABLE?           List names of tables matching LIKE pattern TABLE
.testcase NAME            Begin redirecting output to 'testcase-out.txt'
.timer on|off             Turn SQL timer on or off
.width NUM1 NUM2 ...      Set minimum column widths for columnar output
```

While normal DuckDB queries require a semicolon at the end of each statement, dot commands do not.

The following sections highlight some of the commonly used dot commands.

.database

To view the current database in use, use the .database command:

```
D .database
mydb: mydb.duckdb
```

This command shows that the current database in use is *mydb.duckdb*, with the alias *mydb*.

If you initially run the DuckDB CLI without a filename, you will see the following when you use the .database command:

```
D .database
memory:
```

This indicates that you are now using an in-memory database.

.open

Say you started the DuckDB CLI with no filename specified, and then later you decided that you want to open an existing (or new) DuckDB database. You can do so by using the .open command:

```
% duckdb
v0.10.1 4a89d97db8
Enter ".help" for usage hints.
Connected to a transient in-memory database.
Use ".open FILENAME" to reopen on a persistent database.
D .open mydb2.duckdb
D CREATE TABLE airports as FROM airports.csv;
D show tables;
┌──────────┐
│   name   │
│ varchar  │
├──────────┤
│ airports │
└──────────┘
```

In this example, we first launched the DuckDB CLI without any filename. Then, we opened the database named *mydb2.duckdb* using the .open command. Because *mydb2.duckdb* is a new database file, it will be created in the same directory where you launched the DuckDB CLI.

We then loaded the *airports.csv* file into a newly created table named *airports*.

The .open command closes the existing database and opens a new one. If you want to keep the current database open and work with an additional one, use the ATTACH statement:

```
D ATTACH 'mydb.duckdb';
```

You can optionally specify an alias for the database that you are attaching. The following example is the same as the previous statement. If you don't specify the alias, it will use the filename as the alias by default:

```
D ATTACH 'mydb.duckdb' as mydb;
```

You must enclose the filename in single or double quotes.

You can now verify that you have two databases:

```
D .database
mydb2: mydb2.duckdb
mydb: mydb.duckdb
```

The first database that is listed is the currently active one. To use a particular database, use the USE statement and specify the alias for the database you want to use:

```
D USE mydb2;
```

.table

If you want to quickly look at *all* the tables you have in your databases, use the .table command:

```
D .table
airlines  airports
```

This command shows that there are two tables currently in the two databases—*airlines* and *airports*. This is useful when you have multiple tables in your database.

.dump

If you want to render the content of a table as SQL statements, use the .dump command:

```
D .dump airlines
PRAGMA foreign_keys=OFF;
BEGIN TRANSACTION;
CREATE TABLE airlines(IATA_CODE VARCHAR, AIRLINE VARCHAR);;
INSERT INTO airlines VALUES('UA','United Air Lines Inc.');
INSERT INTO airlines VALUES('AA','American Airlines Inc.');
INSERT INTO airlines VALUES('US','US Airways Inc.');
INSERT INTO airlines VALUES('F9','Frontier Airlines Inc.');
INSERT INTO airlines VALUES('B6','JetBlue Airways');
INSERT INTO airlines VALUES('OO','Skywest Airlines Inc.');
INSERT INTO airlines VALUES('AS','Alaska Airlines Inc.');
INSERT INTO airlines VALUES('NK','Spirit Air Lines');
INSERT INTO airlines VALUES('WN','Southwest Airlines Co.');
INSERT INTO airlines VALUES('DL','Delta Air Lines Inc.');
INSERT INTO airlines VALUES('EV','Atlantic Southeast Airlines');
INSERT INTO airlines VALUES('HA','Hawaiian Airlines Inc.');
INSERT INTO airlines VALUES('MQ','American Eagle Airlines Inc.');
INSERT INTO airlines VALUES('VX','Virgin America');
COMMIT;
```

This command dumps the *airlines* table as a series of SQL statements. This is useful if you need to import the content of a table in DuckDB into a table of another database (such as MySQL).

 The table you are trying to dump must be in the database that you are currently using. If it's not in the current database, use the USE statement to switch to the correct database.

.read

The `.read` command in DuckDB CLI is used to execute SQL commands from a file. Here's an example of how to use it. Suppose you have a text file named *commands.sql* with the following content:

```
CREATE TABLE airports2 as FROM airports.csv;
SELECT * FROM airports2;
```

You can use the `.read` command to read and execute the commands stored in the *commands.sql* file:

```
D .read commands.sql
```

You should now see the content of the *airports2* table:

| IATA_CODE | AIRPORT | ... | COUNTRY | LATITUDE | LONGITUDE |
varchar	varchar		varchar	double	double
ABE	Lehigh Valley Inte…	...	USA	40.65236	-75.4404
ABI	Abilene Regional A…	...	USA	32.41132	-99.6819
ABQ	Albuquerque Intern…	...	USA	35.04022	-106.60919
...					
YAK	Yakutat Airport	...	USA	59.50336	-139.66023
YUM	Yuma International…	...	USA	32.65658	-114.60597
322 rows (40 shown)				7 columns (5 shown)	

Next, you will learn how to persist in-memory databases to disk.

Persisting the In-Memory Database on Disk

Suppose you use an in-memory database with the DuckDB CLI and load the *airports.csv* into a table named *airports*:

```
% duckdb
v0.10.1 4a89d97db8
Enter ".help" for usage hints.
Connected to a transient in-memory database.
Use ".open FILENAME" to reopen on a persistent database.
D CREATE TABLE airports as FROM read_csv_auto(airports.csv);
```

Remember, in-memory databases will be destroyed when you exit the DuckDB CLI. To save them, you need to persist them to disk. To do so, use the EXPORT DATABASE statement:

```
D EXPORT DATABASE 'airports_db';
```

This will create a folder named *airports_db* in the current directory (where you launched the DuckDB CLI), with the files shown in Figure 3-2.

Figure 3-2. The exported database and its files

Within this folder you will find the following files:

airports.csv
> The CSV file from which you loaded the table.

load.sql
> The statement to load the CSV file into the table. It looks like this:

```
COPY airports FROM 'airports_db/airports.csv' (FORMAT 'csv', quote '"',
delimiter ',', header 1);
```

schema.sql
> The SQL statement to create the table in the database. It looks like this:

```
CREATE TABLE airports(IATA_CODE VARCHAR, AIRPORT VARCHAR,
CITY VARCHAR, STATE VARCHAR, COUNTRY VARCHAR, LATITUDE DOUBLE,
LONGITUDE DOUBLE);
```

To load the files contained within the *airports_db* folder into a new DuckDB database, use the following commands (you must run the DuckDB CLI in the directory that contains the *airports_db* folder):

```
$ duckdb mydb3.duckdb
v0.10.1 4a89d97db8
Enter ".help" for usage hints.
D IMPORT DATABASE 'airports_db';
D show tables;
┌──────────┐
│   name   │
│ varchar  │
├──────────┤
│ airports │
└──────────┘
```

Now the *mydb3.duckdb* file contains the *airports* table.

In the next section, you'll learn the syntax of DuckDB SQL and how you can use it to manipulate tables in your databases.

DuckDB SQL Primer

Now that you've familiarized yourself with the DuckDB CLI for managing databases and tables, let's shift our focus to delve deeper into SQL. Rather than delving into the syntax of SQL word by word, a more effective approach to learning SQL is through practical examples. Hence, for this section, we will construct a database for a mini-library. This library database has four tables:

Authors
    Contains information about authors, such as name, nationality, and birth year.

Books
    Contains information about books, such as title, author, genre, and publication year.

Borrowers
    Contains information about book borrowers, such as name, email, and date since becoming members.

Borrowings
    Keeps track of books borrowed by people and contains details such as borrowing date, return date, and status of borrowing.

 DuckDB is largely compatible with SQL standards (particularly SQL:1999) and follows typical SQL syntax for most operations. So, for the most part, the following discussions on DuckDB SQL should be similar to standard SQL.

Figure 3-3 shows the schema of the tables in the DuckDB database.

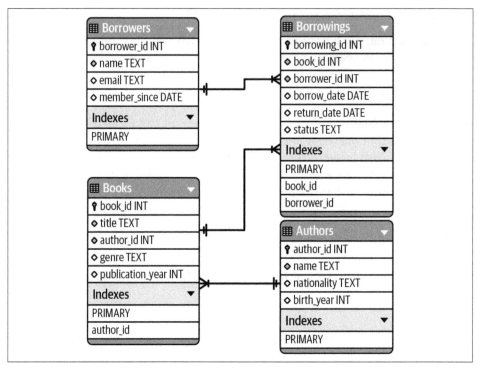

Figure 3-3. The schema of the various tables in the database

In the next few sections, you will learn how to use the DuckDB CLI to create the various tables in the database. You will also learn how to populate them with sample records and use SQL to perform various processes such as retrieval, updating, and deletion.

Creating a Database

Using the DuckDB CLI, create a DuckDB database using the following command:

```
% duckdb library.duckdb
v0.10.1 4a89d97db8
Enter ".help" for usage hints.
D
```

The library in this example is named *library.duckdb*. We will next create the various tables in the DuckDB database.

Creating Tables

Let's first create the four tables using SQL:

```
D CREATE TABLE Authors (
      author_id INTEGER PRIMARY KEY,
      name TEXT NOT NULL,
      nationality TEXT,
      birth_year INTEGER
  );

D CREATE TABLE Borrowers (
      borrower_id INTEGER PRIMARY KEY,
      name TEXT NOT NULL,
      email TEXT,
      member_since DATE
  );

D CREATE TABLE Books (
      book_id INTEGER PRIMARY KEY,
      title TEXT NOT NULL,
      author_id INTEGER NOT NULL,
      genre TEXT,
      publication_year INTEGER,
      FOREIGN KEY (author_id) REFERENCES Authors(author_id)
  );

D CREATE TABLE Borrowings (
      borrowing_id INTEGER PRIMARY KEY,
      book_id INTEGER NOT NULL,
      borrower_id INTEGER NOT NULL,
      borrow_date DATE,
      return_date DATE,
      status TEXT,
      FOREIGN KEY (book_id) REFERENCES Books(book_id),
      FOREIGN KEY (borrower_id) REFERENCES Borrowers(borrower_id)
  );
```

To create a table in SQL, you use the CREATE TABLE statement followed by the table name and a list of columns with their data types and optional constraints.

The FOREIGN KEY and REFERENCES keywords are used in SQL to establish relationships between tables. They enforce referential integrity for the data in the tables. For example, in the following SQL statement, which you used to create the *Books* table:

```
FOREIGN KEY (author_id) REFERENCES Authors(author_id)
```

The FOREIGN KEY statement indicates that the value in the author_id column REFERENCES the author_id column in the *Authors* table. In other words, it ensures that the author_id you specify in a record in the *Books* table must be available in the author_id column of the *Authors* table.

Let's confirm that the tables are created:

```
D show tables;
```

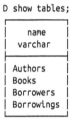

```
┌───────────┐
│   name    │
│  varchar  │
├───────────┤
│ Authors   │
│ Books     │
│ Borrowers │
│ Borrowings│
└───────────┘
```

If you can see the above output, the tables are created correctly.

Viewing the Schemas of Tables

To view the schema of a table, you can use the DESCRIBE statement. For example, let's look at the schema of the *Authors* table:

```
D DESCRIBE Authors;
```

column_name varchar	column_type varchar	null varchar	key varchar	default varchar	extra varchar
author_id	INTEGER	NO	PRI		
name	VARCHAR	NO			
nationality	VARCHAR	YES			
birth_year	INTEGER	YES			

Alternatively, you can use the SHOW statement:

```
D SHOW Authors;
```

If you want to view the schema of the entire database, use the .schema command:

```
D .schema
CREATE TABLE Authors(author_id INTEGER PRIMARY KEY, "name" VARCHAR
NOT NULL, nationality VARCHAR, birth_year INTEGER);
CREATE TABLE Books(book_id INTEGER PRIMARY KEY, title VARCHAR NOT NULL,
author_id INTEGER NOT NULL, genre VARCHAR, publication_year INTEGER,
FOREIGN KEY (author_id) REFERENCES Authors(author_id));
CREATE TABLE Borrowers(borrower_id INTEGER PRIMARY KEY, "name" VARCHAR
NOT NULL, email VARCHAR, member_since DATE);
CREATE TABLE Borrowings(borrowing_id INTEGER PRIMARY KEY, book_id
INTEGER NOT NULL, borrower_id INTEGER NOT NULL, borrow_date DATE,
return_date DATE, status VARCHAR, FOREIGN KEY (book_id) REFERENCES
Books(book_id), FOREIGN KEY (borrower_id) REFERENCES
Borrowers(borrower_id));
```

Dropping a Table

If you need to drop (delete) a table in DuckDB, use the DROP TABLE statement. For example, if you have created a table named *OverdueBorrowers* that is no longer needed, you can drop it as in the following example:

```
D CREATE TABLE OverdueBorrowers (
      borrower_id INTEGER PRIMARY KEY,
      name TEXT NOT NULL,
      email TEXT,
      member_since DATE
   );

D DROP TABLE OverdueBorrowers;
```

If you try to drop a table that is referenced by another table, you'll get an error. For example, if you try to drop the *Authors* table, you'll see the error:

```
Catalog Error: Could not drop the table because this table is
main key table of the table "Books"
```

This is because the *Authors* table contains the `author_id` column that is referenced in the *Books* table.

In the next section, you will learn how to use SQL to work with tables.

Working with Tables

Now that you have seen how to create the database and the tables within it, it's time to populate the tables with some sample records. In the following sections, you'll learn how to:

- Populate tables with records
- Update records within a table
- Delete records within a table
- Query tables
- Join tables
- Perform aggregation of data in tables
- Perform analytics of data in tables

 The first four operations are usually referred to as CRUD operations—create, retrieve, update, and delete.

Let's start with how to populate tables.

Populating Tables with Rows

With the *Authors* table created, let's now insert some rows into it with some author data:

```
D INSERT INTO Authors (author_id, name, nationality, birth_year)
  VALUES
      (1, 'Jane Austen', 'British', 1775),
      (2, 'Charles Dickens', 'British', 1812),
      (3, 'Agatha Christie', 'British', 1890),
      (4, 'J.K. Rowling', 'British', 1965),
      (5, 'Tolkien', 'British', 1892);
```

This statement inserts five rows into the *Authors* table, with each value enclosed within parentheses and separated by commas.

The following statement inserts a single row into the *Authors* table:

```
D INSERT INTO Authors (author_id, name, nationality, birth_year)
  VALUES (6, 'Mark Twain', 'American', 1835);
```

With the records added to the *Authors* table, you can now retrieve them using the SELECT statement:

```
D SELECT * FROM Authors;
```

| author_id | name | nationality | birth_year |
int32	varchar	varchar	int32
1	Jane Austen	British	1775
2	Charles Dickens	British	1812
3	Agatha Christie	British	1890
4	J.K. Rowling	British	1965
5	Tolkien	British	1892
6	Mark Twain	American	1835

With the *Authors* table populated, let's now populate the other tables. First, the *Borrowers* table:

```
D INSERT INTO Borrowers (borrower_id, name, email, member_since)
  VALUES
      (1, 'John Smith', 'john.smith@example.com', '2022-01-01'),
      (2, 'Emma Johnson', 'emma.johnson@example.com', '2021-12-15'),
      (3, 'Michael Brown', 'michael.brown@example.com', '2022-02-20'),
      (4, 'Sophia Wilson', 'sophia.wilson@example.com', '2022-03-10'),
      (5, 'William Taylor', 'william.taylor@example.com', '2022-04-05'),
      (6, 'Jane Doe', 'jane.doe@example.com', '2022-03-05');
```

```
D SELECT * FROM Borrowers;
```

| borrower_id | name | email | member_since |
int32	varchar	varchar	date
1	John Smith	john.smith@example.com	2022-01-01
2	Emma Johnson	emma.johnson@example.com	2021-12-15
3	Michael Brown	michael.brown@example.com	2022-02-20
4	Sophia Wilson	sophia.wilson@example.com	2022-03-10
5	William Taylor	william.taylor@example.com	2022-04-05
6	Jane Doe	jane.doe@example.com	2022-03-05

Then, populate the *Books* table:

```
D INSERT INTO Books (book_id, title, author_id, genre, publication_year)
  VALUES
      (1, 'Pride and Prejudice', 1, 'Classic', 1813),
      (2, 'Oliver Twist', 2, 'Novel', 1837),
      (3, 'Murder on the Orient Express', 3, 'Mystery', 1934),
      (4, 'Harry Potter and the Philosopher''s Stone', 4, 'Fantasy', 1997),
      (5, 'The Hobbit', 5, 'Fantasy', 1937);

D SELECT * FROM Books;
```

book_id int32	title varchar	author_id int32	genre varchar	publication_year int32
1	Pride and Prejudice	1	Classic	1813
2	Oliver Twist	2	Novel	1837
3	Murder on the Orient Ex…	3	Mystery	1934
4	Harry Potter and the Ph…	4	Fantasy	1997
5	The Hobbit	5	Fantasy	1937

Remember that the `author_id` column in the *Books* table references the `author_id` column in the *Authors* table. Hence, the value for `author_id` must be a valid author id—1 to 6 in this example.

Finally, populate the *Borrowings* table:

```
D INSERT INTO Borrowings (borrowing_id, book_id, borrower_id,
  borrow_date, return_date, status)
  VALUES
      (1, 1, 1, '2022-04-10', '2022-04-25', 'Returned'),
      (2, 3, 2, '2022-03-20', NULL, 'On Loan'),
      (3, 4, 3, '2022-04-05', NULL, 'On Loan'),
      (4, 2, 4, '2022-04-15', NULL, 'On Loan'),
      (5, 5, 5, '2022-03-30', '2022-04-20', 'Returned'),
      (6, 1, 3, '2022-04-26', NULL, 'On Loan');

D SELECT * FROM Borrowings;
```

borrowing_id int32	book_id int32	borrower_id int32	borrow_date date	return_date date	status varchar
1	1	1	2022-04-10	2022-04-25	Returned
2	3	2	2022-03-20		On Loan
3	4	3	2022-04-05		On Loan
4	2	4	2022-04-15		On Loan
5	5	5	2022-03-30	2022-04-20	Returned
6	1	3	2022-04-26		On Loan

Again, the `book_id` and `borrower_id` columns reference the `book_id` column in the *Books* table and the `borrower_id` column in the *Borrowers* table, respectively. Hence, for `book_id` the values must be from 1 to 5, and for `borrower_id` the values must be from 1 to 6.

Updating Rows

To update a specific row in a table, use the UPDATE statement together with keywords like SET and WHERE. For this example, let's assume you want to modify the return status of a particular book. Here are the details you want to modify:

- borrowing_id is 3
- Set status to "Returned"
- Set return_date to 2022-04-05

You can now use the following SQL statement to modify the record:

```
D UPDATE Borrowings
  SET return_date = '2022-04-05',
      status = 'Returned'
  WHERE borrowing_id = 3;
```

To be sure that the updates are performed correctly, let's view the updated *Borrowings* table again:

```
D SELECT * FROM Borrowings;
```

borrowing_id int32	book_id int32	borrower_id int32	borrow_date date	return_date date	status varchar
1	1	1	2022-04-10	2022-04-25	Returned
2	3	2	2022-03-20		On Loan
3	4	3	2022-04-05	2022-04-05	Returned
4	2	4	2022-04-15		On Loan
5	5	5	2022-03-30	2022-04-20	Returned
6	1	3	2022-04-26		On Loan

Deleting Rows

To delete a record, you can use the DELETE statement together with the WHERE keyword to specify the condition. For example, the following statement deletes the record from the *Borrowers* table where the borrower name is "Jane Doe":

```
D DELETE FROM Borrowers
  WHERE name = 'Jane Doe';
```

You can now view the records from the *Borrowers* table to confirm that the record has indeed been deleted:

```
D SELECT * FROM borrowers;
```

borrower_id int32	name varchar	email varchar	member_since date
1	John Smith	john.smith@example.com	2022-01-01
2	Emma Johnson	emma.johnson@example.com	2021-12-15
3	Michael Brown	michael.brown@example.com	2022-02-20
4	Sophia Wilson	sophia.wilson@example.com	2022-03-10
5	William Taylor	william.taylor@example.com	2022-04-05

Of course, there are other ways of deleting a record. A more common one is to delete a record based on its borrower_id, like the following example shows (it is also deleting the Jane Doe record):

```
D DELETE FROM Borrowers
   WHERE borrower_id = 6;
```

If you want to delete a record whose name contains the word "Jane", you can use the LIKE keyword together with the % wildcards:

```
D DELETE FROM Borrowers
   WHERE name LIKE '%Jane%';
```

The % symbols are wildcards that match *any* characters before and after "Jane" in the name column, allowing you to delete rows where the name contains "Jane" anywhere in the string.

Querying Tables

So far you have seen how to perform queries with your tables using the SELECT statement. Let's now dive into the SELECT statement in more detail and use it to perform more sophisticated queries.

For a start, let's retrieve all the authors who were born more than 100 years ago:

```
D SELECT *
  FROM Authors
  WHERE (YEAR(CURRENT_DATE) - birth_year) > 100;
```

author_id int32	name varchar	nationality varchar	birth_year int32
1	Jane Austen	British	1775
2	Charles Dickens	British	1812
3	Agatha Christie	British	1890
5	Tolkien	British	1892
6	Mark Twain	American	1835

The `CURRENT_DATE` function returns the current date (at the time of writing it is 2024-04-18). The `YEAR` function extracts the year from the current date. So, the above statement obtains the current year, subtracts the birth year of each author, and then returns all of the rows whose results are greater than 100.

If you want to find all the books belonging to the "Fantasy" genre, you can use the following statement:

```
D SELECT *
  FROM Books
  WHERE genre = 'Fantasy';
```

book_id int32	title varchar	author_id int32	genre varchar	publication_year int32
4	Harry Potter and the Ph…	4	Fantasy	1997
5	The Hobbit	5	Fantasy	1937

For date columns (such as the `member_since` column in the *Borrowers* table), you can perform date comparisons directly. For example, to find all borrowers who were members since the start of 2022, you'd use the following statement to retrieve borrowers who became members on or after January 1, 2022:

```
D SELECT *
  FROM Borrowers
  WHERE member_since >= '2022-01-01';
```

borrower_id int32	name varchar	email varchar	member_since date
1	John Smith	john.smith@example.com	2022-01-01
3	Michael Brown	michael.brown@example.com	2022-02-20
4	Sophia Wilson	sophia.wilson@example.com	2022-03-10
5	William Taylor	william.taylor@example.com	2022-04-05

Joining Tables

Frequently, when extracting data from your database, you'll need to fetch information from multiple tables. To do this, you need to perform *joins*, which allow you to combine data from different tables based on common columns or relationships between them. DuckDB supports the following types of joins:

- Left outer join (commonly known as left join)
- Right outer join (commonly known as right join)
- Inner join
- Full join
- Cross join

Let's dig into these, starting with left join.

Left join

Let's use an example to demonstrate the use of left join. Using the *Books* and *Authors* table, we want to list the title of each book and its associated author. In this case, you can use the following SQL statement:

```
D SELECT b.book_id, b.title, a.name
  FROM Books b
  LEFT JOIN Authors a ON b.author_id = a.author_id;
```

book_id int32	title varchar	name varchar
1	Pride and Prejudice	Jane Austen
2	Oliver Twist	Charles Dickens
3	Murder on the Orient Express	Agatha Christie
4	Harry Potter and the Philosopher's Stone	J.K. Rowling
5	The Hobbit	Tolkien

In this SQL query, `LEFT JOIN Authors a ON b.author_id = a.author_id` performs a left outer join between the *Books* table (b) and the *Authors* table (a). This means that all rows from the *Books* table (which is the left table) will be included in the result set, and matching rows from the *Authors* table will be joined based on the condition `b.author_id = a.author_id`.

If there is no matching author for a book (i.e., `author_id` is NULL in the *Authors* table), the columns from the *Authors* table (`a.name` in this case) will be NULL in the result set. Figure 3-4 shows how the left outer join works. In a left outer join, all rows from the left table are included in the result, regardless of whether they have matching rows in the right table.

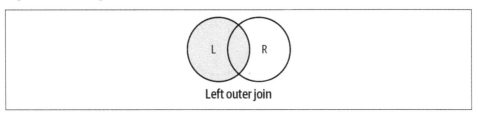

Left outer join

Figure 3-4. Left outer join

Consider the following example, where we flip the order of the tables and make *Authors* the left table:

```
D SELECT a.name, b.book_id, b.title
  FROM Authors a
  LEFT JOIN Books b on a.author_id = b.author_id;
```

name varchar	book_id int32	title varchar
Jane Austen	1	Pride and Prejudice
Charles Dickens	2	Oliver Twist
Agatha Christie	3	Murder on the Orient Express
J.K. Rowling	4	Harry Potter and the Philosopher's Stone
Tolkien	5	The Hobbit
Mark Twain		

Observe that this time around, the result has six rows. The last row contains the author Mark Twain, but since he has no books listed in the *Books* table, the value of the book_id and title columns are both NULL.

Right join

The right join is similar to the left join, except that the right join includes all rows from the right table, even if there are no matching rows in the left table. In other words, the right join ensures that every row from the right table appears in the result set, with NULL values filled in for columns from the left table where there is no match. This type of join is useful when you want to prioritize data from the right table and include all of its rows in the output, regardless of whether they have corresponding matches in the left table.

Figure 3-5 shows how the right join works.

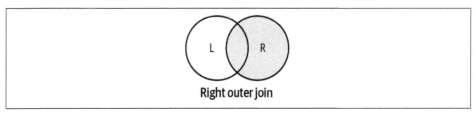

Right outer join

Figure 3-5. Right outer join

Here is an example of a right outer join:

```
D SELECT b.book_id, b.title, a.name
  FROM Books b
  RIGHT JOIN Authors a ON b.author_id = a.author_id;
```

book_id int32	title varchar	name varchar
1	Pride and Prejudice	Jane Austen
2	Oliver Twist	Charles Dickens
3	Murder on the Orient Express	Agatha Christie
4	Harry Potter and the Philosopher's Stone	J.K. Rowling
5	The Hobbit	Tolkien
		Mark Twain

The result contains all the authors in the *Authors* table.

Inner join

The inner join combines rows from two or more tables based on related columns between them. It retrieves only the rows where there is a match between the columns in the specified join condition. Continuing with our example, if you only want to list titles with matching authors, you'd use an inner join:

```
D SELECT b.book_id, b.title, a.name
  FROM Books b
  INNER JOIN Authors a ON b.author_id = a.author_id;
```

book_id int32	title varchar	name varchar
1	Pride and Prejudice	Jane Austen
2	Oliver Twist	Charles Dickens
3	Murder on the Orient Express	Agatha Christie
4	Harry Potter and the Philosopher's Stone	J.K. Rowling
5	The Hobbit	Tolkien

This query returns the book_id, title, and author's name for each book, ensuring that only books with corresponding authors are included in the result set. An inner join includes only the rows that have matching values in both tables. Figure 3-6 shows how inner join works.

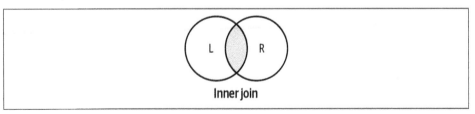

Figure 3-6. Inner join

Full join

The result of a full join will include rows from both tables, regardless of whether there is a match in the join condition. Here's an example:

```
D SELECT b.book_id, b.title, a.name
  FROM Books b
  FULL JOIN Authors a ON b.author_id = a.author_id;
```

| book_id | title | name |
int32	varchar	varchar
1	Pride and Prejudice	Jane Austen
2	Oliver Twist	Charles Dickens
3	Murder on the Orient Express	Agatha Christie
4	Harry Potter and the Philosopher's Stone	J.K. Rowling
5	The Hobbit	Tolkien
		Mark Twain

A full join includes all rows from both tables in the result set, matching rows where they exist and including NULL values for unmatched rows. Figure 3-7 shows how full join works.

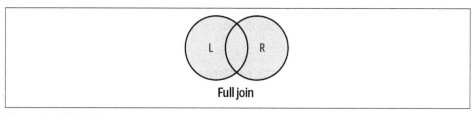

Full join

Figure 3-7. Full join

Multiple table joins

Now that you understand the use of the various joins, let's use them to join multiple tables so that you can explore complex relationships and retrieve comprehensive data from your database.

First, let's find all the books borrowed by John Smith:

```
D SELECT b.title AS book_title
  FROM Books b
  INNER JOIN Borrowings br ON b.book_id = br.book_id
  INNER JOIN Borrowers bw ON br.borrower_id = bw.borrower_id
  WHERE bw.name = 'John Smith';
```

| book_title |
varchar
Pride and Prejudice

This SQL statement performs two inner joins—one between the *Books* and *Borrowings* tables based on the book_id column, and one between *Borrowings* and *Borrowers* based on the borrower_id column. The result is then filtered on the name column in the *Borrowers* table. The result shows that the book borrowed by John Smith is *Pride and Prejudice*.

Next, let's find all books that have been borrowed and list the borrower's name along with the book titles:

```
D SELECT bw.name AS borrower_name, b.title AS book_title
  FROM Borrowings br
  INNER JOIN Books b ON br.book_id = b.book_id
  INNER JOIN Borrowers bw ON br.borrower_id = bw.borrower_id;
```

```
┌────────────────┬───────────────────────────────────────────┐
│ borrower_name  │                book_title                 │
│   varchar      │                 varchar                   │
├────────────────┼───────────────────────────────────────────┤
│ Michael Brown  │ Pride and Prejudice                       │
│ Sophia Wilson  │ Oliver Twist                              │
│ Emma Johnson   │ Murder on the Orient Express              │
│ Michael Brown  │ Harry Potter and the Philosopher's Stone  │
│ William Taylor │ The Hobbit                                │
│ John Smith     │ Pride and Prejudice                       │
└────────────────┴───────────────────────────────────────────┘
```

This query is similar to the previous one, except that you also listed the borrower's name. However, there is no filtering for a particular borrower this time around.

Your results may not be in the same order as shown. To display results in a consistent order, add an ORDER BY statement to the query:

```
SELECT bw.name AS borrower_name, b.title AS book_title
FROM Borrowings br
INNER JOIN Books b ON br.book_id = b.book_id
INNER JOIN Borrowers bw ON
    br.borrower_id = bw.borrower_id
ORDER BY bw.name, b.title;
```

The result will now be sorted alphabetically by the borrower's name, followed by the book title.

To include the author's name along with the book title in the results, you can further join the *Authors* table with the *Books* table based on the author_id column:

```
D SELECT bw.name AS borrower_name, b.title AS book_title, a.name AS author_name
  FROM Borrowings br
  INNER JOIN Books b ON br.book_id = b.book_id
  INNER JOIN Borrowers bw ON br.borrower_id = bw.borrower_id
  INNER JOIN Authors a ON b.author_id = a.author_id;
```

borrower_name varchar	book_title varchar	author_name varchar
Michael Brown	Pride and Prejudice	Jane Austen
Sophia Wilson	Oliver Twist	Charles Dickens
Emma Johnson	Murder on the Orient Express	Agatha Christie
Michael Brown	Harry Potter and the Philosopher's Stone	J.K. Rowling
William Taylor	The Hobbit	Tolkien
John Smith	Pride and Prejudice	Jane Austen

Let's now see which are the books borrowed by Michael Brown, the borrowing dates, and the return status of each book:

```
D SELECT b.book_id, b.title, br.borrow_date, br.return_date
  FROM Borrowings br
  INNER JOIN Books b ON br.book_id = b.book_id
  INNER JOIN Borrowers bw ON br.borrower_id = bw.borrower_id
  WHERE bw.name = 'Michael Brown';
```

book_id int32	title varchar	borrow_date date	return_date date
1	Pride and Prejudice	2022-04-26	
4	Harry Potter and the Philosopher's S…	2022-04-05	2022-04-05

Aggregating Data

Aggregation in SQL refers to the process of summarizing or aggregating multiple rows of data into a single value. Let's learn how to do this using a few examples.

First, let's sum up the number of books borrowed by each borrower:

```
D SELECT bw.name AS borrower_name, COUNT(br.book_id) AS books_borrowed
  FROM Borrowings br
  INNER JOIN Borrowers bw ON br.borrower_id = bw.borrower_id
  GROUP BY bw.name
  ORDER BY bw.name;
```

borrower_name varchar	books_borrowed int64
Emma Johnson	1
John Smith	1
Michael Brown	2
Sophia Wilson	1
William Taylor	1

This SQL statement performs an inner join between the *Borrowings* and *Borrowers* tables based on the borrower_id column. It uses the COUNT function to count the number of book_id entries in the *Borrowings* table and create an alias named books_borrowed. Finally, it groups and sorts the result by the name column of the *Borrowers* table.

You can also use the COUNT function to find out which book is the most borrowed:

```
D SELECT b.book_id, b.title AS book_name, COUNT(*) AS num_borrowings
  FROM Borrowings br
  INNER JOIN Books b ON br.book_id = b.book_id
  GROUP BY b.book_id, b.title
  ORDER BY num_borrowings DESC
  LIMIT 1;
```

| book_id | book_name | num_borrowings |
int32	varchar	int64
1	Pride and Prejudice	2

The ORDER BY num_borrowings DESC line orders the results in descending order based on the number of borrowings, so the book with the highest number of borrowings will appear first. We use LIMIT 1 to limit the result to only the top-most row, which corresponds to the most borrowed book.

Out of curiosity, you might want to know the average age of all the authors, since there is a birth_year column in the *Authors* table. To find the average age of all authors in the *Authors* table, you can find the age of each author using the current year and their birth year, and then use the AVG function to calculate the average of these ages:

```
D SELECT AVG(YEAR(CURRENT_DATE) - birth_year) AS average_age_of_authors
  FROM Authors;
```

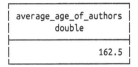

| average_age_of_authors |
double
162.5

Using the AVG function, you can also find the average publication year of all the books:

```
D SELECT AVG(publication_year) AS avg_publication_year
  FROM Books;
```

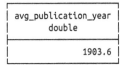

| avg_publication_year |
double
1903.6

If you want to know who the oldest author is, use the MIN function:

```
D SELECT name, birth_year, YEAR(CURRENT_DATE) - birth_year AS age
  FROM Authors
  WHERE birth_year = (SELECT MIN(birth_year) FROM Authors);
```

| name | birth_year | age |
varchar	int32	int64
Jane Austen	1775	249

As you can see from the result, Jane Austen is 249 years old (as of 2024)!

Analytics

Using the techniques you have learned from the previous sections, you can use SQL to perform some interesting analytics on the various tables.

Let's start with finding overdue books. Assuming the loan period for a book is a maximum of 14 days, let's find the names of the borrowers who returned books late. Additionally, we want to determine the number of days the returned book was overdue.

Here, you can use the INNER JOIN statement to join three tables—*Borrowings*, *Books*, and *Borrowers*—so that you can obtain the book name and borrower name, as well as the date of return. To find out how many days the returned book was overdue, you can use the DATEDIFF function to calculate the difference between the return date and borrowing date, and then deduct 14 days from it:

```
D SELECT bw.name AS borrower_name, b.title AS book_title, br.borrow_date,
         br.return_date,
         DATEDIFF('day', br.borrow_date, br.return_date) - 14 AS overdue
  FROM Borrowings br
  INNER JOIN Books b ON br.book_id = b.book_id
  INNER JOIN Borrowers bw ON br.borrower_id = bw.borrower_id
  WHERE br.return_date IS NOT NULL AND
        DATEDIFF('day', br.borrow_date, br.return_date) > 14;
```

| borrower_name | book_title | borrow_date | return_date | overdue |
varchar	varchar	date	date	int64
John Smith	Pride and Prejudice	2022-04-10	2022-04-25	1
William Taylor	The Hobbit	2022-03-30	2022-04-20	7

You can see that John Smith returned his book one day late, while William Taylor returned his book one week late.

The preceding SQL statement could be saved as a *view* (a view is essentially a saved query) so that users can reference it later as if it were a table. You can create a view using the CREATE VIEW statement:

```
D CREATE VIEW overdue_borrowings AS
  SELECT bw.name AS borrower_name,
         b.title AS book_title,
         br.borrow_date,
         br.return_date,
         DATEDIFF('day', br.borrow_date, br.return_date) - 14 AS overdue
  FROM Borrowings br
  INNER JOIN Books b ON br.book_id = b.book_id
  INNER JOIN Borrowers bw ON br.borrower_id = bw.borrower_id
  WHERE br.return_date IS NOT NULL
    AND DATEDIFF('day', br.borrow_date, br.return_date) > 14;
```

The view created is persisted to the DuckDB database. You can now quickly see who returned their books late using this view:

```
D SELECT * FROM overdue_borrowings;
```

Now that we know who has returned books late, we also want to know which books are overdue and by how many days:

```
D SELECT b.book_id, b.title, bw.name AS borrower_name, br.borrow_date,
         DATEDIFF('day', br.borrow_date, CURRENT_DATE()) - 14 AS overdue
  FROM Borrowings br
  INNER JOIN Books b ON br.book_id = b.book_id
  INNER JOIN Borrowers bw ON br.borrower_id = bw.borrower_id
  WHERE br.return_date IS NULL AND
        DATEDIFF('day', br.borrow_date, CURRENT_DATE()) > 14;
```

| book_id | title | borrower_name | borrow_date | overdue |
int32	varchar	varchar	date	int64
1	Pride and Prejudice	Michael Brown	2022-04-26	710
2	Oliver Twist	Sophia Wilson	2022-04-15	721
3	Murder on the Orient Express	Emma Johnson	2022-03-20	747

Because we're calculating from the current date, the values in the overdue column are quite large. If you want to know the books that are overdue on a particular day (say, 2022-06-10), you can replace the CURRENT_DATE() function with a specific date:

```
D SELECT b.book_id, b.title, bw.name AS borrower_name, br.borrow_date,
         DATEDIFF('day', br.borrow_date, '2022-06-10') - 14 AS overdue
  FROM Borrowings br
  INNER JOIN Books b ON br.book_id = b.book_id
  INNER JOIN Borrowers bw ON br.borrower_id = bw.borrower_id
  WHERE br.return_date IS NULL AND
        DATEDIFF('day', br.borrow_date, '2022-06-10') > 14;
```

| book_id | title | borrower_name | borrow_date | overdue |
int32	varchar	varchar	date	int64
1	Pride and Prejudice	Michael Brown	2022-04-26	31
2	Oliver Twist	Sophia Wilson	2022-04-15	42
3	Murder on the Orient Express	Emma Johnson	2022-03-20	68

Finally, let's find out which is the most borrowed book. You want to show the title, who borrowed it, when it was loaned out, and when it was returned:

```
D SELECT b.book_id, b.title AS book_name,
         bw.name AS borrower_name,
         br.borrow_date AS loan_date, br.return_date
  FROM Borrowings br
  INNER JOIN Books b ON br.book_id = b.book_id
  INNER JOIN Borrowers bw ON br.borrower_id = bw.borrower_id
  WHERE b.book_id IN (
      SELECT book_id
      FROM Borrowings
      GROUP BY book_id
      HAVING COUNT(*) = (
          SELECT MAX(num_borrowings)
          FROM (
              SELECT COUNT(*) AS num_borrowings
              FROM Borrowings
              GROUP BY book_id
          ) AS counts
      )
  )
  GROUP BY b.book_id, b.title, br.borrower_id, bw.name, br.borrow_date,
           br.return_date;
```

| book_id | book_name | borrower_name | loan_date | return_date |
int32	varchar	varchar	date	date
1	Pride and Prejudice	John Smith	2022-04-10	2022-04-25
1	Pride and Prejudice	Michael Brown	2022-04-26	

Observe that these SQL statements contain three nested SELECT statements (see also Figure 3-8).

Here's how each statement works:

Innermost SELECT *statement (1)*

The innermost SELECT statement counts the number of borrowings for each book_id in the *Borrowings* table. This query groups the results by book_id and returns a count of borrowings for each book.

Intermediate SELECT *statement (2)*

The second SELECT statement retrieves the maximum borrow count (MAX(num_borrowings)) from the results of the innermost query. This gives the maximum number of borrowings any book has.

Outer WHERE *clause (3)*

The outer WHERE clause uses the IN condition to filter for book_ids from the *Borrowings* table that have a borrowing count equal to this maximum value. This means it identifies all books that have the highest borrowing count in order to account for books that have the same borrow counts.

Outer SELECT *statement (4)*

Finally, the outer SELECT statement retrieves details about these most borrowed books by performing inner joins with the *Borrowings*, *Books*, and *Borrowers* tables. This join connects the data based on book_id and borrower_id, allowing the retrieval of fields such as book title, borrower name, loan date, and return date.

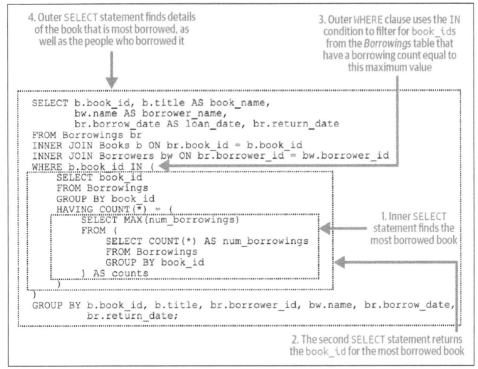

Figure 3-8. The query is made up of three SELECT *statements*

Summary

The chapter offers a thorough examination of DuckDB, beginning with an exploration of its CLI and data import techniques. It discusses dot commands and database persistence to enhance data management and accessibility. The subsequent section serves as a primer on SQL, encompassing topics such as database and table creation, data querying, and different join types for data manipulation. Additionally, you gained insight into data aggregation and advanced analytics techniques using SQL statements, enabling you to extract valuable insights from your DuckDB database.

Understanding the CLI and data import techniques is crucial for efficiently managing your DuckDB environment. The dot commands provide powerful capabilities to streamline your workflow, so make sure to get comfortable with these commands. Database persistence is another key area; ensuring your data is saved and accessible will prevent data loss and improve your ability to manage large datasets.

When it comes to SQL, the foundation you build here will serve you well across many database platforms. Practice creating and manipulating databases and tables, as these skills are fundamental. Pay special attention to different join types, as these will allow you to combine datasets in meaningful ways, unlocking deeper analytical possibilities. These skills will enable you to perform complex analyses and extract valuable insights from your data, driving better decision making.

In the next chapter, you'll learn how to use DuckDB with Polars, a DataFrame library that is designed to be fast and efficient.

## CHAPTER 4

Using DuckDB with Polars

Most data scientists and data analysts are familiar with the pandas library. With pandas, you can organize your dataset into Series or DataFrame structures and employ the diverse array of functions provided by the pandas library for data manipulation. However, one of the main complaints about pandas is its slow speed and inefficiencies when dealing with large datasets. This is because pandas was originally designed to work with tabular data that fits in memory. When dealing with large datasets, it becomes slow because it needs to swap data in and out of memory.

To address the inefficiencies of pandas in working with large datasets, there is a competing library—Polars. The first part of this chapter provides an introduction to Polars and how you can work with it (just like with pandas). The second part of this chapter shows how you can query Polars DataFrames using DuckDB.

Introduction to Polars

Polars is a DataFrame library that is completely written in Rust. Polars is designed with the following in mind:

Speed
Polars leverages Rust, a system programming language known for its performance.

Parallelism
Polars can take advantage of multicore processors, which provide substantial speed improvements for CPU-bound operations.

Memory efficiency
> Polars uses lazy evaluation, which means an operation is not performed until it is needed. In addition, queries can be chained and optimized before execution, resulting in much more efficient execution.

Efficient storage of data
> Polars stores data in columnar format, which is more efficient than the row-based storage in pandas.

Ease of use
> Polars supports a SQL-like syntax for data manipulation, making it immediately accessible to a large group of users. In addition, it has many methods that are similar to pandas, making it very easy for pandas users to migrate to.

To install Polars, use the `pip` command:

```
!pip install polars
```

The version of Polars used in this book is 1.8.2.

In the following sections, you'll learn how to get started with the Polars library and understand the magic behind the efficiencies of Polars—lazy evaluation.

Creating a Polars DataFrame

Let's start off with the basics. Let's create a Polars DataFrame using a Python dictionary. The following code snippet creates a Polars DataFrame containing six columns and eight rows (see Figure 4-1):

```
import polars as pl

df = pl.DataFrame(
    {
        'Model': ['Camry','Corolla','RAV4',
                  'Mustang','F-150','Escape',
                  'Golf','Tiguan'],
        'Year': [1982,1966,1994,1964,1975,2000,1974,2007],
        'Engine_Min':[2.5,1.8,2.0,2.3,2.7,1.5,1.0,1.4],
        'Engine_Max':[3.5,2.0,2.5,5.0,5.0,2.5,2.0,2.0],
        'AWD':[False,False,True,False,True,True,True,True],
        'Company': ['Toyota','Toyota','Toyota','Ford',
                    'Ford','Ford','Volkswagen','Volkswagen'],
    }
)
df
```

shape: (8, 6)

Model	Year	Engine_Min	Engine_Max	AWD	Company
str	i64	f64	f64	bool	str
"Camry"	1982	2.5	3.5	false	"Toyota"
"Corolla"	1966	1.8	2.0	false	"Toyota"
"RAV4"	1994	2.0	2.5	true	"Toyota"
"Mustang"	1964	2.3	5.0	false	"Ford"
"F-150"	1975	2.7	5.0	true	"Ford"
"Escape"	2000	1.5	2.5	true	"Ford"
"Golf"	1974	1.0	2.0	true	"Volkswagen"
"Tiguan"	2007	1.4	2.0	true	"Volkswagen"

Figure 4-1. The Polars DataFrame containing six columns and eight rows

 Just like pandas, Jupyter Notebook will pretty-print the Polars DataFrame when you print it out.

If you observe the output, you should find it similar to a pandas DataFrame, except:

- A Polars DataFrame does not have an index. This is one of the design philosophies behind Polars: the index in a DataFrame is not useful and seldom needed.
- Below the headers of the DataFrame, Polars displays the data type of each column (str, i64, f64, and bool)

To display the full name of the data type of each column in the Polars DataFrame, use the dtypes property:

```
df.dtypes
```

For the DataFrame in Figure 4-1, this statement displays the following result:

```
[String, Int64, Float64, Float64, Boolean, String]
```

To get the column names, use the columns property:

```
df.columns
# ['Model', 'Year', 'Engine_Min', 'Engine_Max', 'AWD', 'Company']
```

If you want to get all the rows of the DataFrame, use the rows() method:

```
df.rows()
```

The rows are returned as a list of tuples:

```
[('Camry', 1982, 2.5, 3.5, False, 'Toyota'),
 ('Corolla', 1966, 1.8, 2.0, False, 'Toyota'),
 ('RAV4', 1994, 2.0, 2.5, True, 'Toyota'),
 ('Mustang', 1964, 2.3, 5.0, False, 'Ford'),
 ('F-150', 1975, 2.7, 5.0, True, 'Ford'),
 ('Escape', 2000, 1.5, 2.5, True, 'Ford'),
 ('Golf', 1974, 1.0, 2.0, True, 'Volkswagen'),
 ('Tiguan', 2007, 1.4, 2.0, True, 'Volkswagen')]
```

With the DataFrame loaded, the next few sections will show you how to select parts (such as columns and rows) of the DataFrame.

Selecting columns

To select a particular column in the DataFrame, use the select() method:

```
df.select(
    'Model'
)
```

This returns the column named Model (see Figure 4-2).

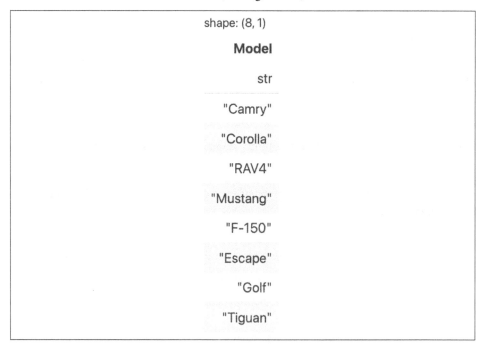

Figure 4-2. The DataFrame with the Model column printed

If you're familiar with pandas, you might be wondering if the square bracket indexing method still works. Well, df['Model'] works just like using the select() method. However, the Polars documentation specifically mentions that the square bracket indexing method is an anti-pattern for Polars because it is sometimes confusing. So, while df['Model'] works, there is a possibility that the square bracket indexing method may be removed in a future version of Polars.

If you need to retrieve more than one column, enclose the column names in a list (or simply specify the additional column names):

```
df.select(
    ['Model','Company']  # or 'Model','Company'
)
```

If you want to retrieve all the string columns (that is, columns of type pl.String) in the DataFrame, you can use an expression within the select() method:

```
df.select(
    pl.col(pl.String)
)
```

The statement pl.col(pl.String) is known as an *expression* in Polars. You can interpret this expression as "get me all the columns whose data type is String".

This statement prints out the Model and Company columns (see Figure 4-3).

shape: (8, 2)

Model	Company
str	str
"Camry"	"Toyota"
"Corolla"	"Toyota"
"RAV4"	"Toyota"
"Mustang"	"Ford"
"F-150"	"Ford"
"Escape"	"Ford"
"Golf"	"Volkswagen"
"Tiguan"	"Volkswagen"

Figure 4-3. The DataFrame with the Model and Company columns printed

Expressions are powerful in Polars. For example, you can pipe together multiple expressions:

```
df.select(
    pl.col(['Year','Model','Engine_Max'])
    .sort_by(['Engine_Max','Year'],descending = [False,True])
)
```

In this code snippet, the first expression selects the three columns Year, Model, and Engine_Max. The result of the first expression is then piped to the second expression, which sorts the column Engine_Max in ascending order and the Year column in descending order. The result is shown in Figure 4-4.

shape: (8, 3)

Year	Model	Engine_Max
i64	str	f64
2007	"Tiguan"	2.0
1974	"Golf"	2.0
1966	"Corolla"	2.0
2000	"Escape"	2.5
1994	"RAV4"	2.5
1982	"Camry"	3.5
1975	"F-150"	5.0
1964	"Mustang"	5.0

Figure 4-4. The DataFrame with the Year, Model, *and* Engine_Max *columns printed*

You can also group multiple expressions in a list. For example the following code snippet lists all the string columns plus the Year column:

```
df.select(
    [pl.col(pl.String), 'Year']
)
```

Selecting rows

If you want to get a particular row in a Polars DataFrame, you can use the row() method and pass in a row number. For example, the following statement retrieves the first row in the table:

```
df.row(0)
# ('Camry', 1982, 2.5, 3.5, False, 'Toyota')
```

If you want to get multiple rows, you can use the square bracket indexing method, though this is not recommended:

```
df[1:3]  # returns the second and third rows
```

 Instead of using square bracket indexing, Polars encourages the use of more explicit forms of querying and functions to manipulate data. In the real world, you often retrieve rows based on certain criteria, instead of specific row numbers. Despite this, Polars still provides support for square bracket indexing (at least for now).

Like pandas, Polars supports common methods like head(), tail(), and sample().

To select rows, Polars recommends using the `filter()` method. For example, if you want to select all the rows that contains cars from Toyota, use the `filter()` method with the following expression:

```
df.filter(
    pl.col('Company') == 'Toyota'
)
```

Figure 4-5 shows all rows containing cars from Toyota.

shape: (3, 6)

Model	Year	Engine_Min	Engine_Max	AWD	Company
str	i64	f64	f64	bool	str
"Camry"	1982	2.5	3.5	false	"Toyota"
"Corolla"	1966	1.8	2.0	false	"Toyota"
"RAV4"	1994	2.0	2.5	true	"Toyota"

Figure 4-5. The DataFrame contains all the cars from Toyota

You can also specify multiple conditions using logical operators. The following example retrieves all cars that are from Toyota or Ford:

```
df.filter(
    (pl.col('Company') == 'Toyota') |
    (pl.col('Company') == 'Ford')
)
```

 Remember to use a pair of parentheses to enclose each condition.

If you want to match multiple brands of cars, it is easier to use the `is_in()` method:

```
df.filter(
    (pl.col('Company').is_in(['Toyota','Ford']))
)
```

The following example retrieves all cars from Toyota that were launched after 1980:

```
df.filter(
    (pl.col('Company') == 'Toyota') &
    (pl.col('Year') > 1980)
)
```

The following example retrieves all the cars other than Toyota:

```
df.filter(
    ~(pl.col('Company') == 'Toyota')
)
```

Alternatively, you can also use the != operator:

```
df.filter(
    (pl.col('Company') != 'Toyota')
)
```

Selecting rows and columns

Now that you have seen how to use the `select()` method to select columns and the `filter()` method to select rows from a Polars DataFrame, let's see how you can chain them together to select specific rows and columns.

For example, if you want to get all the various models from Toyota, you can chain the `filter()` and `select()` methods:

```
df.filter(
    pl.col('Company') == 'Toyota'
).select(
    'Model'
)
```

This code snippet prints out all the models from Toyota (see Figure 4-6).

shape: (3, 1)
Model
str
"Camry"
"Corolla"
"RAV4"

Figure 4-6. The DataFrame contains all the models from Toyota

If you want to select multiple columns, simply contain the column names using a list:

```
df.filter(
    pl.col('Company') == 'Toyota'
).select(
    ['Model','Year']
)
```

Using SQL on Polars

While you can use the various methods in Polars to select rows and columns from the DataFrame, you can also use SQL to directly query a Polars DataFrame. This is done through the `SQLContext` class. In Polars, `SQLContext` provides a way to execute SQL statements against Polars DataFrames using SQL syntax.

Here is an example:

```
ctx = pl.SQLContext(cars = df)
ctx.execute("SELECT * FROM cars", eager=True)
```

`SQLContext` takes a named parameter (`cars` in this case) with its value set to the Polars DataFrame. You use the `SQLContext` object to execute the SQL statement against the Polars DataFrame. Figure 4-7 shows the result returned by the SQL statement.

shape: (8, 6)

Model	Year	Engine_Min	Engine_Max	AWD	Company
str	i64	f64	f64	bool	str
"Camry"	1982	2.5	3.5	false	"Toyota"
"Corolla"	1966	1.8	2.0	false	"Toyota"
"RAV4"	1994	2.0	2.5	true	"Toyota"
"Mustang"	1964	2.3	5.0	false	"Ford"
"F-150"	1975	2.7	5.0	true	"Ford"
"Escape"	2000	1.5	2.5	true	"Ford"
"Golf"	1974	1.0	2.0	true	"Volkswagen"
"Tiguan"	2007	1.4	2.0	true	"Volkswagen"

Figure 4-7. The result of the SQL query

Here's another example using SQL to find the average minimum and maximum engine capacities for each company:

```
ctx.execute('''
    SELECT Company,
           AVG(Engine_Min) AS avg_engine_min,
           AVG(Engine_Max) AS avg_engine_max
    FROM cars
    GROUP BY Company;
''', eager=True)
```

Figure 4-8 shows the output of this query.

shape: (3, 3)

Company	avg_engine_min	avg_engine_max
str	f64	f64
"Toyota"	2.1	2.666667
"Volkswagen"	1.2	2.0
"Ford"	2.166667	4.166667

Figure 4-8. The average minimum and maximum engine capacities of each company's cars

Up to this point, you have seen the techniques to select rows and columns from a Polars DataFrame. But you have not seen the most compelling reason to use Polars yet—lazy evaluation. In the next section, you'll see how Polars uses this technique to improve performance when manipulating DataFrames.

Understanding Lazy Evaluation in Polars

One of the key features of Polars is its support for lazy evaluation. Lazy evaluation is a technique that allows for the construction of query plans that represent a sequence of operations without immediately executing them. Rather, the operations are executed only when the final result is explicitly requested. This approach makes it very efficient when dealing with large datasets or complex transformations because it avoids unnecessary computations.

To really understand why this efficiency measure is so important, you need to first understand how things are done in pandas. In pandas, you usually use the read_csv() function to read a CSV file into a pandas DataFrame:

```
import pandas as pd

df = pd.read_csv('flights.csv')
df
```

If your CSV file is large, you will spend a long time (and a lot of memory) to load all the rows in the CSV file into the pandas DataFrame. The *flights.csv* file has more than 5.8 million rows; hence it takes a significant amount of memory to load the entire file into memory (see Figure 4-9).

	YEAR	MONTH	DAY	DAY_OF_WEEK	AIRLINE	FLIGHT_NUMBER	TAIL_NUMBER	ORIGIN_AIRPORT	DESTINATI
0	2015	1	1	4	AS	98	N407AS	ANC	
1	2015	1	1	4	AA	2336	N3KUAA	LAX	
2	2015	1	1	4	US	840	N171US	SFO	
3	2015	1	1	4	AA	258	N3HYAA	LAX	
4	2015	1	1	4	AS	135	N527AS	SEA	
...	...	...	...	...	...	...	...	...	
5819074	2015	12	31	4	B6	688	N657JB	LAX	
5819075	2015	12	31	4	B6	745	N828JB	JFK	
5819076	2015	12	31	4	B6	1503	N913JB	JFK	
5819077	2015	12	31	4	B6	333	N527JB	MCO	
5819078	2015	12	31	4	B6	839	N534JB	JFK	

5819079 rows × 31 columns

Figure 4-9. Loading a large CSV file using pandas

A typical operation with pandas is to load the CSV file into a DataFrame and then perform some filtering on it:

```
df = pd.read_csv('flights.csv')
df = df[(df['MONTH'] == 5) &
        (df['ORIGIN_AIRPORT'] == 'SFO') &
        (df['DESTINATION_AIRPORT'] == 'SEA')]
df
```

This is inefficient because you must load the entire CSV file into memory only to filter out a subset of it. In Polars, there is a much more efficient way of loading a DataFrame, known as lazy evaluation. There are two types of lazy evaluation:

Implicit lazy evaluation
> This is where you use functions that inherently support lazy evaluation (such as the scan_csv() function, which you'll see in the next section).

Explicit lazy evaluation
> This is where you use functions that do not inherently support lazy evaluation (such as the read_csv() function), and you explicitly make them use lazy evaluation.

Let's dig a little deeper into each of these.

Implicit lazy evaluation

To understand how lazy evaluation works, let's walk through an example. Instead of using the read_csv() function (which also works with Polars), you use the scan_csv() function:

```
import polars as pl

q = pl.scan_csv('flights.csv')
type(q)
```

The scan_csv() function returns an object of type polars.lazyframe.frame.Lazy Frame, which is a representation of a lazy computation graph/query against a Data-Frame. Put simply, when you use the scan_csv() function to load a CSV file, the contents of the CSV file are not loaded immediately. Instead, the function waits for further queries so that it can optimize the entire set of queries before loading the contents of the CSV file.

Contrast this with using the read_csv() function to load a CSV file in Polars:

```
df = pl.read_csv('flights.csv')
type(df)
```

The read_csv() function returns a polars.dataframe.frame.DataFrame object, which is similar to a pandas DataFrame. However, unlike the scan_csv() method, the read_csv() method uses *eager* execution mode, which means that it will immediately load the entire dataset into the DataFrame before you perform any other queries.

Once you have obtained a LazyFrame object, you can apply your queries to it:

```
q = pl.scan_csv('flights.csv')
q = q.select(['MONTH', 'ORIGIN_AIRPORT','DESTINATION_AIRPORT'])
q = q.filter(
    (pl.col('MONTH') == 5) &
    (pl.col('ORIGIN_AIRPORT') == 'SFO') &
    (pl.col('DESTINATION_AIRPORT') == 'SEA'))
```

 The select() and filter() methods work on Polars DataFrames as well as on LazyFrame objects.

For readability, you should ideally use a pair of parentheses to chain up the various methods in Polars:

```
q = (
    pl.scan_csv('flights.csv')
    .select(['MONTH', 'ORIGIN_AIRPORT','DESTINATION_AIRPORT'])
    .filter(
        (pl.col('MONTH') == 5) &
        (pl.col('ORIGIN_AIRPORT') == 'SFO') &
        (pl.col('DESTINATION_AIRPORT') == 'SEA'))
)
```

You can call the show_graph() method to show the execution graph:

```
q.show_graph(optimized=True)
```

Figure 4-10 shows the execution graph of your query. You can see that it first scans the CSV file (top of the graph), and then performs a filter (bottom of the graph).

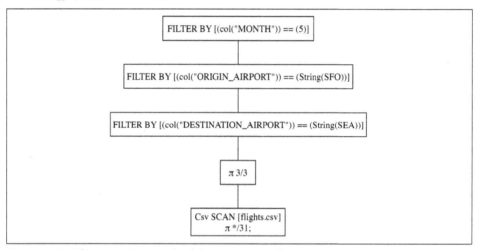

Figure 4-10. The execution graph of the optimized query

In contrast, if you call the show_graph() method with the optimized argument set to False, you will see that it performs a scan of the CSV file, loads all 31 columns, and only then performs the filter one-by-one (see Figure 4-11):

```
q.show_graph(optimized=False)
```

Figure 4-11. The execution graph of the unoptimized query

 By default, show_graph() prints out the query in its optimized format. However, if you print out the q object, it displays the graph in non-optimized mode.

To execute the queries, call the collect() method:

```
q.collect()
```

The collect() method returns the result of the queries as a Polars DataFrame (see Figure 4-12).

```
shape: (674, 3)
```

MONTH	ORIGIN_AIRPORT	DESTINATION_AIRPORT
i64	str	str
5	"SFO"	"SEA"
5	"SFO"	"SEA"
5	"SFO"	"SEA"
5	"SFO"	"SEA"
5	"SFO"	"SEA"
…	…	…
5	"SFO"	"SEA"
5	"SFO"	"SEA"
5	"SFO"	"SEA"
5	"SFO"	"SEA"
5	"SFO"	"SEA"

Figure 4-12. The DataFrame returned by the `collect()` *method*

Explicit lazy evaluation

Earlier I mentioned that if you use the `read_csv()` function to read a CSV file, Polars will use eager execution and immediately load the DataFrame. Consider the following code snippet:

```
df = (
    pl.read_csv('flights.csv')
    .select(['MONTH', 'ORIGIN_AIRPORT','DESTINATION_AIRPORT'])
    .filter(
        (pl.col('MONTH') == 5) &
        (pl.col('ORIGIN_AIRPORT') == 'SFO') &
        (pl.col('DESTINATION_AIRPORT') == 'SEA'))
    )
df
```

Observe that after loading the CSV file, we perform a selection of columns followed by filtering of rows. All these queries are cascaded and are performed one after another. This is because the `read_csv()` function does not implicitly support lazy evaluation.

To ensure that all the subsequent queries after the CSV is loaded can be optimized, use the `lazy()` method immediately after the `read_csv()` function to explicitly indicate that you want the `read_csv()` function to use lazy evaluation:

```
q = (
    pl.read_csv('flights.csv')
    .lazy()
    .select(['MONTH', 'ORIGIN_AIRPORT','DESTINATION_AIRPORT'])
    .filter(
```

```
            (pl.col('MONTH') == 5) &
            (pl.col('ORIGIN_AIRPORT') == 'SFO') &
            (pl.col('DESTINATION_AIRPORT') == 'SEA'))
    )
df = q.collect()
display(df)
```

The lazy() function returns a LazyFrame object, and with that you can chain further queries using methods such as select(), filter(), and so on. All the queries will now be optimized before execution.

Now that you are familiar with the basics of Polars, it's time to see how it can be used together with DuckDB so that we can have the best of both worlds: the ability to harness the efficiency of the Polars database, together with the use of SQL for querying the dataset.

Querying Polars DataFrames Using DuckDB

Despite the ease of use, manipulating Polars DataFrames still requires a bit of practice and has a relatively steep learning curve for beginners. But since most developers are already familiar with SQL, isn't it more convenient to manipulate the DataFrames directly using SQL? Using this approach, developers have the best of both worlds:

- The ability to query Polars DataFrames using all the various functions.
- The ability to use SQL for cases where it is much more natural and easier to extract the data that they want.

The good news is that DuckDB has support for Polars DataFrames through Apache Arrow. This means that you can use SQL to directly query a Polars DataFrame.

 Apache Arrow is a development platform for in-memory analytics. It contains a set of technologies that enable big data systems to store, process, and move data quickly. PyArrow is the Python implementation of Arrow.

Using the sql() Function

Let's now cover how you can use DuckDB to query a Polars DataFrame. For this, we'll use the Polars DataFrame that we created earlier:

```
import polars as pl
df = pl.DataFrame(
    {
        'Model': ['Camry','Corolla','RAV4',
                  'Mustang','F-150','Escape',
                  'Golf','Tiguan'],
        'Year': [1982,1966,1994,1964,1975,2000,1974,2007],
        'Engine_Min':[2.5,1.8,2.0,2.3,2.7,1.5,1.0,1.4],
```

```
        'Engine_Max':[3.5,2.0,2.5,5.0,5.0,2.5,2.0,2.0],
        'AWD':[False,False,True,False,True,True,True,True],
        'Company': ['Toyota','Toyota','Toyota','Ford',
                    'Ford','Ford','Volkswagen','Volkswagen'],
    }
)
```

To use DuckDB to query a Polars DataFrame, you need to install the PyArrow library:

```
pip install pyarrow
```

 You can perform the installation either in Jupyter Notebook or in Terminal/Command Prompt. In Jupyter Notebook, after the installation, remember to restart the kernel.

To select all the rows from df, use the sql() function from the duckdb module:

```
import duckdb

result = duckdb.sql('''
    SELECT *
    FROM df
''')
result
```

The sql() function returns a duckdb.DuckDBPyRelation object, which is displayed as a table when printed in Jupyter Notebook (see Figure 4-13).

Model varchar	Year int64	Engine_Min double	Engine_Max double	AWD boolean	Company varchar
Camry	1982	2.5	3.5	false	Toyota
Corolla	1966	1.8	2.0	false	Toyota
RAV4	1994	2.0	2.5	true	Toyota
Mustang	1964	2.3	5.0	false	Ford
F-150	1975	2.7	5.0	true	Ford
Escape	2000	1.5	2.5	true	Ford
Golf	1974	1.0	2.0	true	Volkswagen
Tiguan	2007	1.4	2.0	true	Volkswagen

Figure 4-13. The result from the sql() function is displayed as a table in Jupyter Notebook

A DuckDBPyRelation object is part of DuckDB's Relational API, which can be used to construct queries. Later in this chapter, we'll discuss this object in more detail.

To convert the `DuckDBPyRelation` object to a Polars DataFrame, use the `pl()` method:

```
result.pl()
```

 To convert the `DuckDBPyRelation` object to a pandas DataFrame, use the `df()` method.

With the `DuckDBPyRelation` object, you can perform several tasks. For example, you can use the `describe()` method to generate some basic statistics (e.g., min, max, median, count) for each column in the DataFrame:

```
result.describe()
```

The result of `describe()` is yet another `DuckDBPyRelation` object, which you can convert to a Polars or pandas DataFrame if you wish.

Figure 4-14 shows the output of the `describe()` method when called on the `result` object.

aggr varchar	Model varchar	Year double	Engine_Min double	Engine_Max double	AWD varchar	Company varchar
count	8	8.0	8.0	8.0	8	8
mean	NULL	1982.75	1.9000000000000001	3.0625	NULL	NULL
stddev	NULL	15.953056133543761	0.5855400437691198	1.293872923766914	NULL	NULL
min	Camry	1964.0	1.0	2.0	false	Ford
max	Tiguan	2007.0	2.7	5.0	true	Volkswagen
median	NULL	1978.5	1.9	2.5	NULL	NULL

Figure 4-14. The output from the `describe()` method

You can sort the result using the `order()` method:

```
result.order('Year')
```

In this example, the result is sorted by year in ascending order (see Figure 4-15).

Model varchar	Year int64	Engine_Min double	Engine_Max double	AWD boolean	Company varchar
Mustang	1964	2.3	5.0	false	Ford
Corolla	1966	1.8	2.0	false	Toyota
Golf	1974	1.0	2.0	true	Volkswagen
F-150	1975	2.7	5.0	true	Ford
Camry	1982	2.5	3.5	false	Toyota
RAV4	1994	2.0	2.5	true	Toyota
Escape	2000	1.5	2.5	true	Ford
Tiguan	2007	1.4	2.0	true	Volkswagen

Figure 4-15. The output when sorted by year

If you want to sort by year in descending order, use the DESC keyword:

```
result.order('Year DESC')
```

You can use the apply() method to apply a function to a particular column, such as if you want to get the minimum value in the Year column:

```
result.apply('min', 'Year')
```

Figure 4-16 shows the output.

min("Year") int64
1964

Figure 4-16. Getting the minimum value in the Year column

While you can use the various methods from the DuckDBPyRelation object to extract data, there are always instances where it is easier to accomplish the same task using SQL. For example, say you want to sort the rows based on company followed by model. It would be very easy to accomplish this using SQL:

```
duckdb.sql('''
    SELECT Company, Model
    FROM df
    ORDER by Company, Model
''').pl()
```

Figure 4-17 shows the result of this query.

Company	Model
str	str
"Ford"	"Escape"
"Ford"	"F-150"
"Ford"	"Mustang"
"Toyota"	"Camry"
"Toyota"	"Corolla"
"Toyota"	"RAV4"
"Volkswagen"	"Golf"
"Volkswagen"	"Tiguan"

shape: (8, 2)

Figure 4-17. Sorting the output by company and model using SQL

Or, if you want to count the number of models for each company, you can use the SQL GROUP BY statement:

```
duckdb.sql('''
    SELECT Company, count(Model) as count
    FROM df
    GROUP BY Company
''').pl()
```

Figure 4-18 shows the output of this query.

Company	count
str	i64
"Toyota"	3
"Ford"	3
"Volkswagen"	2

shape: (3, 2)

Figure 4-18. Using GROUP BY to count the number of models for each company

You can perform the same query in Polars using the following statement:

```
result.pl().select(
    pl.col('Company').value_counts()
).unnest('Company')
```

In the next section, you'll learn more about the DuckDBPyRelation object and how you can use it to perform various DataFrame operations.

Using the DuckDBPyRelation Object

In the previous sections, you saw several mentions of the DuckDBPyRelation object. This object represents an alternative way for you to construct queries to extract data from your databases. Typically, you create DuckDBPyRelation objects from SQL queries or directly from a connection object.

Let's first create a DuckDB connection and then use the connection to create three tables: *customers*, *products*, and *sales*.

The following code snippet shows how this is done:

```
import duckdb

conn = duckdb.connect()

conn.execute('''
    CREATE TABLE customers
    (customer_id INTEGER PRIMARY KEY, name STRING)
''')

conn.execute('''
    CREATE TABLE products
    (product_id INTEGER PRIMARY KEY, product_name STRING)
''')

conn.execute('''
    CREATE TABLE sales
    (customer_id INTEGER, product_id INTEGER, qty INTEGER,
     PRIMARY KEY(customer_id,product_id))
''')
```

Now that the tables are created in DuckDB, you can load a specific table using the table() method from the conn object:

```
customers_relation = conn.table('customers')
```

The result from the `table()` method is a `duckdb.DuckDBPyRelation` object. As you learned earlier in this chapter, you can convert this object to a pandas or Polars DataFrame:

```
# convert to a pandas DataFrame
customers_relation.df()
```

```
# convert to a Polars DataFrame
customers_relation.pl()
```

Inserting rows

Using the `DuckDBPyRelation` object, you can call the `insert()` function to insert a new row into the table. The following code snippet inserts three rows into the *customers* table:

```
customers_relation.insert([1, 'Alice'])
customers_relation.insert([2, 'Bob'])
customers_relation.insert([3, 'Charlie'])
```

At the same time, let's also insert rows into the *products* and *sales* tables:

```
products_relation = conn.table('products')
products_relation.insert([10, 'Paperclips'])
products_relation.insert([20, 'Staple'])
products_relation.insert([30, 'Notebook'])

sales_relation = conn.table("sales")
sales_relation.insert([1,20,1])
sales_relation.insert([1,10,2])
sales_relation.insert([2,30,7])
sales_relation.insert([3,10,3])
sales_relation.insert([3,20,2])
```

Joining tables

Now that we have three `DuckDBPyRelation` objects representing the three tables, we can perform joins between the tables using the `join()` method:

```
result = customers_relation.join(
    sales_relation,
    condition = "customer_id",
    how = "inner"
).join(
    products_relation,
    condition = "product_id",
    how = "inner"
)
```

In this code snippet, the *customers* table is joined to the *sales* table, and the result is then joined with the *products* table.

To see the resultant table after the joins, simply print out the value of `result`. Figure 4-19 shows the result.

customer_id int32	name varchar	product_id int32	qty int32	product_name varchar
1	Alice	20	1	Staple
1	Alice	10	2	Paperclips
2	Bob	30	7	Notebook
3	Charlie	10	3	Paperclips
3	Charlie	20	2	Staple

Figure 4-19. The output of the join operation

Filtering rows

After you have performed a join on the tables, you can use the result to extract the rows that you want using the `filter()` method:

```
result.filter('customer_id = 1')
```

Figure 4-20 shows the products bought by Alice (customer ID 1).

customer_id int32	name varchar	product_id int32	qty int32	product_name varchar
1	Alice	10	2	Paperclips
1	Alice	20	1	Staple

Figure 4-20. The result shows the products bought by Alice

Alternatively, you can use the `execute()` method and pass in a SQL statement:

```
# execute a query on the result to fetch and print the joined data
conn.execute('''
    SELECT *
    FROM result
    WHERE customer_id = 1
''').pl()
```

Aggregating rows

You can also perform aggregation using a `DuckDBPyRelation` object. Suppose you want to sum up the purchases for all customers. You can use the `aggregate()` method like this:

```
result.aggregate('customer_id, MAX(name) AS Name, ' +
                 'SUM(qty) as "Total Qty"',
                 'customer_id')
```

The first argument takes in an aggregate expression, while the second argument takes in a group expression. The result is shown in Figure 4-21.

customer_id int32	Name varchar	Total Qty int128
1	Alice	3
2	Bob	7
3	Charlie	5

Figure 4-21. The total quantity of items bought by each customer

This aggregate function is identical to the following GROUP BY statement:

```
SELECT customer_id as 'Customer ID', MAX(name) AS Name,
       sum(qty) as 'Total Qty'
FROM result
GROUP BY customer_id
```

Projecting columns

Using the DuckDBPyRelation object, you can select specific columns to display using the project() method:

```
result.project('name, qty, product_name')
```

This statement displays the three columns—name, qty, and product_name—in the result (see Figure 4-22).

name varchar	qty int32	product_name varchar
Alice	1	Staple
Alice	2	Paperclips
Bob	7	Notebook
Charlie	3	Paperclips
Charlie	2	Staple

Figure 4-22. Displaying specific columns using the project() method

Limiting rows

To limit the number of rows returned, use the limit() method:

```
result.limit(3)
```

Figure 4-23 shows the first three rows in the result object.

customer_id int32	name varchar	product_id int32	qty int32	product_name varchar
1	Alice	20	1	Staple
1	Alice	10	2	Paperclips
2	Bob	30	7	Notebook

Figure 4-23. Use the `limit()` method to specify the number of rows to return

If you want to start with the third row and display the next three rows, specify the number of rows to display, followed by the offset:

```
result.limit(3,2)  # display 3 rows, starting at offset 2 (third row)
```

The result is shown in Figure 4-24.

customer_id int32	name varchar	product_id int32	qty int32	product_name varchar
2	Bob	30	7	Notebook
3	Charlie	10	3	Paperclips
3	Charlie	20	2	Staple

Figure 4-24. Displaying three rows, starting from offset 2 (third row)

Summary

In this chapter, you have learned about the Polars DataFrame library, including the basics of extracting rows and columns, followed by an explanation of how lazy evaluation works in Polars. More importantly, you also learned how DuckDB and Polars can be used together to query DataFrames. Utilizing both libraries gives you the best of both worlds—you can manipulate your data using methods that you are already familiar with and you can use a familiar querying language (SQL) to query an efficient DataFrame.

In the next chapter, you'll learn how to perform exploratory data analysis with DuckDB using a real-world dataset!

## CHAPTER 5

Performing EDA with DuckDB

By this point, you should have a pretty good grip on the basics of DuckDB. You have seen how to load up your DuckDB databases from data stored in file formats such as CSV and Parquet, and have also learned how to load it up from database servers, such as MySQL. In this chapter, we'll apply DuckDB in practical scenarios, utilizing it for conducting exploratory data analysis.

EDA is an approach to analyzing and visualizing datasets to summarize their main characteristics. The key goal of EDA is to understand the patterns, trends, and relationships within the data. In EDA, we often use the following techniques on our data:

Data summarization
    Uses descriptive statistics (such as mean, median, standard deviation, and more) to understand the distribution of the dataset.

Data visualization
    Uses libraries such as Matplotlib and Seaborn to plot various types of charts (such as bar charts, pie charts, and more) to visually inspect the distribution of data and the relationships between different types of data.

Trends identification
    Identifies the patterns, trends, and anomalies within the data and provides insights into potential factors affecting these observations.

In this chapter, you will learn how to use DuckDB to explore and visualize the 2015 Flight Delays dataset. In particular, you will learn about *geospatial analysis*, where you will learn how to:

- Display a map
- Display all the airports on a map

- Use the `spatial` extension in DuckDB
- Convert latitude and longitude to the `Point` data type
- Find nearby airports

You will also perform *descriptive analytics*, where you will learn how to:

- Find the airports for each state and city
- Aggregate the total number of airports in each state
- Obtain the flight counts for each pair of origin and destination airports
- Get the canceled flights from airlines
- Get the flight count for each day of the week
- Find the most common timeslot for flight delays
- Find the airlines with the most and fewest delays

Let's start by loading our dataset.

Our Dataset: The 2015 Flight Delays Dataset

For consistency reasons, we will be using the 2015 Flight Delays and Cancellations dataset that you saw in Chapter 2 for all the examples in this chapter. If you recall, this dataset contains three CSV files:

airlines.csv
> A list of American airlines

airports.csv
> A list of airports in the US

flights.csv
> A list of flight details for the various airlines in 2015

We'll be loading these three CSV files into our DuckDB database. So let's start by creating a DuckDB connection:

```
import duckdb
conn = duckdb.connect()
```

Once the connection is created, let's load the three CSV files into the DuckDB database. First, load the *flights.csv* file:

```
conn.execute('''
    CREATE TABLE flights
    as
    SELECT
        *
```

```
        FROM read_csv_auto('flights.csv')
    ''')
```

Then, load the *airports.csv* file:

```
conn.execute('''
    CREATE TABLE airports
    as
    SELECT
        *
    FROM read_csv_auto('airports.csv')
''')
```

And, finally, the *airlines.csv* file:

```
conn.execute('''
    CREATE TABLE airlines
    as
    SELECT
        *
    FROM read_csv('airlines.csv')
''')
```

You now should have three tables in your DuckDB database. You can confirm this by
using the following statement:

```
display(conn.execute('SHOW TABLES').df())
```

Figure 5-1 shows the three tables in the database.

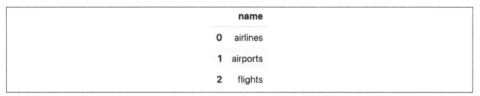

Figure 5-1. The three tables in the DuckDB database

With the three tables loaded, let's start performing some geospatial analysis using the
airports table. The next section will demonstrate how to plot the locations of each airport on a map, as well as how to use the `spatial` extension in DuckDB to work with
geospatial data.

Geospatial Analysis

Geospatial analysis—also known as *spatial analysis* or *geographic information system
(GIS) analysis*—is a field of study that involves examining, interpreting, and visualizing spatial data to understand patterns, relationships, and trends within geographical
areas. A common use case for geospatial analysis is in urban planning and transportation. For example, a city's public transportation department wants to optimize bus
routes to improve efficiency and reduce travel time. To achieve this, they use geospatial analysis to analyze the city's bus stops, traffic patterns, and population density.

Since the *airports* table contains locations of airports, this is a good time for us to do some geospatial analysis.

Let's plot the location of each airport on a map. This would be useful for us to visualize the geolocation of each airport on the map. For this purpose, we will use the *folium* library, a Python wrapper for the *leaflet.js* library, which is a JavaScript library for plotting interactive maps. Using folium, you can now easily add geospatial visualization to your Python projects, directly in a Jupyter Notebook.

To install folium, use the `pip` command in Jupyter Notebook:

```
!pip install folium
```

Once the library is installed, you are ready to display a map. The following few sections will show you how to use folium to display a map and then add markers to it.

Displaying a Map

Let's first display a map using folium. For this, we want to position the US at the center of the map, and so we select a latitude and longitude of 47.116386 and -101.299591, respectively, and then pass those values to the `Map` class of the folium library:

```
import folium

mymap = folium.Map(location = [47.116386, -101.299591],
                   width = 950,
                   height = 550,
                   zoom_start = 3,
                   tiles = 'openstreetmap')
mymap
```

Figure 5-2 shows the United States in the center of the map.

In this code snippet, observe the following:

- You set the location using the `location` parameter and pass in the latitude and longitude using a list.
- You set the size of the map using the `width` and `height` parameters.
- The `zoom_start` parameter sets the initial zoom level of the map; the higher the number, the more zoomed in the map is.
- The `tiles` parameter specifies the *tileset* (a collection of map tiles that are used to create a continuous map display) to use; the default is `openstreetmap`.

Figure 5-2. Displaying the United States in the center of the folium map

For the `tiles` parameter, besides `openstreetmap` you can use one of the following built-in tilesets:

- cartodbpositron
- cartodbdark_matter

Instead of fixing the map to use a particular tileset through the `tiles` parameter, you can add different tilesets to the map using the `TileLayerclass`. The following statements in bold add two tilesets to the current map:

```
import folium
mymap = folium.Map(location = [47.116386, -101.299591],
                   width = 950,
                   height = 550,
                   zoom_start = 3,
                   tiles = 'openstreetmap')

folium.TileLayer('cartodbpositron',
                 attr = 'cartodbpositron',
                 show = False).add_to(mymap)
folium.TileLayer('cartodbdark_matter',
                 attr = 'cartodbdark_matter',
                 show = False).add_to(mymap)

folium.LayerControl().add_to(mymap)

mymap
```

You can switch between the different tilesets by clicking the tiles icon at the top right corner of the map (see Figure 5-3) and selecting the one that you want to display.

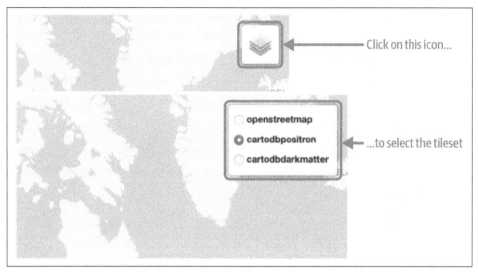

Figure 5-3. Selecting the tileset to use for the folium map

Now that you know how to display a map using folium, it's time to display the airport locations stored in the *airports* table on the map.

Displaying All Airports on the Map

First, extract all the airports and store the result in the df variable:

```
df = conn.execute('''
    SELECT
        latitude as lat,
        longitude as lng,
        airport as airport
    FROM airports
    WHERE
        (lat is not null) or
        (lng is not null)
''').df()
```

Then, iterate through all the rows in the DataFrame to extract the latitude, longitude, and name of the airport, and add a marker to the map using the CircleMarker class:

```
import math

for lat, lng, airport in zip(df['lat'], df['lng'], df['airport']):
    airport = folium.CircleMarker(
                location = [lat, lng],   # location of the marker
                radius = 4,              # size of the marker
                color = 'red',           # color of the marker
                fill = True,             # fill the marker with color
                fill_color = 'yellow',   # fill the marker with yellow color
                fill_opacity = 0.5,      # make the marker translucent
                popup = airport)         # name of the airport

    # add the circle marker to the map
    airport.add_to(mymap)
mymap
```

Figure 5-4 shows the map with the markers in the OpenStreetMap tile.

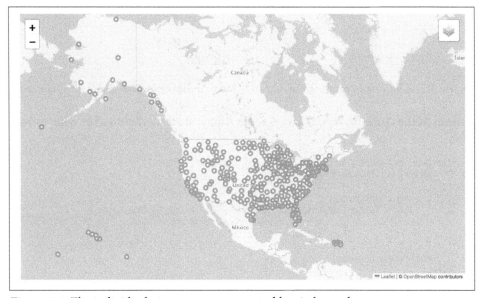

Figure 5-4. The individual airports are represented by circle markers

When you click on a marker, a pop-up displaying the airport name will appear (see Figure 5-5).

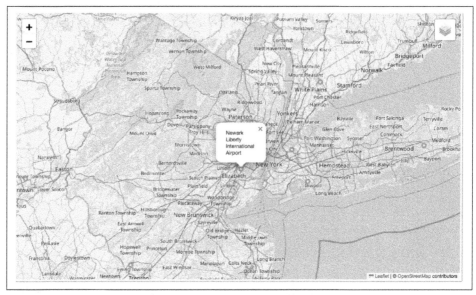

Figure 5-5. Zooming in on the map and clicking on a marker to reveal the airport name

Instead of the circle marker, you can add a simple stock Leaflet marker with an icon in it:

```
for lat, lng, airport in zip(df['lat'], df['lng'], df['airport']):
    airport = folium.Marker(
        location = [lat, lng],
        popup = airport,
        icon = folium.Icon(color = 'lightgray',      # icon to display in
                           icon = 'plane-arrival',   # the marker
                           prefix = 'fa'),
        )
    airport.add_to(mymap)
mymap
```

The list of icons you can display inside the marker is available at Font Awesome (*https://oreil.ly/nbBVx*).

Figure 5-6 shows a sample of the marker with the icon and the pop-up showing the name of the airport.

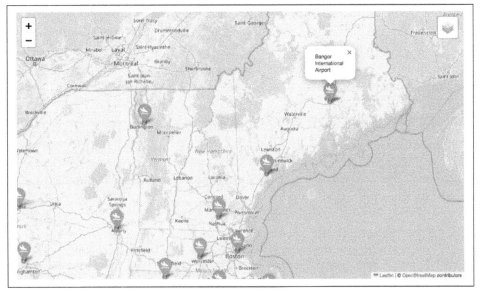

Figure 5-6. Using the stock Leaflet marker with an icon in it

So far, plotting the various airports locations on the map has been easy and fun. How about finding airports that are nearest to a particular location? Well, DuckDB has the `spatial` extension that makes this task a walk in the park. The next section will walk you through some of the things you can do with the `spatial` extension in DuckDB.

Using the spatial Extension in DuckDB

DuckDB provides the `spatial` extension to support geospatial processing. Using this extension, you can perform a number of spatial processing tasks easily in DuckDB, such as:

- Finding the distance between points
- Determining if two locations are within a specified distance from each other

> For more information on the `spatial` extension (*https://oreil.ly/teXax*) in DuckDB, see the documentation.

Let's use the `spatial` extension in DuckDB to see how we can perform some spatial processing with the *airports* table.

First, let's load the *airports.csv* file into a pandas DataFrame:

```
import pandas as pd
df = pd.read_csv('airports.csv')
```

Next, you need to perform some conversions with the latitudes and longitudes so that the `spatial` extension can work with them.

Converting latitude and longitude to the Point data type

The *airports* table has two location-specific columns—`latitude` and `longitude`. To work with the `spatial` extension in DuckDB, we need to add a new column to the DataFrame. This column will contain the values of the location represented in the `Point` data type.

 The `Point` data type represents a single point in space represented in various coordinate systems, such as the Cartesian coordinate system, geographic coordinates (longitude, latitude), polar coordinates, etc.

There are two ways to convert latitude and longitude to the `Point` data type:

- Use the Shapely library
- Use the `spatial` extension in DuckDB

Let's first see how you can use the Shapely library, a Python package for manipulation and analysis of geometric objects. You can install Shapely using the `pip` command:

```
!pip install shapely
```

Using the `Point` class in the `geometry` module (from the Shapely library), convert the latitude and longitude values into a `Point` object and save it in WKT (well-known text) format:

```
from shapely.geometry import Point

df['geometry'] = df.apply(
    lambda row: Point(row['LONGITUDE'], row['LATITUDE']).wkt, axis=1)
df
```

WKT is a text-based format for representing geometric objects in a human-readable form. The location in this example is stored in the EPSG:4326 format.

EPSG:4326 is a specific coordinate reference system (CRS) often used in geospatial applications and GIS. The EPSG (European Petroleum Survey Group, now known as the Geomatics Committee of the International Association of Oil and Gas Producers) maintains a database of coordinate reference systems and related parameters. An example of EPSG:4326 format is POINT (-75.4404 40.65236). The EPSG:4326 system is also known as WGS 84 (World Geodetic System 1984).

Figure 5-7 shows how the DataFrame looks after the conversion, with the additional of the geometry column.

	IATA_CODE	AIRPORT	CITY	STATE	COUNTRY	LATITUDE	LONGITUDE	geometry
0	ABE	Lehigh Valley International Airport	Allentown	PA	USA	40.65236	-75.44040	POINT (-75.4404 40.65236)
1	ABI	Abilene Regional Airport	Abilene	TX	USA	32.41132	-99.68190	POINT (-99.6819 32.41132)
2	ABQ	Albuquerque International Sunport	Albuquerque	NM	USA	35.04022	-106.60919	POINT (-106.60919 35.04022)
3	ABR	Aberdeen Regional Airport	Aberdeen	SD	USA	45.44906	-98.42183	POINT (-98.42183 45.44906)
4	ABY	Southwest Georgia Regional Airport	Albany	GA	USA	31.53552	-84.19447	POINT (-84.19447 31.53552)
...	...	...	...	...	...	...	...	...
317	WRG	Wrangell Airport	Wrangell	AK	USA	56.48433	-132.36982	POINT (-132.36982 56.48433)
318	WYS	Westerly State Airport	West Yellowstone	MT	USA	44.68840	-111.11764	POINT (-111.11764 44.6884)
319	XNA	Northwest Arkansas Regional Airport	Fayetteville/Springdale/Rogers	AR	USA	36.28187	-94.30681	POINT (-94.30681 36.28187)
320	YAK	Yakutat Airport	Yakutat	AK	USA	59.50336	-139.66023	POINT (-139.66023 59.50336)
321	YUM	Yuma International Airport	Yuma	AZ	USA	32.65658	-114.60597	POINT (-114.60597 32.65658)

322 rows × 8 columns

Figure 5-7. The DataFrame with the added geometry column

Now that we've updated the DataFrame, we'll load it into the DuckDB database and name it "airports_2":

```
conn.execute("CREATE TABLE airports_2 AS SELECT * FROM df")
```

For the second approach to converting latitude and longitude, we'll perform the conversion directly in DuckDB using the spatial extension. To use the spatial extension, you need to first install and load it:

```
conn.execute('INSTALL spatial;')
conn.execute('LOAD spatial;')
```

Then, use the `ST_AsPoint()` function to convert the latitude and longitude to `Point` objects:

```
conn.execute('''
    DROP TABLE IF EXISTS airports_2 ;
    CREATE TABLE airports_2 as
    SELECT
        *,
        ST_AsText(ST_Point(LONGITUDE,LATITUDE)) as geometry
    FROM airports
''')
```

Using either approach, the DuckDB database now contains a new table named *airports_2.*

Converting a pandas DataFrame to a GeoPandas GeoDataFrame

To perform spatial analysis on the `geometry` column, you need to convert the pandas DataFrame to a GeoPandas `GeoDataFrame`.

 A `GeoDataFrame` is a tabular data structure in the geospatial library GeoPandas, which extends the capabilities of a regular pandas DataFrame to handle spatial data. GeoPandas is built on top of the pandas and Shapely libraries, combining the tabular data manipulation capabilities of pandas with the geometric operations provided by Shapely.

To convert a pandas DataFrame to a `GeoDataFrame`, we will use the *leafmap* library, a Python library designed for interactive geospatial data visualization. You can install leafmap in Jupyter Notebook using the `pip` command:

```
!pip install leafmap
```

In addition, install the `mapclassify` and `geopandas` packages:

```
!pip install mapclassify
!pip install geopandas
```

You can now perform the conversion using the `df_to_gdf()` function:

```
import leafmap
    df_airports_gdf = leafmap.df_to_gdf(
        conn.execute('SELECT * FROM airports_2').df(),
        geometry = 'geometry',
        src_crs="EPSG:4326",
        dst_crs="EPSG:4326")
```

In this statement, we specified the original location format as EPSG:4326 and the destination format to convert to also as EPSG:4326. The column to convert (geometry) is indicated by the geometry parameter. Essentially, this operation converts the data type of the geometry column from object to geometry.

With the DataFrame converted, you can now use it to perform some cool geospatial visualization, as the next few sections illustrate.

Displaying airport locations on the map

You can now call the explore() method on GeoDataFrame to create an interactive map based on folium and *leaflet.js*:

```
df_airports_gdf.explore()
```

Figure 5-8 shows a folium map displaying circle markers depicting all the airports in the US.

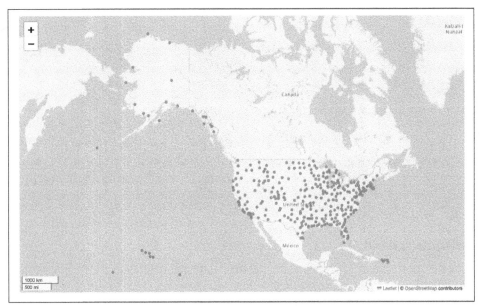

Figure 5-8. A folium map displaying all the airports in the US

Clicking on a marker displays the airport details (see Figure 5-9).

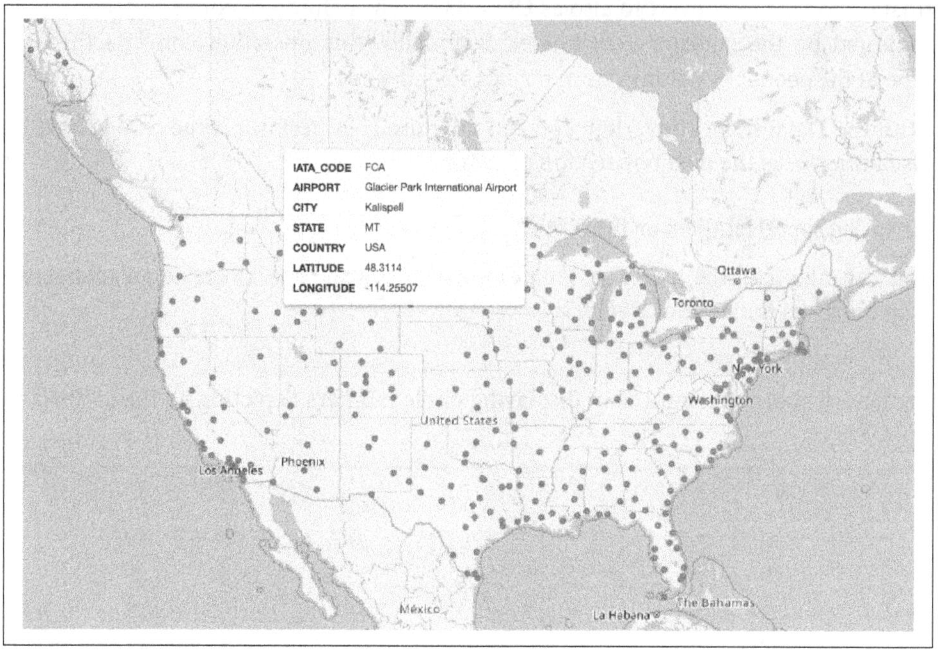

Figure 5-9. Clicking the marker displays the airport details

At this point, you can see that using a GeoDataFrame makes it very easy to display the various airports on the map—you don't even need to know how to create the map as everything is done automatically for you. But that's not all to using a GeoDataFrame. How about finding the nearest airports, or calculating the distance between two locations? The next section shows you how!

Finding nearby airports

Suppose you have a location in Miami (latitude 25.7824017 and longitude -80.2706578; see the location on Google Maps as shown in Figure 5-10). Say you want to find some of the nearest airports closest to this location.

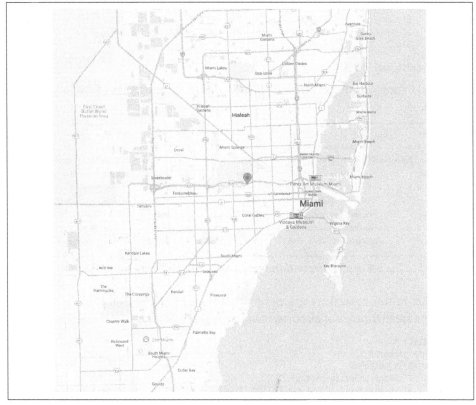

Figure 5-10. The location in Miami as shown in Google Maps

The spatial extension in DuckDB has a number of functions that you can use to do this. Here are two you can use:

- ST_DWithin() determines whether two geometries are within a specified distance of each other.

- ST_Distance() calculates the distance between two geometries

Let's first use the ST_DWithin() function to find airports that are within three degrees of the location in Miami:

```
conn.execute('INSTALL spatial;')
conn.execute('LOAD spatial;')

# miami
LOCATION_LNGLAT = (-80.2706578, 25.7824017)

# within 3 degrees
df_airports_near_miami = conn.sql(f"""
    SELECT *
    FROM airports_2
```

```
WHERE ST_DWithin(
    ST_GeomFromText(geometry),
    ST_GeomFromText('POINT ({LOCATION_LNGLAT[0]} {LOCATION_LNGLAT[1]})'),
    3);
""").df()
df_airports_near_miami
```

Figure 5-11 shows the list of airports that are within three degrees of the location you specified.

	IATA_CODE	AIRPORT	CITY	STATE	COUNTRY	LATITUDE	LONGITUDE	geometry
0	EYW	Key West International Airport	Key West	FL	USA	24.55611	-81.75956	POINT (-81.75956 24.55611)
1	FLL	Fort Lauderdale-Hollywood International Airport	Ft. Lauderdale	FL	USA	26.07258	-80.15275	POINT (-80.15275 26.07258)
2	MCO	Orlando International Airport	Orlando	FL	USA	28.42889	-81.31603	POINT (-81.31603 28.42889)
3	MIA	Miami International Airport	Miami	FL	USA	25.79325	-80.29056	POINT (-80.29056 25.79325)
4	MLB	Melbourne International Airport	Melbourne	FL	USA	28.10275	-80.64581	POINT (-80.64581 28.10275)
5	PBI	Palm Beach International Airport	West Palm Beach	FL	USA	26.68316	-80.09559	POINT (-80.09559 26.68316)
6	RSW	Southwest Florida International Airport	Ft. Myers	FL	USA	26.53617	-81.75517	POINT (-81.75517 26.53617)
7	SRQ	Sarasota-Bradenton International Airport	Sarasota	FL	USA	27.39533	-82.55411	POINT (-82.55411 27.39533)

Figure 5-11. The list of airports within three degrees of the location in Miami

Notice that in this case, there are eight airports nearest to our location in Miami. If you want a smaller range of airports, change the three degrees to two degrees:

```
SELECT *
FROM airports_2
WHERE ST_DWithin(
    ST_GeomFromText(geometry),
    ST_GeomFromText('POINT ({LOCATION_LNGLAT[0]} {LOCATION_LNGLAT[1]})'),
    2);
```

You will now get only five airports.

What if you want to get the three closest airports? In this case, you are better off using the ST_Distance() function:

```
df_airports_near_miami = conn.sql(f"""
    SELECT *,
        ST_Distance(ST_GeomFromText(geometry),
        ST_GeomFromText('POINT (
            {LOCATION_LNGLAT[0]}
            {LOCATION_LNGLAT[1]})')') as distance
    FROM airports_2;
""").df()
df_airports_near_miami
```

The ST_Distance() function calculates the distance between two geometries. Figure 5-12 shows the DataFrame with a new column named distance, representing the distance of each airport from our location in Miami.

	IATA_CODE	AIRPORT	CITY	STATE	COUNTRY	LATITUDE	LONGITUDE	geometry	distance
0	ABE	Lehigh Valley International Airport	Allentown	PA	USA	40.65236	-75.44040	POINT (-75.4404 40.65236)	15.634803
1	ABI	Abilene Regional Airport	Abilene	TX	USA	32.41132	-99.68190	POINT (-99.6819 32.41132)	20.511920
2	ABQ	Albuquerque International Sunport	Albuquerque	NM	USA	35.04022	-106.60919	POINT (-106.60919 35.04022)	27.918193
3	ABR	Aberdeen Regional Airport	Aberdeen	SD	USA	45.44906	-98.42183	POINT (-98.42183 45.44906)	26.762707
4	ABY	Southwest Georgia Regional Airport	Albany	GA	USA	31.53552	-84.19447	POINT (-84.19447 31.53552)	6.963812
...	...	...	...	...	...	...	...	...	...
317	WRG	Wrangell Airport	Wrangell	AK	USA	56.48433	-132.36982	POINT (-132.36982 56.48433)	60.472565
318	WYS	Westerly State Airport	West Yellowstone	MT	USA	44.68840	-111.11764	POINT (-111.11764 44.6884)	36.179733
319	XNA	Northwest Arkansas Regional Airport	Fayetteville/Springdale/Rogers	AR	USA	36.28187	-94.30681	POINT (-94.30681 36.28187)	17.528617
320	YAK	Yakutat Airport	Yakutat	AK	USA	59.50336	-139.66023	POINT (-139.66023 59.50336)	68.295127
321	YUM	Yuma International Airport	Yuma	AZ	USA	32.65658	-114.60597	POINT (-114.60597 32.65658)	35.016682

322 rows × 9 columns

Figure 5-12. The DataFrame with the new `distance` *column*

If you want the top three nearest airports, sort the `distance` column in ascending order and get the top three:

```
df_airports_near_miami = conn.sql(f"""
    SELECT *,
        ST_Distance(ST_GeomFromText(geometry),
        ST_GeomFromText('POINT (
            {LOCATION_LNGLAT[0]}
            {LOCATION_LNGLAT[1]})')) as distance
    FROM airports_2
    ORDER by distance
    LIMIT 3
""").df()
df_airports_near_miami
```

Figure 5-13 now shows the three nearest airports to our location in Miami.

	IATA_CODE	AIRPORT	CITY	STATE	COUNTRY	LATITUDE	LONGITUDE	geometry	distance
0	MIA	Miami International Airport	Miami	FL	USA	25.79325	-80.29056	POINT (-80.29056 25.79325)	0.022667
1	FLL	Fort Lauderdale-Hollywood International Airport	Ft. Lauderdale	FL	USA	26.07258	-80.15275	POINT (-80.15275 26.07258)	0.313218
2	PBI	Palm Beach International Airport	West Palm Beach	FL	USA	26.68316	-80.09559	POINT (-80.09559 26.68316)	0.917613

Figure 5-13. The three nearest airports to our location in Miami

To plot the airports on a map, convert the result to the `GeoDataFrame` object and call the `explore()` function:

```
import leafmap

df_airports_near_miami_gdf = leafmap.df_to_gdf(df_airports_near_miami)
folium_map = df_airports_near_miami_gdf.explore()
folium_map
```

Figure 5-14 shows the three airports on the map (with the callouts added).

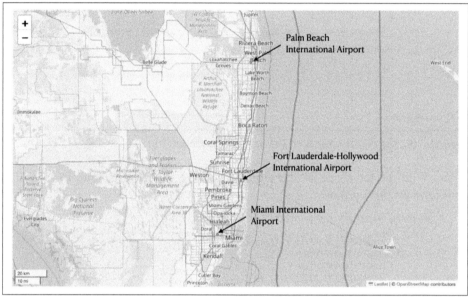

Figure 5-14. The three airports closest to our location in Miami

Using the reference to the folium map returned by the `explore()` function, let's add a marker to our location in Miami:

```
import folium

# add a popup at Miami
folium.Marker(location = [LOCATION_LNGLAT[1],LOCATION_LNGLAT[0]],
              popup='Miami').add_to(folium_map)
folium_map
```

Figure 5-15 shows the marker added to the map.

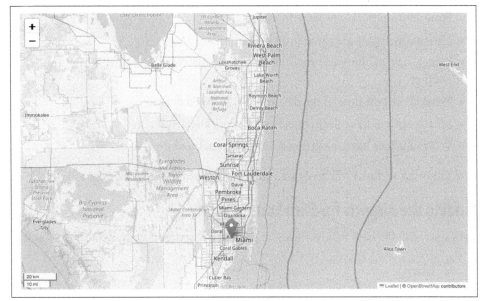

Figure 5-15. The marker showing our location in Miami

So far, we have learned how to:

- Display a map using the folium library
- Display multiple tilesets in our maps
- Display all the airports on a map using markers
- Use the `spatial` extension in DuckDB
- Convert the latitude and longitude to the `Point` data type using the Shapely library and the `spatial` extension in DuckDB
- Display the airport locations using a `GeoDataFrame` object
- Find nearby airports by degrees and distance

In the next section, we'll turn our attention to using the dataset for descriptive analytics. This will allow us to gain additional insights that would not be possible otherwise.

Performing Descriptive Analytics

Now that you have seen how to use the `spatial` extension in DuckDB for geospatial analysis, let's turn our attention to descriptive analytics. *Descriptive analytics* involves the interpretation and summary of historical data to understand patterns, trends, and insights about past events. Using the Flight Delays dataset, we can use descriptive analytics to obtain answers to the following questions:

- How many airports are there in each state?
- How many flights are there from one airport to another?
- Which day of the week has the fewest number of flights from one airport to another?
- What is the best time of the day to travel to avoid delays?
- Which airlines have the greatest number of canceled flights?
- Which airlines have the greatest number of delayed flights?

The following sections will show you how to get the answers to these questions!

Finding the Airports for Each State and City

Let's start with the easy one. We want to group all the airports based on state and city:

```
df_city_state = conn.execute('''
    SELECT
        *
    FROM airports
    ORDER BY STATE, CITY
''').df()

df_city_state
```

Figure 5-16 shows the resulting DataFrame containing the airports details grouped by state and city.

	IATA_CODE	AIRPORT	CITY	STATE	COUNTRY	LATITUDE	LONGITUDE
0	ADK	Adak Airport	Adak	AK	USA	51.87796	-176.64603
1	ANC	Ted Stevens Anchorage International Airport	Anchorage	AK	USA	61.17432	-149.99619
2	BRW	Wiley Post-Will Rogers Memorial Airport	Barrow	AK	USA	71.28545	-156.76600
3	BET	Bethel Airport	Bethel	AK	USA	60.77978	-161.83800
4	CDV	Merle K. (Mudhole) Smith Airport	Cordova	AK	USA	60.49183	-145.47765
...	...	...	...	...	...	...	...
317	COD	Yellowstone Regional Airport	Cody	WY	USA	44.52019	-109.02380
318	GCC	Gillette-Campbell County Airport	Gillette	WY	USA	44.34890	-105.53936
319	JAC	Jackson Hole Airport	Jackson	WY	USA	43.60732	-110.73774
320	LAR	Laramie Regional Airport	Laramie	WY	USA	41.31205	-105.67499
321	RKS	Rock Springs-Sweetwater County Airport	Rock Springs	WY	USA	41.59422	-109.06519

322 rows × 7 columns

Figure 5-16. The DataFrame containing all the airport details grouped by state and city

We can use the `set_index()` method to make this a multi-index DataFrame:

```
df_city_state.set_index(['STATE','CITY'], inplace = True)
df_city_state
```

Figure 5-17 shows the DataFrame with the STATE and CITY as its index.

STATE	CITY	IATA_CODE	AIRPORT	COUNTRY	LATITUDE	LONGITUDE
AK	Adak	ADK	Adak Airport	USA	51.87796	-176.64603
	Anchorage	ANC	Ted Stevens Anchorage International Airport	USA	61.17432	-149.99619
	Barrow	BRW	Wiley Post-Will Rogers Memorial Airport	USA	71.28545	-156.76600
	Bethel	BET	Bethel Airport	USA	60.77978	-161.83800
	Cordova	CDV	Merle K. (Mudhole) Smith Airport	USA	60.49183	-145.47765
...	...	...	...	...	...	...
WY	Cody	COD	Yellowstone Regional Airport	USA	44.52019	-109.02380
	Gillette	GCC	Gillette-Campbell County Airport	USA	44.34890	-105.53936
	Jackson	JAC	Jackson Hole Airport	USA	43.60732	-110.73774
	Laramie	LAR	Laramie Regional Airport	USA	41.31205	-105.67499
	Rock Springs	RKS	Rock Springs-Sweetwater County Airport	USA	41.59422	-109.06519

322 rows × 5 columns

Figure 5-17. The DataFrame converted to a multi-index DataFrame

If you want to find all the airports in California (CA), you can simply specify "CA" using the `loc[]` indexer:

```
df_city_state.loc['CA']
```

Figure 5-18 shows all the airports in California.

CITY	IATA_CODE	AIRPORT	COUNTRY	LATITUDE	LONGITUDE
Arcata/Eureka	ACV	Arcata Airport	USA	40.97812	-124.10862
Bakersfield	BFL	Meadows Field	USA	35.43360	-119.05677
Burbank	BUR	Bob Hope Airport (Hollywood Burbank Airport)	USA	34.20062	-118.35850
Crescent City	CEC	Del Norte County Airport (Jack McNamara Field)	USA	41.78016	-124.23653
Fresno	FAT	Fresno Yosemite International Airport	USA	36.77619	-119.71814
Long Beach	LGB	Long Beach Airport (Daugherty Field)	USA	33.81772	-118.15161
Los Angeles	LAX	Los Angeles International Airport	USA	33.94254	-118.40807
Mammoth Lakes	MMH	Mammoth Yosemite Airport	USA	37.62405	-118.83777
Monterey	MRY	Monterey Regional Airport (Monterey Peninsula ...	USA	36.58698	-121.84295
Oakland	OAK	Oakland International Airport	USA	37.72129	-122.22072
Ontario	ONT	Ontario International Airport	USA	34.05600	-117.60119
Palm Springs	PSP	Palm Springs International Airport	USA	33.82922	-116.50625
Redding	RDD	Redding Municipal Airport	USA	40.50898	-122.29340
Sacramento	SMF	Sacramento International Airport	USA	38.69542	-121.59077
San Diego	CLD	McClellan-Palomar Airport	USA	33.12723	-117.27873
San Diego	SAN	San Diego International Airport (Lindbergh Field)	USA	32.73356	-117.18966
San Francisco	SFO	San Francisco International Airport	USA	37.61900	-122.37484
San Jose	SJC	Norman Y. Mineta San José International Airport	USA	37.36186	-121.92901
San Luis Obispo	SBP	San Luis Obispo County Regional Airport (McChe...	USA	35.23706	-120.64239
Santa Ana	SNA	John Wayne Airport (Orange County Airport)	USA	33.67566	-117.86822
Santa Barbara	SBA	Santa Barbara Municipal Airport (Santa Barbara...	USA	34.42621	-119.84037
Santa Maria	SMX	Santa Maria Public Airport (Capt G. Allan Hanc...	USA	34.89925	-120.45758

Figure 5-18. All the airports in California

If you want to locate an airport in a specific city in California, such as San Francisco, then pass the state and city as a tuple to the loc[] indexer:

```
df_city_state.loc[('CA','San Francisco')]
```

Figure 5-19 now shows you the airport in San Francisco, California.

STATE	CITY	IATA_CODE	AIRPORT	COUNTRY	LATITUDE	LONGITUDE
CA	San Francisco	SFO	San Francisco International Airport	USA	37.619	-122.37484

Figure 5-19. The airport in San Francisco, California

The next section will show you how to tally up the number of airports in each state.

Aggregating the Total Number of Airports in Each State

Let's now make a count of all the airports in each state and then order the count in decreasing order:

```
df_airports_state = conn.execute('''
    SELECT
        STATE,
        count(*) as COUNT
    FROM airports
    GROUP BY STATE
    ORDER BY Count DESC
''').df()
df_airports_state.head()
```

Figure 5-20 shows the top five states by airport count.

	STATE	COUNT
0	TX	24
1	CA	22
2	AK	19
3	FL	17
4	MI	15

Figure 5-20. The top five states by airport count

It would be interesting to plot this as a pie chart:

```
import matplotlib.pyplot as plt
import seaborn

palette_color = seaborn.color_palette('pastel')
plt.figure(figsize = (7, 7))
plt.pie(df_airports_state['COUNT'],
        labels = df_airports_state['STATE'],
        colors = palette_color,
        autopct = '%.0f%%',)

plt.legend(df_airports_state['STATE'], loc = "best")
```

Since there is quite a long list of states, the pie chart looks kind of messy (see Figure 5-21).

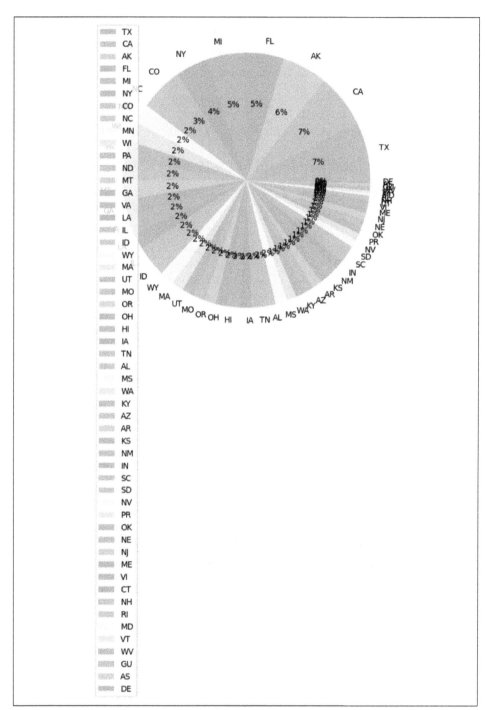

Figure 5-21. The pie chart showing the distribution of airports in each state

To clean this up a bit, it might be useful to reduce the data to the top ten states with the most airports using the `LIMIT 10` statement:

```
SELECT
    STATE,
    count(*) as COUNT
FROM airports
GROUP BY STATE
ORDER BY Count DESC
LIMIT 10
```

When you replot, you will see the pie chart as shown in Figure 5-22.

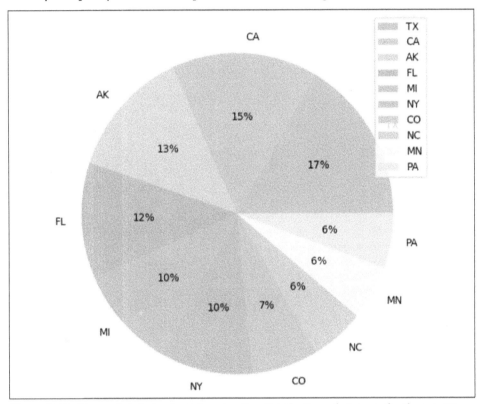

Figure 5-22. The updated pie chart showing the distribution of airports for the top 10 states

But there is still room for improvement. It doesn't make a lot of sense to show the percentage of each slice—we actually want to know how many airports there are in each state. To do that, let's define a function named `fmt()` to help format the pie chart. Pass the `fmt()` function into the `autopct` parameter of the `pie()` function:

```
# total number of airports
total = df_airports_state['COUNT'].sum()
```

```
def fmt(x):
    return '{:.1f}%\n({:.0f} airports)'.format(x, total * x / 100)

palette_color = seaborn.color_palette('pastel')
plt.figure(figsize = (7, 7))

plt.pie(df_airports_state['COUNT'],
        labels = df_airports_state['STATE'],
        colors = palette_color,
        autopct = fmt)

plt.legend(df_airports_state['STATE'], loc = "best")
```

When plotting the pie chart, Matplotlib calls the fmt() function for each slice that it is plotting. The value of x is the percentage of each slice. So multiplying the percentage by the total count of airports will give the actual airport count for each slice.

Figure 5-23 shows the updated pie chart with the total number of airports for each state.

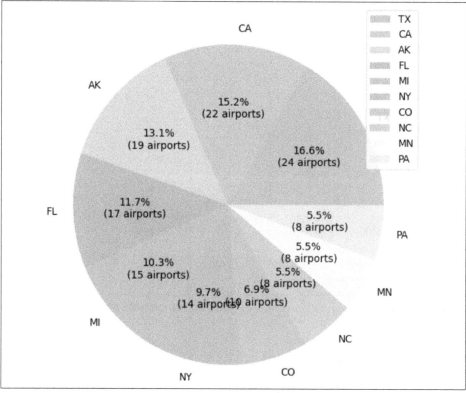

Figure 5-23. The updated pie chart showing the number of airports for each state

While a pie chart may look appealing, some may argue that pie charts are problematic (see "Why Pie Charts Are Evil" (*https://oreil.ly/A41ud*) for arguments as to why). Another way to present this information is with a bar chart:

```
# create the bar chart
plt.bar(df_airports_state['STATE'],
        df_airports_state['COUNT'],
        color='skyblue')

plt.xlabel('State')
plt.ylabel('Number of Airports')
plt.title('Top 10 States with Most Airports')
plt.xticks(rotation = 45)
```

Figure 5-24 shows the bar chart plotted using this code snippet.

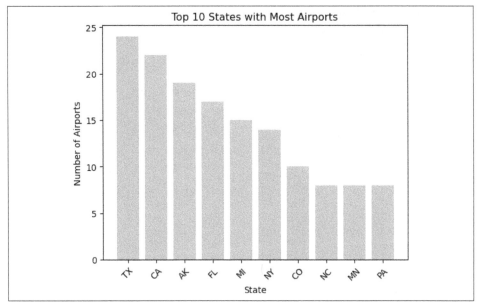

Figure 5-24. The bar chart showing the number of airports for each state

The next thing we want to do is to find out more details about the flights, such as:

- The count of flights departing from each airport
- The number of flights for each combination of origin and destination airports

The next section will dive into these in detail.

Obtaining the Flight Counts for Each Pair of Origin and Destination Airports

Let's start with the simplest task—getting the number of flights for each origin airport:

```
conn.execute('''
    SELECT
        ORIGIN_AIRPORT, COUNT(ORIGIN_AIRPORT) as COUNT
    FROM flights
    GROUP BY ORIGIN_AIRPORT
    ORDER BY COUNT DESC
''').df()
```

Figure 5-25 shows the departing flight count for each origin airport. For example, there were 346,846 flights departing from ATL (Hartsfield–Jackson Atlanta International Airport), 285,884 flights departing from ORD (O'Hare International Airport), and so on.

	ORIGIN_AIRPORT	COUNT
0	ATL	346836
1	ORD	285884
2	DFW	239551
3	DEN	196055
4	LAX	194673
...	...	...
623	13541	11
624	10165	9
625	14222	9
626	13502	6
627	11503	4

628 rows × 2 columns

Figure 5-25. The total number of flights from each originating airport

A more interesting task is to obtain the flight count for each pair of origin and destination airports:

```
conn.execute('''
    SELECT
        ORIGIN_AIRPORT, DESTINATION_AIRPORT,
        COUNT(*) as COUNT
    FROM flights
    GROUP BY ORIGIN_AIRPORT, DESTINATION_AIRPORT
    ORDER BY COUNT DESC
''').df()
```

Figure 5-26 shows that flights between SFO (San Francisco International Airport) and LAX (Los Angeles International Airport) are the most frequent.

	ORIGIN_AIRPORT	DESTINATION_AIRPORT	COUNT
0	SFO	LAX	13744
1	LAX	SFO	13457
2	JFK	LAX	12016
3	LAX	JFK	12015
4	LAS	LAX	9715
...	...	...	...
8604	TUL	AUS	1
8605	GCC	RAP	1
8606	10685	13487	1
8607	IAD	MSN	1
8608	OAK	FLL	1

8609 rows × 3 columns

Figure 5-26. The count of flights from one airport to another

What if we limit the selection to flights exclusively provided by Delta Air Lines (DL)? Here we go:

```
conn.execute('''
    SELECT
        ORIGIN_AIRPORT, DESTINATION_AIRPORT,
        COUNT(*) as COUNT
    FROM flights
    WHERE AIRLINE='DL'
    GROUP BY ORIGIN_AIRPORT, DESTINATION_AIRPORT
    ORDER BY COUNT DESC
''').df()
```

Figure 5-27 shows that the most popular flight from Delta Air Lines is from LGA (LaGuardia Airport) to ATL.

	ORIGIN_AIRPORT	DESTINATION_AIRPORT	COUNT
0	LGA	ATL	5303
1	ATL	LGA	5298
2	MCO	ATL	5250
3	ATL	MCO	5247
4	FLL	ATL	4780
...	...	...	...
1659	10423	12892	1
1660	SLC	MIA	1
1661	MYR	DTW	1
1662	MHT	LGA	1
1663	JFK	SAV	1

1664 rows × 3 columns

Figure 5-27. The flight count for each origin-destination airport pair on Delta

Using the same SQL statement, you can modify the airline code to get the flights provided by any particular airline.

In the next section, we're going to find out which airline has the most canceled flights.

Getting the Canceled Flights from Airlines

In the *flights* table, all canceled flights have the CANCELLED field set to 1. Using this, let's find out how many flights have been canceled by Delta Air Lines in 2015:

```
conn.execute('''
    SELECT
        ORIGIN_AIRPORT, DESTINATION_AIRPORT,
        COUNT(*) as COUNT
    FROM flights
    WHERE AIRLINE='DL' AND CANCELLED = 1
    GROUP BY ORIGIN_AIRPORT, DESTINATION_AIRPORT
    ORDER BY COUNT DESC
'''
).df()
```

Figure 5-28 shows the flights canceled by Delta Air Lines.

	ORIGIN_AIRPORT	DESTINATION_AIRPORT	COUNT
0	BOS	LGA	146
1	LGA	BOS	146
2	LGA	ATL	87
3	ATL	LGA	78
4	BOS	ATL	58
...	...	...	...
454	LAX	SJC	1
455	ATL	BTV	1
456	SLC	STL	1
457	MCO	SLC	1
458	FAR	MSP	1

459 rows × 3 columns

Figure 5-28. The number of flights canceled by Delta Air Lines

Understanding the percentage of flights canceled is more meaningful than knowing the absolute number:

```
conn.execute('''
    SELECT
        ORIGIN_AIRPORT, DESTINATION_AIRPORT,
        (SUM(CANCELLED) * 100.0) / COUNT(*) as CANCELLED_PERCENT
    FROM flights
    WHERE AIRLINE = 'DL'
    GROUP BY ORIGIN_AIRPORT, DESTINATION_AIRPORT
    ORDER BY CANCELLED_PERCENT DESC
'''
).df()
```

Figure 5-29 shows the canceled percentage for Delta Air Lines.

	ORIGIN_AIRPORT	DESTINATION_AIRPORT	CANCELLED_PERCENT
0	BOS	LGA	4.500617
1	LGA	BOS	4.490926
2	SRQ	LGA	4.040404
3	LGA	SRQ	4.040404
4	RSW	JFK	3.636364
...	...	...	...
1659	SLC	TPA	0.000000
1660	CVG	BNA	0.000000
1661	13487	14683	0.000000
1662	12892	13796	0.000000
1663	JFK	CLE	0.000000

1664 rows × 3 columns

Figure 5-29. The result showing the percentage of flights canceled by Delta Air Lines

It looks like flights from BOS (Boston Logan International Airport) to LGA, and vice versa, have had high cancellations.

Finally, if you want to know overall what percentage of flights from Delta Air Lines have been canceled:

```
conn.execute('''
    SELECT
        (SUM(CANCELLED) * 100.0) / COUNT(*) as CANCELLED_PERCENT
    FROM flights
    WHERE AIRLINE = 'DL'
'''
).df()
```

Figure 5-30 shows that Delta Air Lines canceled 0.44% of all its flights in 2015.

	CANCELLED_PERCENT
0	0.436589

Figure 5-30. The percentage of flights canceled by Delta Air Lines

But just showing the cancellation percentage of one airline does not really give you an idea of how good or how bad the cancellation rate is; it is more useful to be able to compare across all the airlines. And here we go:

```
import matplotlib.pyplot as plt

df = conn.execute('''
    SELECT AIRLINE,
        (SUM(CANCELLED) * 100.0) / COUNT(*) as CANCELLED_PERCENT
    FROM flights
    -- WHERE AIRLINE = 'DL'
    GROUP BY AIRLINE
    ORDER BY CANCELLED_PERCENT DESC
'''
).df()
display(df)
```

The `--` in the SQL statement comments out the `WHERE` condition, and so the result now is the cancellation percentages for all airlines (see Figure 5-31).

	AIRLINE	CANCELLED_PERCENT
0	MQ	5.099582
1	EV	2.662869
2	US	2.046650
3	NK	1.707290
4	OO	1.692861
5	B6	1.601210
6	AA	1.504028
7	UA	1.274521
8	WN	1.271382
9	VX	0.862640
10	F9	0.647320
11	DL	0.436589
12	AS	0.387779
13	HA	0.224198

Figure 5-31. The flights cancellation percentages for all airlines

You can see that Delta Air Lines is not that bad after all; in terms of cancellation it is third from the last. Let's plot a bar chart to see how all the other airlines fared:

```
df.plot(kind='bar', x='AIRLINE', y='CANCELLED_PERCENT')
plt.xlabel('Airlines')
plt.ylabel('Cancellation Percentage')
plt.title('Cancellation Percentage for Different Airlines')
```

Figure 5-32 shows you the cancellation percentage for all the airlines.

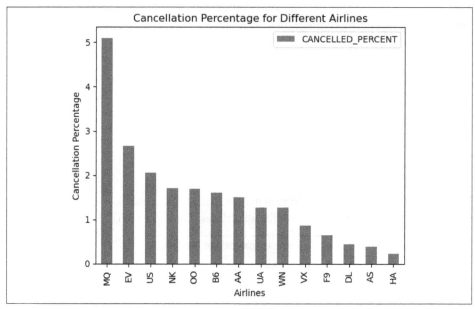

Figure 5-32. The cancellation percentage for all airlines

Note that the labels for the x-axis are the airline codes. It would be better to display the airline names in full. For this, you need to do a JOIN operation with the *airlines* table:

```python
import matplotlib.pyplot as plt

df = conn.execute('''
    SELECT
        a.AIRLINE,
        (SUM(f.CANCELLED) * 100.0) / COUNT(*) as CANCELLED_PERCENT
    FROM flights f
    JOIN airlines a ON f.AIRLINE = a.IATA_CODE
    GROUP BY a.AIRLINE
    ORDER BY CANCELLED_PERCENT DESC
'''
).df()

df.plot(kind='bar', x='AIRLINE', y='CANCELLED_PERCENT')
plt.xlabel('Airlines')
plt.ylabel('Cancellation Percentage')
plt.title('Cancellation Percentage for Different Airlines')
```

Figure 5-33 shows the updated bar chart with the airline names displayed on the x-axis.

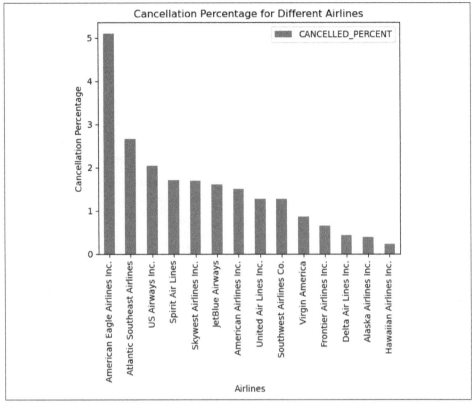

Figure 5-33. The updated bar chart with the airline names displayed on the x-axis

It would also be useful to display the cancellation percentages using a pie chart:

```
ax = df.plot(kind='pie',
             x='AIRLINE',
             y='CANCELLED_PERCENT',
             labels = df['AIRLINE'],
             autopct = '%.0f%%',
             legend=False
)
ax.get_yaxis().set_visible(False)
plt.xlabel('Airlines')
plt.title('Cancellation Percentage for Different Airlines')
```

Figure 5-34 shows the pie chart of cancellation percentages.

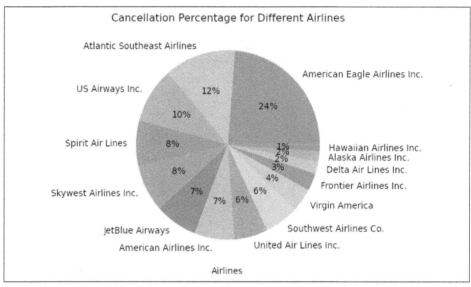

Figure 5-34. Using a pie chart to display the percentage of flights canceled by all airlines

Another set of statistics that would be very useful to us is the number of flights for each day of the week. We'll examine this set in the next section.

Getting the Flight Count for Each Day of the Week

For each flight combination (origin to destination airport), we want to know the flight count for each day of the week to see if certain days have fewer flights.

Let's create the DataFrame that groups all the flight combinations by day of week:

```
df_flights_day_of_week = conn.execute('''
    SELECT
        day_of_week,
        origin_airport,
        destination_airport,
        COUNT(*) AS flight_count
    FROM
        flights
    WHERE
        CANCELLED = 0  -- Exclude cancelled flights
    GROUP BY
        day_of_week,
        origin_airport,
        destination_airport
    ORDER BY
        day_of_week,
        origin_airport,
        destination_airport;
''').df()

df_flights_day_of_week
```

Figure 5-35 shows the result.

	DAY_OF_WEEK	ORIGIN_AIRPORT	DESTINATION_AIRPORT	flight_count
0	1	10135	10397	12
1	1	10135	11433	12
2	1	10135	13930	11
3	1	10136	11298	28
4	1	10140	10397	12
...	...	...	...	...
57262	7	XNA	ORD	271
57263	7	XNA	SFO	8
57264	7	YAK	CDV	47
57265	7	YAK	JNU	48
57266	7	YUM	PHX	278

57267 rows × 4 columns

Figure 5-35. The count for each flight combination grouped by day of week

Verifying Airport Codes

Upon reviewing the results, you'll notice that in the first five rows, both the ORIGIN_AIRPORT and DESTINATION_AIRPORT fields contain numeric values for airport codes rather than alphabetic ones. In fact, this pattern is consistent throughout the entire month of October 2015. You can confirm this by checking for non-numeric values in both columns using the following query:

```
conn.execute('''
    SELECT YEAR, MONTH, DAY, ORIGIN_AIRPORT, DESTINATION_AIRPORT
    FROM flights
    WHERE ORIGIN_AIRPORT NOT SIMILAR TO '[A-Za-z]+'
        OR DESTINATION_AIRPORT NOT SIMILAR TO '[A-Za-z]+';
''').df()
```

As shown in Figure 5-36, the result confirms that in October 2015, both the ORIGIN_AIRPORT and DESTINATION_AIRPORT columns contain numeric values.

	YEAR	MONTH	DAY	ORIGIN_AIRPORT	DESTINATION_AIRPORT
0	2015	10	1	14747	11298
1	2015	10	1	14771	13487
2	2015	10	1	12889	13487
3	2015	10	1	12892	13303
4	2015	10	1	14771	11057
...	...	...	...	...	...
486160	2015	10	31	11292	12478
486161	2015	10	31	12478	10732
486162	2015	10	31	12478	14843
486163	2015	10	31	14747	12266
486164	2015	10	31	12892	12266

486165 rows × 5 columns

Figure 5-36. Numeric values in the `ORIGIN_AIRPORT` *and* `DESTINATION_AIRPORT` *columns for October*

Numeric values in the fields `ORIGIN_AIRPORT` and `DESTINATION_AIRPORT` typically represent special cases, such as system-assigned codes for smaller airports, freight-only hubs, or unspecified locations. These codes may also appear in cases of diversions or operational exceptions where specific airport codes were unavailable. For simplicity, we'll consider these numeric values as distinct airport codes.

The result in Figure 5-35 itself contains all the flight combinations. So, let's plot the flight count for all the flights from SFO to LAX using a bar chart:

```
from_airport = 'SFO'
to_airport = 'LAX'

df_flights_result = df_flights_day_of_week.query(
    f'ORIGIN_AIRPORT=="{from_airport}" & DESTINATION_AIRPORT=="{to_airport}"')

df_flights_result.plot(kind='bar',
                    x = 'DAY_OF_WEEK',
                    y = 'flight_count',
                    legend = False)

plt.xlabel('Day of Week')
plt.ylabel('Number of Flights')
plt.title(f'Number of Flights from {from_airport} to {to_airport}')
plt.xticks(df_flights_result['DAY_OF_WEEK'] - 1,
        ['Mon', 'Tue', 'Wed', 'Thu', 'Fri', 'Sat', 'Sun'])
plt.show()
```

Figure 5-37 shows that there seem to be fewer flights from SFO to LAX on Saturdays and Sundays.

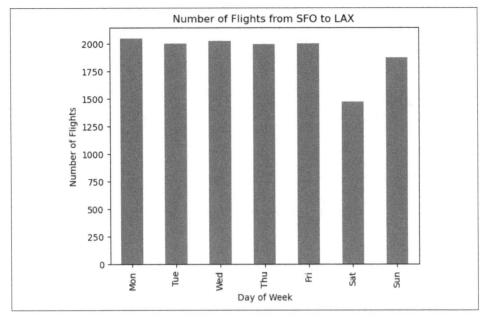

Figure 5-37. The total number of flights from SFO to LAX on each day of the week

Instead of just counting the number of flights for each flight combination for each day of the week, you could compute the percentage.

The following query calculates the percentage of flights on each weekday for given origin and destination airports, excluding canceled flights. It achieves this by using two common table expressions (CTEs) to first gather the flight counts by day of the week and then gather the total flight counts for each origin-destination pair:

```
df_flights_weekday = conn.execute('''
    with t1 as (
        SELECT
            day_of_week,
            origin_airport,
            destination_airport,
            COUNT(*) AS flight_count_per_weekday
        FROM
            flights
        WHERE
            CANCELLED = 0 -- Exclude cancelled flights
        GROUP BY
            day_of_week,
            origin_airport,
            destination_airport
        ORDER BY
            day_of_week,
            origin_airport,
```

```
              destination_airport
    ),
    t2 as (
        SELECT
            origin_airport,
            destination_airport,
            count(*) as total_flight_count
        FROM
            flights
        WHERE
            CANCELLED = 0 -- Exclude cancelled flights
        GROUP BY
            origin_airport,
            destination_airport
    )
    SELECT
        t1.origin_airport,
        t1.destination_airport,
        t1.day_of_week,
        t2.total_flight_count,
        100. * (t1.flight_count_per_weekday / t2.total_flight_count) as
            percent_flights_on_weekday
    FROM t1
    JOIN t2
    ON
        t1.origin_airport = t2.origin_airport AND
        t1.destination_airport = t2.destination_airport
''').df()
df_flights_weekday
```

Figure 5-38 shows the result returned by the query.

	ORIGIN_AIRPORT	DESTINATION_AIRPORT	DAY_OF_WEEK	total_flight_count	percent_flights_on_weekday
0	IAH	BOI	3	327	14.373089
1	IAH	BOS	3	1643	14.972611
2	IAH	BRO	3	1268	14.037855
3	IAH	BTR	3	2275	15.208791
4	IAH	BWI	3	979	15.321757
...	...	...	...	...	...
57262	13931	13232	6	62	16.129032
57263	14108	11433	6	31	16.129032
57264	12898	13930	6	31	16.129032
57265	13851	11292	6	190	13.684211
57266	12982	14107	6	29	31.034483

57267 rows × 5 columns

Figure 5-38. The percentage of flight counts for each flight combination grouped by day of week

You can now plot the result as a bar chart:

```
from_airport = 'SFO'
to_airport = 'LAX'

# step 1: Filter the DataFrame for SFO to LAX
sfo_to_las_flights = df_flights_weekday.query(
    f'ORIGIN_AIRPORT=="{from_airport}" & DESTINATION_AIRPORT=="{to_airport}"')

# step 2: Plotting
plt.figure(figsize=(10, 6))
plt.bar(sfo_to_las_flights['DAY_OF_WEEK'],
        sfo_to_las_flights['percent_flights_on_weekday'],
        color='skyblue')

plt.xticks(sfo_to_las_flights['DAY_OF_WEEK'].sort_values(),
           ['Mon', 'Tue', 'Wed', 'Thu', 'Fri', 'Sat', 'Sun'])

plt.title(f'Percentage of Flights from {from_airport} ' +
          f'to {to_airport} by Day of the Week')
plt.xlabel('Day of the Week')
plt.ylabel('Percentage of Flights')
plt.xticks(rotation=45)
plt.grid(axis='y')
```

Figure 5-39 shows the same result as a bar chart.

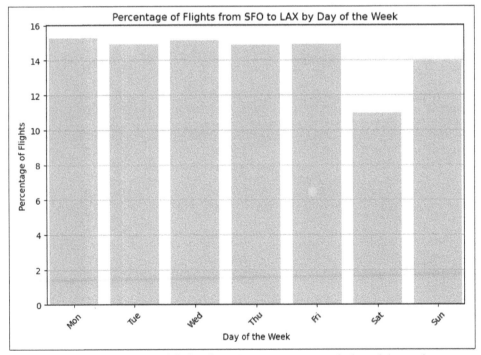

Figure 5-39. The percentage of flights from SFO to LAX on each day of the week

Another interesting statistic to gather would be the time of the day delays occur most often. You will learn how to do this in the next section.

Finding the Most Common Timeslot for Flight Delays

To find the time where delays occur most often, we will divide the day into four time slots:

- 12 a.m. to 6 a.m.
- 6 a.m. to 12 p.m.
- 12 p.m. to 6 p.m.
- 6 p.m. to 12 a.m.

Using these time slots, we can create a SQL query that finds the flight delays for each slot:

```
df_delays_by_week = conn.execute('''
SELECT
    DAY_OF_WEEK,
    CASE
        WHEN SCHEDULED_DEPARTURE BETWEEN '0000' AND '0559' THEN '00:00-06:00'
        WHEN SCHEDULED_DEPARTURE BETWEEN '0600' AND '1159' THEN '06:00-12:00'
        WHEN SCHEDULED_DEPARTURE BETWEEN '1200' AND '1759' THEN '12:00-18:00'
        WHEN SCHEDULED_DEPARTURE BETWEEN '1800' AND '2400' THEN '18:00-24:00'
        ELSE 'Other'
    END AS DEPARTURE_TIME_INTERVAL,
    AVG(ARRIVAL_DELAY) AS AVG_ARRIVAL_DELAY
FROM
    flights
WHERE
    ARRIVAL_DELAY > 0
GROUP BY
    DAY_OF_WEEK,
    CASE
        WHEN SCHEDULED_DEPARTURE BETWEEN '0000' AND '0559' THEN '00:00-06:00'
        WHEN SCHEDULED_DEPARTURE BETWEEN '0600' AND '1159' THEN '06:00-12:00'
        WHEN SCHEDULED_DEPARTURE BETWEEN '1200' AND '1759' THEN '12:00-18:00'
        WHEN SCHEDULED_DEPARTURE BETWEEN '1800' AND '2400' THEN '18:00-24:00'
        ELSE 'Other'
    END
ORDER BY
    DAY_OF_WEEK, DEPARTURE_TIME_INTERVAL;
''').df()

df_delays_by_week
```

If you wish, you can divide the day into more time slots, but for now Figure 5-40 shows the result.

	DAY_OF_WEEK	DEPARTURE_TIME_INTERVAL	AVG_ARRIVAL_DELAY
0	1	00:00-06:00	32.348575
1	1	06:00-12:00	31.576553
2	1	12:00-18:00	37.778949
3	1	18:00-24:00	39.396041
4	2	00:00-06:00	30.334905
5	2	06:00-12:00	29.191015
6	2	12:00-18:00	35.259384
7	2	18:00-24:00	37.801541
8	3	00:00-06:00	29.617457
9	3	06:00-12:00	28.237131
10	3	12:00-18:00	33.427170
11	3	18:00-24:00	34.349877
12	4	00:00-06:00	25.404742
13	4	06:00-12:00	27.648437
14	4	12:00-18:00	34.133880
15	4	18:00-24:00	36.982575
16	5	00:00-06:00	26.451996
17	5	06:00-12:00	26.634905
18	5	12:00-18:00	32.529718
19	5	18:00-24:00	35.998932
20	6	00:00-06:00	30.042233
21	6	06:00-12:00	27.598548
22	6	12:00-18:00	33.975286
23	6	18:00-24:00	36.418688
24	7	00:00-06:00	29.783261
25	7	06:00-12:00	29.875063
26	7	12:00-18:00	34.226615
27	7	18:00-24:00	36.372640

Figure 5-40. The DataFrame containing the flight delays for each time slot grouped by day of week

Just looking at the DataFrame is not very useful. And so we'll plot a bar chart to show the delays for each time slot. But before you begin, you need to pivot (reshape) the DataFrame so that the index of the DataFrame is the DAY_OF_WEEK and the columns are the time slots:

```
df_delays_by_week_pivot = df_delays_by_week.pivot(
    index = 'DAY_OF_WEEK',
    columns = 'DEPARTURE_TIME_INTERVAL',
    values = 'AVG_ARRIVAL_DELAY')
df_delays_by_week_pivot
```

Figure 5-41 shows the reshaped DataFrame.

DEPARTURE_TIME_INTERVAL	00:00-06:00	06:00-12:00	12:00-18:00	18:00-24:00
DAY_OF_WEEK				
1	32.348575	31.576553	37.778949	39.396041
2	30.334905	29.191015	35.259384	37.801541
3	29.617457	28.237131	33.427170	34.349877
4	25.404742	27.648437	34.133880	36.982575
5	26.451996	26.634905	32.529718	35.998932
6	30.042233	27.598548	33.975286	36.418688
7	29.783261	29.875063	34.226615	36.372640

Figure 5-41. The result of reshaping the DataFrame

You can now plot a bar chart:

```
# plotting a bar chart
df_delays_by_week_pivot.plot(kind='bar',
                             stacked=False,
                             figsize=(10, 6))

# updating the x-ticks to show the days of the week
days_of_week = ['Monday', 'Tuesday', 'Wednesday',
                'Thursday', 'Friday', 'Saturday', 'Sunday']
plt.xticks(ticks=range(len(days_of_week)), labels=days_of_week, rotation=0)

plt.title('Average Arrival Delay by Departure Time and Day of Week')
plt.xlabel('Day of Week')
plt.ylabel('Average Arrival Delay (minutes)')
plt.legend(title='Departure Time Interval', bbox_to_anchor=(1, 1))
plt.tight_layout()  # Adjust layout to avoid clipping of labels
plt.show()
```

Figure 5-42 shows that for all flights that have delays:

- The evening time slot (6 p.m. to 12 a.m.) has the longest mean delay.

- On most days (except Thursday, Friday, and Sunday), the morning time slot (6 a.m. to 12 p.m.) has the shortest mean delay.

- If you want to have minimum flight delays, try to travel on Thursday or Friday, in the very early morning (from 12 a.m. to 6 a.m.).

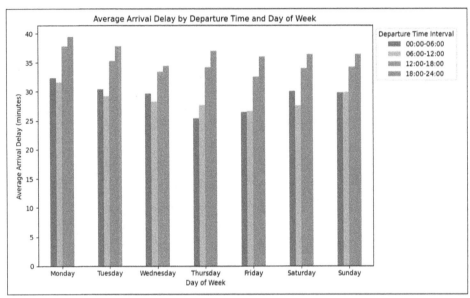

Figure 5-42. Mean arrival delays based on departure time for each day of the week

Now that we know what is the best time to travel in order to avoid delays, let's see which airlines have the most and fewest delays.

Finding the Airlines with the Most and Fewest Delays

Let's first sum up the number of delays for each airline:

```
df_most_delays = conn.execute('''
    SELECT
        count(airlines.AIRLINE) as Count,
        airlines.AIRLINE
    FROM flights, airlines
    WHERE airlines.IATA_CODE = flights.AIRLINE AND flights.ARRIVAL_DELAY > 0
    GROUP BY airlines.AIRLINE
    ORDER BY COUNT DESC
''').df()
df_most_delays
```

Figure 5-43 shows the total number of flights that have delays for each airline.

	Count	AIRLINE
0	470767	Southwest Airlines Co.
1	252191	American Airlines Inc.
2	250840	Delta Air Lines Inc.
3	222435	Skywest Airlines Inc.
4	213217	Atlantic Southeast Airlines
5	186227	United Air Lines Inc.
6	103505	American Eagle Airlines Inc.
7	101998	JetBlue Airways
8	76285	US Airways Inc.
9	56953	Alaska Airlines Inc.
10	56887	Spirit Air Lines
11	41232	Frontier Airlines Inc.
12	30179	Hawaiian Airlines Inc.
13	24180	Virgin America

Figure 5-43. The total number of flights from each airline that were delayed

If you simply counted the number of delayed flights for an airline and use this number to determine which airline has the most delayed flights, it might not be fair. Imagine an airline only has two flights per day and one of them is delayed. While it only has one delayed flight, its delayed flights percentage is actually 50%!

A much more accurate way to determine which airline has the most delays is to calculate the percentage of flight delays for each airline. You can do so via the following SQL query:

```
df_percent_delay = conn.execute('''
    WITH flight_delays AS (
        SELECT
            AIRLINE,
            1.0 * count(*) as TotalFlights,
            1.0 * sum(case when ARRIVAL_DELAY > 0 then 1 else 0 end) as Delays,
            (1.0 * sum(case when ARRIVAL_DELAY > 0 then 1 else 0 end) /
            count(*)) * 100 as Percentage
        FROM flights
        GROUP BY AIRLINE
    )
    SELECT
        flight_delays.Percentage,
        airlines.IATA_CODE,
        airlines.AIRLINE
    FROM flight_delays
```

```
    JOIN airlines ON airlines.IATA_CODE = flight_delays.AIRLINE
    ORDER BY flight_delays.Percentage DESC;
''').df()
```

```
df_percent_delay
```

Figure 5-44 shows the result.

	Percentage	IATA_CODE	AIRLINE
0	48.464376	NK	Spirit Air Lines
1	45.391695	F9	Frontier Airlines Inc.
2	39.567600	HA	Hawaiian Airlines Inc.
3	39.061112	VX	Virgin America
4	38.389150	US	US Airways Inc.
5	38.194632	B6	JetBlue Airways
6	37.806385	OO	Skywest Airlines Inc.
7	37.307535	WN	Southwest Airlines Co.
8	37.277198	EV	Atlantic Southeast Airlines
9	36.109888	UA	United Air Lines Inc.
10	35.130264	MQ	American Eagle Airlines Inc.
11	34.737818	AA	American Airlines Inc.
12	33.012213	AS	Alaska Airlines Inc.
13	28.638594	DL	Delta Air Lines Inc.

Figure 5-44. The percentage of delayed flights for each airline

Let's plot the result using a bar chart:

```
plt.bar(df_percent_delay['AIRLINE'],
        df_percent_delay['Percentage'],
        color='skyblue')
plt.title('Percentage of Delayed Flights by Airline')
plt.xlabel('Airlines')
plt.ylabel('Percentage of Delayed Flights')
plt.xticks(rotation = 90)
plt.grid(axis='y')
```

Figure 5-45 shows the result.

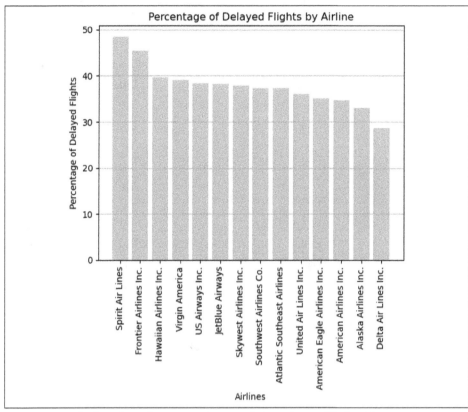

Figure 5-45. The bar chart showing airlines and their share of flight delays

For now, Spirit Air Lines is the leader when it comes to delays—48.46% of its flights were not on time. And if you want to find the airlines that are always on time (and even arrived earlier)? Easy, just swap the sign from > to <=:

```
df_percent_on_time = conn.execute('''
    WITH flight_delays AS (
        SELECT
            AIRLINE,
            1.0 * count(*) as TotalFlights,
            1.0 * sum(case when ARRIVAL_DELAY <= 0 then 1 else 0 end) as
                OnTimeFlights,
            (1.0 * sum(case when ARRIVAL_DELAY <= 0 then 1 else 0 end) /
                count(*)) * 100 as Percentage
        FROM flights
        GROUP BY AIRLINE
    )
    SELECT
        flight_delays.Percentage,
        airlines.IATA_CODE,
        airlines.AIRLINE
```

```
    FROM flight_delays
    JOIN airlines ON airlines.IATA_CODE = flight_delays.AIRLINE
    ORDER BY flight_delays.Percentage DESC;
''').df()
```

df_percent_on_time

Figure 5-46 shows the result.

	Percentage	IATA_CODE	AIRLINE
0	70.721365	DL	Delta Air Lines Inc.
1	66.360617	AS	Alaska Airlines Inc.
2	63.464760	AA	American Airlines Inc.
3	62.346453	UA	United Air Lines Inc.
4	61.150925	WN	Southwest Airlines Co.
5	60.232378	OO	Skywest Airlines Inc.
6	60.129536	HA	Hawaiian Airlines Inc.
7	59.930799	B6	JetBlue Airways
8	59.880781	VX	Virgin America
9	59.711317	EV	Atlantic Southeast Airlines
10	59.493198	MQ	American Eagle Airlines Inc.
11	59.350326	US	US Airways Inc.
12	53.787045	F9	Frontier Airlines Inc.
13	49.673281	NK	Spirit Air Lines

Figure 5-46. The percentage of on-time flights for each airline

Let's plot the bar chart:

```
plt.bar(df_percent_on_time['AIRLINE'],
        df_percent_on_time['Percentage'],
        color='skyblue')
plt.title('Percentage of Ontime Flights by Airline')
plt.xlabel('Airlines')
plt.ylabel('Percentage of Flights Ontime')
plt.xticks(rotation = 90)
plt.grid(axis='y')
```

Figure 5-47 shows that Delta Air Lines takes the lead, with 70.72% of its flights arriving on time (or early).

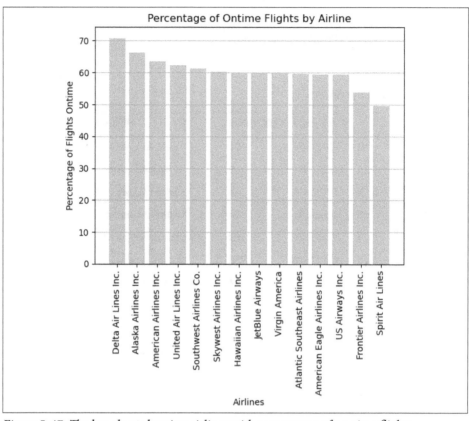

Figure 5-47. The bar chart showing airlines with percentages of on-time flights

Summary

This chapter taught us some of the exciting practical applications of DuckDB through exploratory data analysis of the 2015 Flight Delays dataset. Our journey started with mapping all airport locations onto the folium map. Then, we harnessed DuckDB's `spatial` extension for geospatial analysis, finding that the `spatial` extension's functions significantly streamline such analyses. The `spatial` extension offers a multitude of possibilities, and this chapter merely scratches the surface. The latter part of the chapter shifted focus to the descriptive analytics aspect, revealing valuable insights into flight delays, cancellations, and flight frequencies across different days of the week.

The methodologies and tools used here can be applied to diverse datasets, offering valuable perspectives for decision making in fields such as transportation management, business planning, and data-driven strategies across various industries. In the next chapter, you'll learn how to work with JSON files in DuckDB and how to manipulate JSON files that have complex structures.

## CHAPTER 6

Using DuckDB with JSON Files

In Chapter 2, you learned how to load data in different formats— CSV, Parquet, Excel files, and MySQL databases—into DuckDB. Another important file format that is popular among developers is JSON (JavaScript Object Notation).

One of the notable features of JSON is its flexible and dynamic structure: there is no fixed schema that you need to follow, and you are able to use dynamic key/value pairs to represent your own data. In DuckDB, there are several techniques you can use to work with JSON files, and hence JSON deserves a dedicated chapter.

In this chapter, we'll examine the various ways you can load JSON files into DuckDB. We will look at a few JSON files with different structures and provide recommendations on which function you can use for loading them.

Primer on JSON

This section is a quick primer for those who are new to the JSON file format. If you're already familiar with JSON, feel free to jump straight to the next section.

JSON is a lightweight data representation format that's easy for humans to read and interpret, and very efficient for computers to manipulate and generate. JSON supports the following data types:

- Object
- String
- Boolean
- Number
- Array
- null

The following sections will elaborate on each of the data types.

Object

An *object* is an unordered collection of key/value pairs enclosed in a pair of curly braces ({}). Here is an example:

```
{
    "key": "value"
}
```

Objects can also contain no key/value pairs. These objects are known as *empty objects*. The following is an example of an empty object:

```
{}
```

String

The key in an object must be a string, while the value can be a string, Boolean, number, array, null, or another object. The following shows an object with one key/value pair:

```
{
    "firstName": "John"
}
```

An object can have multiple key/value pairs, for example:

```
{
    "firstName": "John",
    "lastName": "Doe"
}
```

Each key/value pair must be separated by a comma (,). Note that no comma is needed after the last key/value pair.

Each key in the object must be unique. For example, the following example is not a valid JSON string since there are two firstName keys in the object:

```
{
    "firstName": "John",
    "firstName": "Doe"
}
```

Boolean

A Boolean value can be either true or false, as the following example shows:

```
{
    "firstName": "John",
    "lastName": "Doe",
    "isMember": true,
    "single": false,
}
```

Number

A number value can either be an integer or a floating-point number:

```json
{
    "firstName": "John",
    "lastName": "Doe",
    "isMember": true,
    "single": false,
    "weight": 79.5,
    "height": 1.73,
    "children": 3
}
```

Nested Object

The value of a key can be another object, as the following example shows:

```json
{
    "firstName": "John",
    "lastName": "Doe",
    "isMember": true,
    "single": false,
    "weight": 79.5,
    "height": 1.73,
    "children": 3,
    "address": {
        "line1": "123 Street",
        "line2": "San Francisco",
        "state": "CA",
        "postal": "12345"
    }
}
```

Array

An *array* is an ordered sequence of objects:

```json
{
    "firstName": "John",
    "lastName": "Doe",
    "isMember": true,
    "single": false,
    "weight": 79.5,
    "height": 1.73,
    "children": 3,
    "address": {
        "line1": "123 Street",
        "line2": "San Francisco",
        "state": "CA",
        "postal": "12345"
    },
    "phone": [
        {
            "type": "work",
            "number": "1234567"
        },
        {
```

```
            "type": "home",
            "number": "8765432"
        },
        {
            "type": "mobile",
            "number": "1234876"
        }
    ]
}
```

Note that arrays are denoted with a pair of square brackets ([]), and all the objects are separated by commas (,).

null

When a key has no value, you can assign a null to it:

```
{
    "firstName": "John",
    "lastName": "Doe",
    "isMember": true,
    "single": false,
    "weight": 79.5,
    "height": 1.73,
    "children": 3,
    "address": {
        "line1": "123 Street",
        "line2": "San Francisco",
        "state": "CA",
        "postal": "12345"
    },
    "phone": [
        {
            "type": "work",
            "number": "1234567"
        },
        {
            "type": "home",
            "number": "8765432"
        },
        {
            "type": "mobile",
            "number": "1234876"
        }
    ],
    "oldMembershipNo": null
}
```

With this knowledge of JSON, you are now ready to see how you can load a JSON file into DuckDB. The next section shows you the various ways to do just that.

Loading JSON Files into DuckDB

Having acquainted yourself with the JSON syntax, it is now time to learn how to work with it in DuckDB. For a demonstration, let's examine the contents of a file called *json1.json*, which contains the following data:

```
[
    {
        "id": 1,
        "name": "Sarah Johnson",
        "address": "4321 Oak Street Apartment 304 Los Angeles, CA 90001",
        "email":"sarah_johnson478@gmail.com",
        "weight": 140.50
    },
    {
        "id": 2,
        "name": "David Martinez",
        "address": "789 Maple Avenue Suite 102 New York, NY 10001",
        "email":"david_martinez431@gmail.com",
        "weight": 155.0
    },
    {
        "id": 3,
        "name": "Emily Wilson",
        "address": "567 Pine Road Unit 5B Chicago, IL 60601",
        "email":"emily_wilson998@gmail.com",
        "weight": 200.1
    }
]
```

In this JSON file, there is an array of JSON objects, each containing the following fields:

- id
- name
- address
- email
- weight

In the coming sections, you will learn how to load JSON files of different structures into DuckDB using the following:

- read_json_auto()
- read_json()
- COPY-FROM

Let's get started with the read_json_auto() function first.

Using the read_json_auto() Function

To load the JSON file using DuckDB, use the `read_json_auto()` function:

```
import duckdb
conn = duckdb.connect()
conn.execute('''
    SELECT
        *
    FROM read_json_auto('json1.json')
''').df()
```

This code snippet returns a table with five fields, as shown in Figure 6-1.

	id	name	address	email	weight
0	1	Sarah Johnson	4321 Oak Street Apartment 304 Los Angeles, CA ...	sarah_johnson478@gmail.com	140.5
1	2	David Martinez	789 Maple Avenue Suite 102 New York, NY 10001	david_martinez431@gmail.com	155.0
2	3	Emily Wilson	567 Pine Road Unit 5B Chicago, IL 60601	emily_wilson998@gmail.com	200.1

Figure 6-1. The JSON file is loaded into DuckDB and a five-column table is created

To save the table in DuckDB, you can modify the query as follows:

```
conn.execute('''
    CREATE TABLE People
    as
    FROM 'json1.json'
''')
```

The `read_json_auto()` function automatically parses the various key/value pairs in the JSON file and then loads it into DuckDB. Observe that the result (Figure 6-1) is a table with five columns, which match the key/value pairs in the JSON file.

Recall that in Chapter 3 we discussed the DuckDB CLI. Using the DuckDB CLI, if you use the following SQL query to load the JSON file, you will see the following output:

```
D SELECT *
  FROM read_json_auto('json1.json');
┌───────┬────────────────┬─────┬─────────────────────┬────────┐
│  id   │     name       │ ... │       email         │ weight │
│ int64 │    varchar     │     │      varchar        │ double │
├───────┼────────────────┼─────┼─────────────────────┼────────┤
│     1 │ Sarah Johnson  │ ... │ sarah_johnson478@g… │  140.5 │
│     2 │ David Martinez │ ... │ david_martinez431@… │  155.0 │
│     3 │ Emily Wilson   │ ... │ emily_wilson998@gm… │  200.1 │
├───────┴────────────────┴─────┴─────────────────────┴────────┤
│ 3 rows                                  5 columns (4 shown)  │
└─────────────────────────────────────────────────────────────┘
```

In particular, note that the output shows the data type for each column. This is especially helpful when we need to know the type of data that is loaded.

What if you want to load each object as a row and then put all the key/value pairs in a single column? To do that, set the records parameter to false:

```
conn.execute('''
    SELECT
        *
    FROM read_json_auto('json1.json', records = false)
''').df()
```

Figure 6-2 shows the result. All the key/value pairs are now stored in a single column.

	json
0	{'id': 1, 'name': 'Sarah Johnson', 'address': ...
1	{'id': 2, 'name': 'David Martinez', 'address':...
2	{'id': 3, 'name': 'Emily Wilson', 'address': '...

Figure 6-2. Using the records parameter to control how the key/value pairs are loaded

By default, records is set to true. Because the JSON extension expects JSON objects, it unpacks the fields into individual columns automatically.

Using the DuckDB CLI, the output looks like this:

```
D SELECT *
  FROM read_json_auto('json1.json', records = false);
┌──────────────────────────────────────────────────────────────────────┐
│                                  json                                  │
│   struct(id bigint, "name" varchar, address varchar, email varchar, weight d… │
├──────────────────────────────────────────────────────────────────────┤
│ {'id': 1, 'name': Sarah Johnson, 'address': 4321 Oak Street Apartment 304 … │
│ {'id': 2, 'name': David Martinez, 'address': 789 Maple Avenue Suite 102 Ne… │
│ {'id': 3, 'name': Emily Wilson, 'address': 567 Pine Road Unit 5B Chicago, … │
└──────────────────────────────────────────────────────────────────────┘
```

You can also selectively load specific fields from the JSON file. For example, say you only want to load the name and email key/value pairs:

```
conn.execute('''
    SELECT
        name, email
    FROM read_json_auto('json1.json')
''').df()
```

Figure 6-3 shows that only the name and email fields are loaded.

	name	email
0	Sarah Johnson	sarah_johnson478@gmail.com
1	David Martinez	david_martinez431@gmail.com
2	Emily Wilson	emily_wilson998@gmail.com

Figure 6-3. Loading only the name and email key/value pairs

In most cases, the `read_json_auto()` function in DuckDB will do the job of loading your JSON files. However, in some special cases, you may need to manually load a JSON file. You can do this by using the `read_json()` function, which we will discuss next.

Using the read_json() Function

The `read_json_auto()` function is actually an alias for the `read_json()` function, with auto detection turned on. In most cases, you should use the `read_json_auto()` function. In some rare cases, that function is not able to automatically detect the format of your file, in which case you should use the `read_json()` function and specify the format and schema of your data.

The following sections will take a look at a few examples of different JSON file structures and show you how to use the `read_json()` function to load them correctly.

Array of JSON objects

Earlier you saw that *json1.json* contains an array of JSON objects. Using the `read_json()` function, you can read the content by setting the `format` to `auto`, and then specifying which columns (and their types) you want to load:

```
conn.execute('''
    SELECT
        *
    FROM read_json('json1.json',
    format = 'auto',
    columns =
        {
            id:'INTEGER',
            name:'STRING',
            weight:'FLOAT'
        })
''').df()
```

For the `format` parameter, you can specify one of the following values:

- `array`
- `newline_delimited` or `nd`
- `unstructured`
- `auto`

Figure 6-4 shows the three columns that are loaded into DuckDB.

	id	name	weight
0	1	Sarah Johnson	140.500000
1	2	David Martinez	155.000000
2	3	Emily Wilson	200.100006

Figure 6-4. The table loaded into DuckDB

Using the DuckDB CLI, you can verify the types of each column:

```
D SELECT *
  FROM read_json('json1.json',
      format = 'auto',
      columns =
          {
              id:'INTEGER',
              name:'STRING',
              weight:'FLOAT'
          });
```

```
| id    |     name       | weight |
| int32 |    varchar     | float  |
|-------|----------------|--------|
|     1 | Sarah Johnson  |  140.5 |
|     2 | David Martinez |  155.0 |
|     3 | Emily Wilson   |  200.1 |
```

If you want to read all the key/value pairs, simply omit the `columns` parameter:

```
conn.execute('''
    SELECT
        *
    FROM read_json('json1.json',
    format = 'auto')
''').df()
```

Figure 6-5 shows the output of all the key/value pairs loaded into columns.

	id	name	address	email	weight
0	1	Sarah Johnson	4321 Oak Street Apartment 304 Los Angeles, CA ...	sarah_johnson478@gmail.com	140.5
1	2	David Martinez	789 Maple Avenue Suite 102 New York, NY 10001	david_martinez431@gmail.com	155.0
2	3	Emily Wilson	567 Pine Road Unit 5B Chicago, IL 60601	emily_wilson998@gmail.com	200.1

Figure 6-5. Loading all the key/value pairs

What about the other formats? The next section shows when to use the new `line_delimited` format.

Newline-delimited (ND) JSON

Suppose you have another file named *json1_a.json* that contains three lines of JSON objects, each separated by a newline character:

```
{"id": 1, "name": "Sarah Johnson", "address":
    {"line1":"4321 Oak Street Apartment","line2":"304 Los Angeles",
     "state":"CA", "zip":90001}, "email":"sarah_johnson478@gmail.com",
     "weight": 140.50}
{"id": 2, "name": "David Martinez", "address":
    {"line1":"789 Maple Avenue ","line2":"Suite 102 New York",
     "state":"NY","zip":10001},   "email":"david_martinez431@gmail.com",
     "weight": 155.0}
{"id": 3, "name": "Emily Wilson", "address":
    {"line1":"567 Pine Road Unit 5B Chicago",
     "state":"IL", "zip":60601}, "email":"emily_wilson998@gmail.com",
     "weight": 200.1}
```

This is known as a *newline-delimited* JSON file. To load this JSON file using the `read_json()` function, set the format to `newline_delimited`:

```
conn.execute('''
    SELECT
       *
    FROM read_json('json1_a.json',
    format = 'newline_delimited',
    columns =
        {
            id:'INTEGER',
            name:'STRING',
            weight:'FLOAT'
        })
''').df()
```

In addition to the `newline_delimited` format, you can also use the `nd` or `unstructured` format. The `unstructured` format can include any type of JSON, including newline-delimited JSON, as well as more free-form or irregular JSON.

An alternative way of reading a newline-delimited JSON file is to use the `read_ndjson_auto()` function, which does not require you to specify the format parameter:

```
conn.execute('''
    SELECT
       *
    FROM read_ndjson_auto('json1_a.json',
    columns =
        {
            id:'INTEGER',
            name:'STRING',
            weight:'FLOAT'
        })
''').df()
```

This code snippet produces the same output as Figure 6-4.

Nested JSON

Let's consider another example JSON file (*json2.json*) where the objects are nested (highlighted in bold):

```
[
    {
        "id": 1,
        "name": "Sarah Johnson",
        "address": {
            "line1":"4321 Oak Street Apartment",
            "line2":"304 Los Angeles",
            "state":"CA",
            "zip":90001
        },
        "email":"sarah_johnson478@gmail.com",
        "weight": 140.50
    },
    {
        "id": 2,
        "name": "David Martinez",
        "address": {
            "line1":"789 Maple Avenue ",
            "line2":"Suite 102 New York",
            "state":"NY",
            "zip":10001
        },
        "email":"david_martinez431@gmail.com",
        "weight": 155.0
    },
    {
        "id": 3,
        "name": "Emily Wilson",
        "address": {
            "line1":"567 Pine Road Unit 5B Chicago",
            "state":"IL",
            "zip":60601
        },
        "email":"emily_wilson998@gmail.com",
        "weight": 200.1
    }
]
```

Here, you can see that the value of the `address` key is further split into four more keys: `line1`, `line2`, `state`, and `zip`. The exception is the third object, where the value of the `address` key does not have the `line2` key.

Let's use the `read_json()` function to load this file:

```
conn.execute('''
    SELECT
        *
    FROM read_json('json2.json')
''').df()
```

You will see that the value of the address field is now contained in a single column, as shown in Figure 6-6.

	id	name	address	email	weight
0	1	Sarah Johnson	{'line1': '4321 Oak Street Apartment', 'line2'...	sarah_johnson478@gmail.com	140.5
1	2	David Martinez	{'line1': '789 Maple Avenue ', 'line2': 'Suite...	david_martinez431@gmail.com	155.0
2	3	Emily Wilson	{'line1': '567 Pine Road Unit 5B Chicago', 'li...	emily_wilson998@gmail.com	200.1

Figure 6-6. The value of the address field is now contained within a single column

What if you want the value of the address field to be represented in individual columns? In this example, you want to have four columns: line1, line2, state, and zip. You can accomplish this by specifying the individual keys in the SQL statement:

```
conn.execute('''
    SELECT
        id,
        name,
        address['line1'] as line1,
        address['line2'] as line2,
        address['state'] as state,
        address['zip'] as zip,
        email,
        weight
    FROM read_json('json2.json')
''').df()
```

Figure 6-7 shows the contents of the address field now represented in four columns.

	id	name	line1	line2	state	zip	email	weight
0	1	Sarah Johnson	4321 Oak Street Apartment	304 Los Angeles	CA	90001	sarah_johnson478@gmail.com	140.5
1	2	David Martinez	789 Maple Avenue	Suite 102 New York	NY	10001	david_martinez431@gmail.com	155.0
2	3	Emily Wilson	567 Pine Road Unit 5B Chicago	None	IL	60601	emily_wilson998@gmail.com	200.1

Figure 6-7. The value of the address field is now represented in four columns

What happens if there is another nested object in the address key? The following example (*json2_a.json*) shows that within the value of the address key, there is another location key, which contains three more key/value pairs:

```
[
    {
        "id": 1,
        "name": "Sarah Johnson",
        "address": {
            "line1":"4321 Oak Street Apartment",
            "line2":"304 Los Angeles",
```

```
            "location" : {
                "state":"CA",
                "city":"Calexico",
                "zip":90001
            }
        },
        "email":"sarah_johnson478@gmail.com",
        "weight": 140.50
    },
    {
        "id": 2,
        "name": "David Martinez",
        "address": {
            "line1":"789 Maple Avenue ",
            "line2":"Suite 102 New York",
            "location" : {
                "state":"NY",
                "city":"Coney Island",
                "zip":10001
            }
        },
        "email":"david_martinez431@gmail.com",
        "weight": 155.0
    },
    {
        "id": 3,
        "name": "Emily Wilson",
        "address": {
            "line1":"567 Pine Road Unit 5B Chicago",
            "location" : {
                "state":"IL",
                "city":"Brookfield",
                "zip":60601
            }
        },
        "email":"emily_wilson998@gmail.com",
        "weight": 200.1
    }
]
```

In this case, you simply modify your SQL statement like this:

```
conn.execute('''
    SELECT
        address['line1'] as line1,
        address['line2'] as line2,
        address['location']['state'] as state,
        address['location']['city'] as city,
        address['location']['zip'] as zip,
        email,
        weight
    FROM read_json('json2_a.json')
''').df()
```

Figure 6-8 shows the output.

	line1	line2	state	city	zip	email	weight
0	4321 Oak Street Apartment	304 Los Angeles	CA	Calexico	90001	sarah_johnson478@gmail.com	140.5
1	789 Maple Avenue	Suite 102 New York	NY	Coney Island	10001	david_martinez431@gmail.com	155.0
2	567 Pine Road Unit 5B Chicago	None	IL	Brookfield	60601	emily_wilson998@gmail.com	200.1

Figure 6-8. The contents of the `location` field are now represented in three columns

What if your JSON file contains specific structures where there are no clear repeating patterns? The next section shows you how to work with it.

Custom JSON file

Consider the following JSON file (*json3.json*), which contains the `people` key whose value is an array of JSON objects:

```json
{
    "people": [
    {
        "id": 1,
        "name": "Sarah Johnson",
        "address": {
            "line1":"4321 Oak Street Apartment",
            "line2":"304 Los Angeles",
            "state":"CA",
            "zip":90001
        },
    "email":"sarah_johnson478@gmail.com",
        "weight": 140.50
    },
    {
        "id": 2,
        "name": "David Martinez",
        "address": {
            "line1":"789 Maple Avenue ",
            "line2":"Suite 102 New York",
            "state":"NY",
            "zip":10001
        },
        "email":"david_martinez431@gmail.com",
        "weight": 155.0
    },
    {
        "id": 3,
        "name": "Emily Wilson",
        "address": {
            "line1":"567 Pine Road Unit 5B Chicago",
            "state":"IL",
            "zip":60601
        },
        "email":"emily_wilson998@gmail.com",
```

```
        "weight": 200.1
    }
    ]
}
```

Let's try to load it into DuckDB using the `read_json()` function:

```
conn.execute('''
    SELECT
        *
    FROM read_json('json3.json')
''').df()
```

Figure 6-9 shows the output. Interestingly, the value of the `people` key is loaded into a single column.

people
0   [{'id': 1, 'name': 'Sarah Johnson', 'address':...

Figure 6-9. The value of the `people` key is loaded as a single column

Since the `people` key in the JSON file contains a JSON array of objects, let's try to use the `unnest()` function in SQL to transform each element in the array into rows:

```
conn.execute('''
    SELECT unnest(people) p
    FROM read_json('json3.json')
''').df()
```

Figure 6-10 shows the output. Things are looking better now—at least each object is transformed into a row.

p
0   {'id': 1, 'name': 'Sarah Johnson', 'address': ...
1   {'id': 2, 'name': 'David Martinez', 'address':...
2   {'id': 3, 'name': 'Emily Wilson', 'address': {...

Figure 6-10. Each object in the `people` key is now represented as a row

The next step would be to unpack the contents of each row. We can do that with the variable p, which contains the contents of each row:

```
conn.execute('''
    SELECT
        p.id,
        p.name,
        p.address['line1'] as line1,
        p.address['line2'] as line2,
        p.address['state'] as state,
        p.address['zip'] as zip,
        p.email,
        p.weight
```

```
    FROM
    (
        SELECT unnest(people) p
        FROM read_json('json3.json')
    )
''').df()
```

Note that this query can also be written as follows, with the contents of each row wrapped in square brackets:

```
conn.execute('''
    SELECT
        p['id'],
        p['name'],
        p['address']['line1'] as line1,
        p['address']['line2'] as line2,
        p['address']['state'] as state,
        p['address']['zip'] as zip,
        p['email'],
        p['weight']
    FROM
    (
        SELECT unnest(people) p
        FROM read_json('json3.json')
    )
''').df()
```

Figure 6-11 shows that the contents of each row are now unpacked into their individual columns.

	id	name	line1	line2	state	zip	email	weight
0	1	Sarah Johnson	4321 Oak Street Apartment	304 Los Angeles	CA	90001	sarah_johnson478@gmail.com	140.5
1	2	David Martinez	789 Maple Avenue	Suite 102 New York	NY	10001	david_martinez431@gmail.com	155.0
2	3	Emily Wilson	567 Pine Road Unit 5B Chicago	None	IL	60601	emily_wilson998@gmail.com	200.1

Figure 6-11. The contents of each row, unpacked into individual columns

The next section will discuss how you can load multiple JSON files into DuckDB using the `read_json()` function.

Loading multiple JSON files

So far, we have been loading individual JSON files into DuckDB. However, oftentimes you may need to load multiple JSON files all at once. Let's discuss how you can do that.

Consider the following JSON file (*json4.json*):

```
[
    {
        "id": 1,
        "name": "Sarah Johnson",
        "address": "4321 Oak Street Apartment 304 Los Angeles, CA 90001",
        "email":"sarah_johnson478@gmail.com",
        "weight": 140.50
    },
    {
        "id": 2,
        "name": "David Martinez",
        "address": "789 Maple Avenue Suite 102 New York, NY 10001",
        "email":"david_martinez431@gmail.com",
        "weight": 155.0
    }
]
```

And consider this additional JSON file (*json5.json*):

```
[
    {
        "id": 3,
        "name": "Emily Wilson",
        "address": {
            "line1":"567 Pine Road Unit 5B Chicago",
            "state":"IL",
            "zip":60601
        },
        "height": 66
    }
]
```

Observe that both files have the same general structure—an array of objects. The key difference is the composition of each object: the `weight` and `email` keys are missing in the second JSON file and the contents of the `address` key are different for the two files.

Let's now load the two files together by passing a list of filenames to the `read_json()` function:

```
conn.execute('''
    SELECT
        *
    FROM read_json(['json4.json','json5.json'])
''').df()
```

When you load multiple JSON files in DuckDB and a field has a string value in one file but a numeric value in another, DuckDB will attempt to infer the data type for that field. If there's a type conflict, DuckDB might cast the numeric value to a string to maintain consistency, resulting in the entire column being treated as strings. In some cases, if the type conflict is severe, it may throw an error. To avoid this, ensure data type consistency across files or explicitly cast the field to a desired type in the query.

Figure 6-12 shows the output.

	id	name	address	email	weight	height
0	1	Sarah Johnson	"4321 Oak Street Apartment 304 Los Angeles, CA...	sarah_johnson478@gmail.com	140.5	NaN
1	2	David Martinez	"789 Maple Avenue Suite 102 New York, NY 10001"	david_martinez431@gmail.com	155.0	NaN
2	3	Emily Wilson	{"line1":"567 Pine Road Unit 5B Chicago","stat...	None	NaN	66.0

Figure 6-12. The result of loading two JSON files

Observe the following:

- The result is the combination of the two files loaded.
- The resultant columns match the names of the keys in the JSON files. The order of the keys in the JSON files is not important.
- For fields that are missing in each row, a NaN value is inserted for numeric fields, while a None value is inserted for string fields.

In general, when loading multiple files, you should ideally ensure that all the files have the same structure.

 You can always write a Python script to ensure that two JSON files have the same structure.

Rather than supplying a list of filenames to load, you can optionally use the *glob syntax* (commonly known as *wildcard syntax*). You can use the following wildcards to read multiple JSON files:

Wildcard symbol	What it does
*	Matches any number of any characters (including none)
**	Matches any number of subdirectories (including none)
?	Matches any single character
[abc]	Matches one character given in the brackets
[a-z]	Matches one character from the range given in the brackets

The following code snippet loads all the files in the current directory whose filenames begin with "json" and end with a ".json" extension:

```
conn.execute('''
    SELECT
        *
    FROM read_json('json*.json')
''').df()
```

If you only want to load JSON files in the current directory whose filenames begin with "json," followed by a single character, and then end with ".json," use the ? wildcard character:

```
conn.execute('''
    SELECT
        *
    FROM read_json('json?.json')
''').df()
```

This code snippet loads *json1.json*, *json2.json*, *json3.json*, *json4.json*, and *json5.json*.

Now that we have seen how to use the `read_json()` and `read_json_auto()` functions, let's look at the third way to load JSON files into DuckDB.

Using the COPY-FROM Statement

The third way to load JSON files into DuckDB is to use the `COPY-FROM` statement. This offers significant advantages over `read_json()`, particularly when dealing with large datasets. `COPY-FROM` is optimized for performance and scalability. It enables more efficient handling of large files by loading data in batches, which reduces memory consumption and improves speed. `COPY-FROM` takes full advantage of DuckDB's parallel processing capabilities, further boosting performance when loading gigabytes of data. Additionally, `COPY-FROM` integrates more smoothly into database workflows by directly loading data into tables with minimal preprocessing and automatic schema inference, ensuring data consistency.

In contrast, `read_json()` loads the entire file into memory, which can cause performance bottlenecks with large files and often requires additional steps to enforce schema consistency or insert the data into a database. Therefore, `COPY-FROM` is better suited for high-performance, large-scale data ingestion, while `read_json()` is more appropriate for smaller, interactive tasks.

To use the `COPY-FROM` statement to load a JSON file, you need to first create a table with the correct schema to match the JSON structure, and then use `COPY-FROM` to load the file. The following code snippet creates a *people* table in DuckDB to store the contents of the *json1.json* file:

```
conn = duckdb.connect()
conn.execute('''
    CREATE TABLE people (id INT, name STRING, address STRING,
                         email STRING, weight FLOAT);
    COPY people FROM 'json1.json' (FORMAT JSON, AUTO_DETECT true);
    SELECT * FROM people;
''').df()
```

This code snippet produces the result shown in Figure 6-13.

	id	name	address	email	weight
0	1	Sarah Johnson	4321 Oak Street Apartment 304 Los Angeles, CA ...	sarah_johnson478@gmail.com	140.500000
1	2	David Martinez	789 Maple Avenue Suite 102 New York, NY 10001	david_martinez431@gmail.com	155.000000
2	3	Emily Wilson	567 Pine Road Unit 5B Chicago, IL 60601	emily_wilson998@gmail.com	200.100006

Figure 6-13. Loading the JSON file using the COPY-FROM statement

You need to use the (`FORMAT JSON, AUTO_DETECT true`) statement to load the JSON file properly. If your JSON file has a complex structure (such as *json5.json*), this method is not recommended.

In the next section, you will learn how to export DuckDB tables to JSON.

Exporting Tables to JSON

Often, we might want to persist the tables that we have in DuckDB to a JSON file. This is useful when you want to exchange data with other platforms, or simply as a way to back up your data. You can export your data to JSON easily using the COPY statement that we discussed in the previous section.

Consider the following code snippet, where a table named *people* is loaded from a JSON file:

```
conn = duckdb.connect()
conn.execute('''
    CREATE OR REPLACE TABLE people
    as
    SELECT
        name,
        weight
    FROM read_ndjson_auto('json1_a.json')
''')
display(conn.execute('SELECT * FROM people').df())
```

Figure 6-14 shows the content of the *people* table.

	name	weight
0	Sarah Johnson	140.5
1	David Martinez	155.0
2	Emily Wilson	200.1

Figure 6-14. The content of the people *table*

To write the content of the *people* table to a file named *people.json*, use the COPY-TO statement and specify FORMAT JSON (optional, as DuckDB deduces the file type based on the file extension):

```
conn.execute('''
    COPY people
    TO
    'people.json' (FORMAT JSON);
''')
```

The content of *people.json* looks like this:

```
{"id":1,"name":"Sarah Johnson","weight":140.5}
{"id":2,"name":"David Martinez","weight":155.0}
{"id":3,"name":"Emily Wilson","weight":200.1}
```

Observe that the content is not strictly standard JSON; it is actually a newline-delimited JSON file, where each line contains a separate JSON object. If you want the output to be strictly JSON, specify ARRAY TRUE:

```
conn.execute('''
    COPY people
    TO
    'people_array.json' (ARRAY TRUE);
''')
```

The content of *people_array.json* will look like this:

```
[
    {"name":"Sarah Johnson","weight":140.5},
    {"name":"David Martinez","weight":155.0},
    {"name":"Emily Wilson","weight":200.1}
]
```

This is a valid JSON string.

Summary

In this chapter, you learned several methods for loading JSON files into DuckDB:

- Use the read_json_auto() function. This method is the most direct, and you should always try this method first.

- Use the read_json() function. If your JSON file has some complex structure and the read_json_auto() function is not able to load it properly, you should try using the read_json() function to load your file.

- Use the COPY-FROM statement. To use this method, you need to manually create a table in DuckDB first before loading the JSON file. Use this method if the structure of your JSON file is relatively simple; otherwise, you should always try to use the read_json_auto() or read_json() functions.

Finally, you also learned how to export the tables in your DuckDB to a JSON file using the COPY-TO statement.

In the next chapter, you will learn how to use JupySQL, a SQL client for Jupyter Notebook. Using JupySQL enables you to access your datasets directly in Jupyter Notebook using SQL.

## CHAPTER 7

Using DuckDB with JupySQL

Traditionally, data scientists use Jupyter Notebook to pull data from database servers or from external datasets (such as CSV, JSON files, etc.) and store it into pandas Data-Frames (see Figure 7-1).

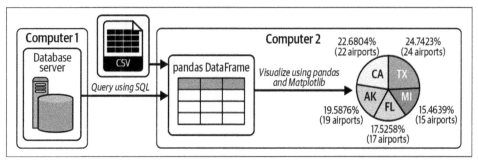

Figure 7-1. Traditional way of querying data as pandas DataFrames and then using them for data visualization

They then use the DataFrames for visualization purposes. This approach has a couple of drawbacks:

- Querying a database server may degrade the performance of the database server, which may not be optimized for analytical workloads.

- Loading the data into DataFrames takes up precious resources, including memory and compute. For example, if the intention is to visualize certain aspects of the dataset, you need to load the entire dataset into memory before you can perform visualization on it.

- Plotting visualizations using Matplotlib also uses a significant amount of memory. Behind the scenes, Matplotlib maintains various objects such as figures, axes, lines, text, and other graphical elements in memory. Each of these elements consumes resources as they are created and rendered. Additionally, Matplotlib handles data arrays used for plotting and temporarily stores them in memory for processing. If you're creating multiple plots or figures, each figure and its associated data remain in memory until explicitly closed or cleared, leading to increased memory usage. Furthermore, backends used for rendering (e.g., interactive or static backends) also play a role, with some backends requiring more memory to handle complex visual elements and graphical interfaces. This can be especially noticeable when working with high-resolution plots, multiple subplots, or large datasets.

While tools like Power BI, Domo, Tableau, and Excel simplify the process of loading and visualizing data, pandas remains an excellent choice for quick, in-line visualizations during EDA due to its built-in plotting features. With minimal effort, users can generate basic visualizations such as line plots, bar charts, histograms, and scatter plots directly from pandas DataFrames or Series. This makes it convenient for quickly visualizing data distributions, trends, and patterns while working on data manipulation—without needing to switch to other libraries or perform extra steps.

To improve performance, ideally the processing of the data (all the data wrangling and filtering) should be offloaded to a client that is able to perform the data analytics efficiently and return the result to be used for visualization. And this is the topic of this chapter—JupySQL.

 While DuckDB also allows you to access your datasets directly using SQL, operations with JupySQL can be done as SQL cells in the Notebook.

What Is JupySQL?

JupySQL is a SQL client for Jupyter Notebook, enabling you to access your datasets directly in Jupyter Notebook using SQL. The main idea of JupySQL is to run SQL in a Jupyter Notebook, hence its name. JupySQL is a fork of ipython-sql, which adds SQL cells to Jupyter. It is currently actively maintained and enhanced by the team at Ploomber.

JupySQL enables you to query your dataset using SQL, without your needing to maintain the DataFrame to store your dataset. For example, you could use JupySQL to connect to a database server (such as MySQL or PostgreSQL) or CSV files through the DuckDB engine. The result of your query can then be directly used for visualization. Figure 7-2 shows how JupySQL works.

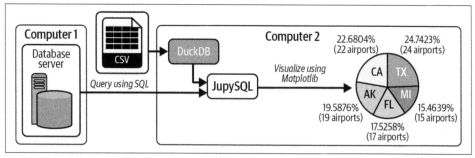

Figure 7-2. How JupySQL works with DuckDB to query various data sources and use them for data visualization

In the following sections, you will learn how to install JupySQL, use it in your Jupyter Notebook, and use it with DuckDB.

Installing JupySQL

To use JupySQL in your Jupyter Notebook, you need to install the `jupysql` package. In addition, to work with DuckDB within JupySQL, you also need to install the `duckdb-engine` package. The following statement installs both:

```
!pip install jupysql duckdb-engine
```

The `duckdb-engine` package is the SQLAlchemy driver for DuckDB. SQLAlchemy is an open source Python library for working with relational databases. It provides a set of high-level and low-level tools for interacting with databases in a flexible and efficient manner. You should also install the SQLAlchemy library:

```
!pip install SQLAlchemy
```

You can use the following magic commands (denoted by a % symbol) in your Jupyter Notebook to use JupySQL to interact with your data sources.

Option	What it does
%sql	A line magic command to execute an SQL statement
%%sql	A cell magic command to execute multiline SQL statements
%sqlplot	A line magic command to plot a chart

Loading the sql Extension

With the necessary packages installed, let's see how you can use SQL directly in your Jupyter Notebook using JupySQL.

First, create a new Jupyter Notebook. Next, create a new cell and load the `sql` extension using the `%load_ext` line magic command (see Figure 7-3):

```
%load_ext sql
```

Figure 7-3. Loading the sql extension using %load_ext line magic command

One important point to note here: do not put your comments in the same line as the `%load_ext` magic command. This will cause errors on your SQL statement. For example, suppose you want to put a comment on the preceding statement, such as:

```
%load_ext sql  # load the sql extension
```

This will try to load the module named "sql # load the sql extension," resulting in an error. To add a comment, put it on a separate line:

```
# load the sql extension
%load_ext sql
```

Integrating with DuckDB

With the `sql` extension loaded, you need to load a database engine in which you can use it to process your data. For this section, you will use DuckDB. The following statement starts a DuckDB in-memory database:

```
%sql duckdb://
```

This statement uses a SQLAlchemy-style connection string to connect to the database engine—in this case, the DuckDB engine. If you want to use a persistent DuckDB database, specify the name of the file, like this:

```
%sql duckdb:///MyDB.db
```

JupySQL generally manages the connection for you. When you run SQL commands using `%sql`, it opens a connection, executes the command, and closes the connection automatically after execution.

If you need help with JupySQL, you can always use the %sql? line magic command to display the docstring (see Figure 7-4):

```
%sql?
```

```
Docstring:
::

  %execute [-l] [-x CLOSE] [-c CREATOR] [-s SECTION] [-p] [-P] [-n]
           [--append] [-a CONNECTION_ARGUMENTS] [-f FILE] [-S SAVE]
           [-w WITH_] [-N] [-A ALIAS] [--interact INTERACT]
           [line ...]

Runs SQL statement against a database, specified by
SQLAlchemy connect string.

If no database connection has been established, first word
should be a SQLAlchemy connection string, or the user@db name
of an established connection.

Examples::

  %%sql postgresql://me:mypw@localhost/mydb
  SELECT * FROM mytable

  %%sql me@mydb
  DELETE FROM mytable

  %%sql
  DROP TABLE mytable

SQLAlchemy connect string syntax examples:

  postgresql://me:mypw@localhost/mydb
  sqlite://
  mysql+pymysql://me:mypw@localhost/mydb
```

Figure 7-4. Displaying the docstring for JupySQL

Performing Queries

Let's start off by using the %sql magic command in Jupyter Notebook to perform a query on the CSV file *airlines.csv*:

```
%sql SELECT * FROM airlines.csv
```

You will see the result of loading the *airlines.csv* file in Figure 7-5.

IATA_CODE	AIRLINE
UA	United Air Lines Inc.
AA	American Airlines Inc.
US	US Airways Inc.
F9	Frontier Airlines Inc.
B6	JetBlue Airways
OO	Skywest Airlines Inc.
AS	Alaska Airlines Inc.
NK	Spirit Air Lines
WN	Southwest Airlines Co.
DL	Delta Air Lines Inc.

Truncated to displaylimit of 10.

Figure 7-5. The CSV file is loaded into DuckDB

The result of the `%sql` magic command is a `sql.run.ResultSet` object. You can convert the result into a pandas DataFrame if you wish:

```
rs = %sql SELECT * FROM 'airlines.csv'
df = rs.DataFrame()    # convert to pandas DataFrame
```

Note that there is a default display limit of 10 rows for the result. If you want to display all the rows, use the following statement:

```
%config SqlMagic.displaylimit = None       # or set to 0
```

Configuration details can also be read from a file (*https://oreil.ly/ 2Vf_N*) (e.g., at ~/.jupysql/config), which requires installation of the toml package (`pip install toml`).

If your query spans multiple lines, use the `%%sql` cell magic command:

```
%%sql
SELECT
    count(*) as Count, STATE
FROM airports.csv
GROUP BY STATE
ORDER BY Count
```

The result is shown in Figure 7-6.

Count	STATE
1	CT
1	VT
1	RI
1	WV
1	AS
1	NH
1	MD
1	GU
1	DE
2	VI

Truncated to displaylimit of 10.

Figure 7-6. Counting the number of airports for each state

While the preceding queries can load CSV files into DuckDB, the data is not persisted as tables in the DuckDB database. If you want to make use of the *airlines* content, you must perform the query again. To persist the table in the DuckDB database, you need to use the CREATE TABLE statement:

```
%%sql
CREATE TABLE airlines
as
FROM 'airlines.csv'
```

The content of *airlines.csv* is now saved in the table named *airlines* (within the *MyDB.db* file since we are using a file-backed DuckDB database). To retrieve the content of the *airlines* table, use the following statement:

```
%sql SELECT * FROM airlines
```

Note that if you open the DuckDB database with a persistent database, the tables are automatically saved in the database. The next time you open the database, the tables will still be there. For in-memory DuckDB databases, all the tables will be lost when you restart the Jupyter kernel.

To check the tables in the DuckDB database, use the %sqlcmd command:

```
%sqlcmd tables
```

Figure 7-7 shows the *airlines* table in the DuckDB database.

Name
airlines

Figure 7-7. The airlines *table stored in the DuckDB database*

To view the schema for the table, use the `%sqlcmd columns` command with the `-t` argument:

```
%sqlcmd columns -t airlines
```

Figure 7-8 shows the schema for the *airlines* table.

name	type	nullable	default	autoincrement	comment
IATA_CODE	VARCHAR	True	None	False	None
AIRLINE	VARCHAR	True	None	False	None

Figure 7-8. Viewing the schema for the airlines *table*

If you want to generate statistics about the table, use the `%sqlcmd profile` command with the `-t` argument:

```
%sqlcmd profile -t airlines
```

Figure 7-9 shows the statistics for the *airlines* table.

	IATA_CODE	AIRLINE
count	14	14
unique	14	14
top	WN	Skywest Airlines Inc.
freq	1	1
min	nan	nan
max	nan	nan

Figure 7-9. Generating statistics for the airlines *table*

Storing Snippets

Besides saving the result of your queries as tables in your DuckDB database, you can also save the queries (known as *snippets*) so that you can invoke them again later.

The following example saves a snippet and names it `state_count`:

```
%%sql --save state_count
SELECT
    count(*) as Count, STATE
FROM airports.csv
GROUP BY STATE
ORDER BY Count DESC
LIMIT 10
```

Figure 7-10 shows the result of this query.

Count	STATE
24	TX
22	CA
19	AK
17	FL
15	MI
14	NY
10	CO
8	WI
8	MT
8	MN

Truncated to displaylimit of 10.

Figure 7-10. JupySQL runs the snippet that you created

Stored snippets are not persisted to DuckDB databases (even with persistent databases).

To run this snippet again, you just use the snippet name:

```
%sql SELECT * FROM state_count
```

Figure 7-11 shows JupySQL is running the query from the stored snippet.

Count	STATE
24	TX
22	CA
19	AK
17	FL
15	MI
14	NY
10	CO
8	WI
8	MT
8	MN

Truncated to displaylimit of 10.

Figure 7-11. The output of running the stored snippet

If you do not want to execute the query when you define the snippet, use the `no-execute` option:

```
%%sql --save state_count --no-execute
SELECT
    count(*) as Count, STATE
FROM airports.csv
GROUP BY STATE
ORDER BY Count
```

Now that you have learned how to use JupySQL to work with your data sources, it is time for you to visualize your data using JupySQL! The next section will discuss the various types of plots you can create using JupySQL.

Visualization

JupySQL enables you to plot charts using the `%sqlplot` line magic command. In the following sections, you will learn how to plot:

- Histograms
- Box plots
- Pie charts
- Bar plots

Histograms

Let's start by plotting a histogram. Before you start plotting, you need to ensure that the Matplotlib package is installed on your computer:

```
!pip install matplotlib
```

Next, create and save a query and name it `airports_A`:

```
%%sql --save airports_A --no-execute
SELECT
*
FROM airports.csv
WHERE state LIKE 'A%'
```

This query finds all the airports belong to states with names starting with "A"—that is, AK, AL, AR, AS, and AZ. The `--no-execute` option prevents the query from being executed immediately, so no data is retrieved or processed at this time.

To plot a histogram showing the number of airports for each of the states starting with "A", use the `%sqlplot` line magic command:

```
%sqlplot histogram --table airports_A --column STATE
```

Here are the options used:

Option	What it does
`--table`	Specifies the table/query to use for plotting.
`--column`	Specifies the field name to use as the column for the plot.

The histogram also supports the following options:

Option	What it does
`-s/--schema`	Schema to use. No need to pass if using a default schema.
`-b/--bins`	Number of bins. The default is 50.
`-B/--breaks`	Custom bin intervals.
`-W/--binwidth`	Width of each bin.
`-w/--with`	Use a previously saved query as input data.

Figure 7-12 shows the histogram.

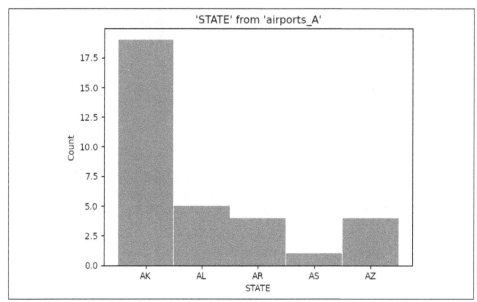

Figure 7-12. Histogram showing the number of airports in states starting with "A"

Let's try another query—this time from the Boston housing dataset (*https://oreil.ly/ W9Wxr*) (Licensing: CC0: Public Domain (*https://oreil.ly/Rq8FR*)). Let's create a query to load the *boston.csv* file:

```
%%sql --save boston
SELECT
    *
FROM boston.csv
```

Figure 7-13 shows the content of the Boston dataset.

column00	crim	zn	indus	chas	nox	rm	age	dis	rad	tax	ptratio	black	lstat	medv
1	0.00632	18.0	2.31	0	0.538	6.575	65.2	4.09	1	296	15.3	396.9	4.98	24.0
2	0.02731	0.0	7.07	0	0.469	6.421	78.9	4.9671	2	242	17.8	396.9	9.14	21.6
3	0.02729	0.0	7.07	0	0.469	7.185	61.1	4.9671	2	242	17.8	392.83	4.03	34.7
4	0.03237	0.0	2.18	0	0.458	6.998	45.8	6.0622	3	222	18.7	394.63	2.94	33.4
5	0.06905	0.0	2.18	0	0.458	7.147	54.2	6.0622	3	222	18.7	396.9	5.33	36.2
6	0.02985	0.0	2.18	0	0.458	6.43	58.7	6.0622	3	222	18.7	394.12	5.21	28.7
7	0.08829	12.5	7.87	0	0.524	6.012	66.6	5.5605	5	311	15.2	395.6	12.43	22.9
8	0.14455	12.5	7.87	0	0.524	6.172	96.1	5.9505	5	311	15.2	396.9	19.15	27.1
9	0.21124	12.5	7.87	0	0.524	5.631	100.0	6.0821	5	311	15.2	386.63	29.93	16.5
10	0.17004	12.5	7.87	0	0.524	6.004	85.9	6.5921	5	311	15.2	386.71	17.1	18.9

Truncated to displaylimit of 10.

Figure 7-13. The content of the Boston dataset

Specifically, we want to plot the distribution of age and median dollar value of owner-occupied homes in thousands (medv):

```
%sqlplot histogram --column age medv --table boston
```

Figure 7-14 shows the histogram. For this histogram, you used two fields, age and medv.

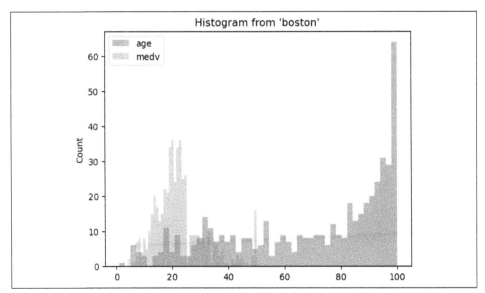

Figure 7-14. The histogram for the age and medv fields

The next dataset you will use is the Titanic dataset from Kaggle (*https://oreil.ly/Kyv6X*) (*titanic_train.csv*; licensing: Database Contents License (DbCL) v1.0).

As usual, let's first create a query for it:

```
%%sql --save titanic
SELECT
    *
FROM titanic_train.csv
WHERE age NOT NULL AND embarked NOT NULL
```

Figure 7-15 shows the Titanic dataset.

PassengerId	Survived	Pclass	Name	Sex	Age	SibSp	Parch	Ticket	Fare	Cabin	Embarked
1	0	3	Braund, Mr. Owen Harris	male	22.0	1	0	A/5 21171	7.25	None	S
2	1	1	Cumings, Mrs. John Bradley (Florence Briggs Thayer)	female	38.0	1	0	PC 17599	71.2833	C85	C
3	1	3	Heikkinen, Miss. Laina	female	26.0	0	0	STON/O2. 3101282	7.925	None	S
4	1	1	Futrelle, Mrs. Jacques Heath (Lily May Peel)	female	35.0	1	0	113803	53.1	C123	S
5	0	3	Allen, Mr. William Henry	male	35.0	0	0	373450	8.05	None	S
7	0	1	McCarthy, Mr. Timothy J	male	54.0	0	0	17463	51.8625	E46	S
8	0	3	Palsson, Master. Gosta Leonard	male	2.0	3	1	349909	21.075	None	S
9	1	3	Johnson, Mrs. Oscar W (Elisabeth Vilhelmina Berg)	female	27.0	0	2	347742	11.1333	None	S
10	1	2	Nasser, Mrs. Nicholas (Adele Achem)	female	14.0	1	0	237736	30.0708	None	C
11	1	3	Sandstrom, Miss. Marguerite Rut	female	4.0	1	1	PP 9549	16.7	G6	S

Truncated to *displaylimit* of 10.

Figure 7-15. The content of the Titanic dataset

Let's plot the distribution of age in the Titanic dataset, with the age grouped into 10 bins:

```
%sqlplot histogram --column age --bins 10 --table titanic
```

A *bin* in a histogram is the range of values used to group data points, with the height of each bin representing the frequency of data within that range.

Figure 7-16 shows the distribution of age in the Titanic dataset. As you can see from the histogram, most passengers were in their thirties.

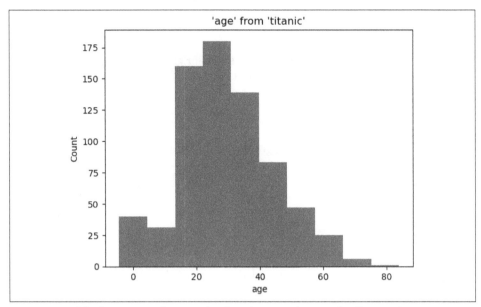

Figure 7-16. The histogram showing the distribution of age in the Titanic dataset

You can also customize the plot by assigning the it to a variable, which is of type `matplotlib.axes._subplots.AxesSubplot`:

```
ax = %sqlplot histogram --column age --bins 10 --table titanic
```

By doing this, you gain more control over various aspects of the plot. For example, you can adjust the title, labels, gridlines, and tick marks, as well as modify the legend, customize colors and styles of lines, markers, or bars, and even add annotations or additional subplots. This approach enables you to fine-tune every element of the plot, making it highly tailored to your specific needs and preferences.

To customize the plot, install the Seaborn package:

```
!pip install seaborn
```

Using the `AxesSubplot` object, you can obtain the patches within the plot and then set their properties, such as alpha, color, and edge color:

```
ax = %sqlplot histogram --column age --bins 10 --table titanic

import seaborn

# https://seaborn.pydata.org/generated/seaborn.color_palette.html
palette_color = seaborn.color_palette('pastel')

for i, bar in enumerate(ax.patches):
    bar.set_alpha(0.8)
    bar.set_color(palette_color[i])
    bar.set_edgecolor('black')
```

```
ax.set_title("Distribution of Age on Titanic")
ax.set_xlabel("Age")
```

 In Matplotlib, patches are 2-D shapes or graphical objects that can be added to a plot to represent geometric forms including rectangles, circles, polygons, ellipses, and more.

Figure 7-17 shows the modified histogram with the bars set to different colors.

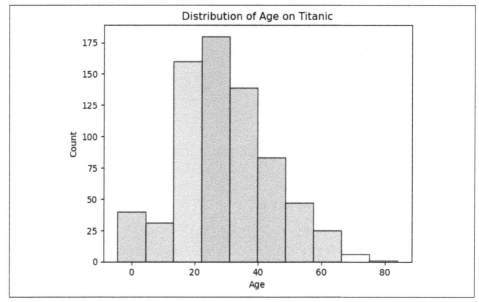

Figure 7-17. The modified histogram with the bars set to different colors

Box Plots

Another popular plot that you can create with JupySQL is a *box plot*. A box plot, also known as a *whisker plot*, is typically used to display the distribution of a dataset by summarizing its minimum, first quartile (Q1), median (Q2), third quartile (Q3), and maximum values. It visually represents the spread and skewness of the data while highlighting potential outliers. The central box encompasses the interquartile range (IQR), which contains the middle 50% of the data, while the lines extending from the box (whiskers) indicate the range of the data outside the quartiles, excluding outliers. Box plots are particularly useful for comparing distributions across different groups and quickly identifying variability and symmetry in the data.

Using the *titanic* table that we saved in the previous section, let's now use a box plot to show the distribution of the **age** field:

```
%sqlplot boxplot --column age --table titanic
```

Figure 7-18 shows the box plot showing the distribution of age. The circles are the outliers.

Outliers are data points that significantly deviate from the other observations in a dataset. They are typically defined as values that lie outside the general distribution of the data, often being much higher or lower than the rest of the data points. Outliers can occur due to variability in the data, measurement errors, or they may indicate a novel phenomenon.

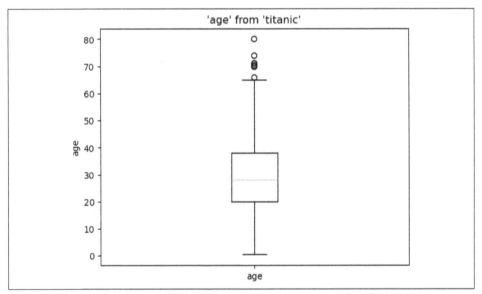

Figure 7-18. The box plot showing the distribution of the age in the Titanic dataset

boxplot supports the following options:

Option	What it does
-t/--table	Table to use. If using DuckDB, you can provide a file path (such as a CSV or JSON file) to query directly as a table.
-s/--schema	Schema to use. No need to pass if using a default schema.
-c/--column	Columns to plot. You may pass more than one value (e.g., -c a b c).
-o/--orient	Boxplot orientation (h for horizontal, v for vertical).
-w/--with	Use a previously saved query as input data.

To plot the box horizontally, use the `--orient` option:

```
%sqlplot boxplot --column age --table titanic --orient h
```

Figure 7-19 shows the box plot in a horizontal orientation.

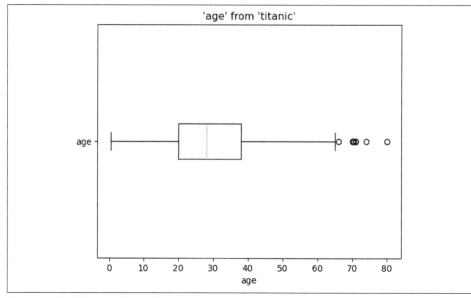

Figure 7-19. The box plot in horizontal orientation

Pie Charts

JupySQL can also plot pie charts. Using the *airports.csv* file, create the following query to get the number of airports for each state:

```
%%sql --save airports_by_state
SELECT count(*) as Count, STATE
FROM airports.csv
GROUP BY STATE
ORDER BY Count
DESC LIMIT 5
```

To make the pie chart manageable, we'll extract only the top five states (see Figure 7-20).

Count	STATE
24	TX
22	CA
19	AK
17	FL
15	MI

Figure 7-20. The top five states with the most airports

To display a pie chart, use the following statement:

```
%sqlplot pie --table airports_by_state --column STATE count --show-numbers
```

The pie chart supports the following options:

Option	What it does
-t/--table	The table to use. If using DuckDB, you can provide a file path (such as a CSV or JSON file) to query directly as a table.
-s/--schema	The schema to use. No need to pass if using a default schema.
-c/--column	The columns to plot.
-w/--with	Use a previously saved query as input data.
-S/--show-numbers	Show the percentages on the pie.

The `--show-numbers` option shows the percentage on each slice of the pie (see Figure 7-21).

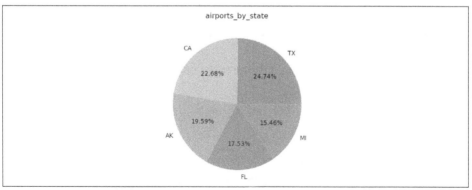

Figure 7-21. The pie chart showing the percentage of airports for five states

Bar Plots

The last type of plot we want to discuss in this section is the bar plot.

First, let's use the `airports_by_state` snippet that we have saved in the previous section to plot a bar chart showing the number of airports in each state:

```
%sqlplot bar --table airports_by_state --column STATE Count --show-numbers
```

The `--show-numbers` option displays the number on top of each bar (see Figure 7-22).

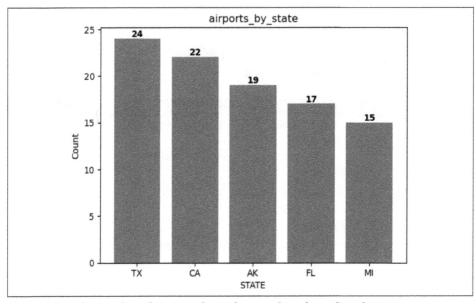

Figure 7-22. The number of airports for each state plotted as a bar chart

Like the examples earlier, you can customize the bars by using the `patches` property of the `AxesSubplot` object:

```
ax = %sqlplot bar --table airports_by_state --column STATE Count --show-numbers

import seaborn

palette_color = seaborn.color_palette('pastel')

# iterate through each bar
for i, bar in enumerate(ax.patches):
    bar.set_alpha(0.8)                  # set the transparency
    bar.set_color(palette_color[i])     # set the color
    bar.set_edgecolor('black')          # set the border color

ax.set_title("Number of airports for each state")
ax.set_xlabel("State")
```

Figure 7-23 shows the bars in different colors, as well as the change in the x-axis label and the title of the plot.

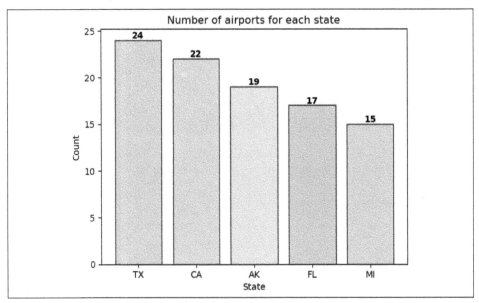

Figure 7-23. Each bar in the bar chart has its own color

Let's return to the Titanic dataset. Suppose you want to look at the survival rates across different age groups to determine whether age influenced likelihood of survival. To do this, you need to define the various age groups and then count how many survived and how many did not for each group:

```
%%sql --save titanic_age_groups
SELECT
    AgeGroup,
    SUM(CASE WHEN Survived = 1 THEN 1 ELSE 0 END) AS SurvivedCount,
    SUM(CASE WHEN Survived = 0 THEN 1 ELSE 0 END) AS NotSurvivedCount
FROM (
    SELECT
        CASE
            WHEN Age >= 0 AND Age < 10 THEN '0-9'
            WHEN Age >= 10 AND Age < 20 THEN '10-19'
            WHEN Age >= 20 AND Age < 30 THEN '20-29'
            WHEN Age >= 30 AND Age < 40 THEN '30-39'
            WHEN Age >= 40 AND Age < 50 THEN '40-49'
            WHEN Age >= 50 AND Age < 60 THEN '50-59'
            ELSE '60+' -- Assuming age 60 and above
        END AS AgeGroup,
        Survived
    FROM titanic_train.csv
) AS AgeGroups
GROUP BY AgeGroup
ORDER BY AgeGroup;
```

This query returns the output shown in Figure 7-24.

AgeGroup	SurvivedCount	NotSurvivedCount
0-9	38	24
10-19	41	61
20-29	77	143
30-39	73	94
40-49	34	55
50-59	20	28
60+	59	144

Figure 7-24. The output of the query to determine survival by age

Let's plot the bar chart for those who survived (see Figure 7-25 for the output):

```
ax1 = %sqlplot bar --column AgeGroup SurvivedCount --table titanic_age_groups
for i, bar in enumerate(ax1.patches):
    bar.set_alpha(0.4)
    bar.set_edgecolor('black')
```

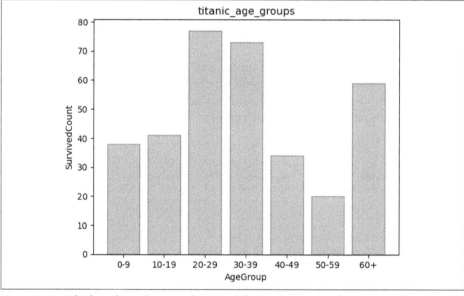

Figure 7-25. The bar chart showing the age of those who survived

We can overlay a second bar chart by adding another block of statements plotting those who did not survive (bolded code):

```
ax1 = %sqlplot bar --column AgeGroup SurvivedCount --table titanic_age_groups
for i, bar in enumerate(ax1.patches):
    bar.set_alpha(0.4)
    bar.set_edgecolor('black')

ax2 = %sqlplot bar --column AgeGroup NotSurvivedCount --table titanic_age_groups
ax2.legend(["Survived", "Did not survive"],loc='upper left')
for i, bar in enumerate(ax2.patches):
    bar.set_alpha(0.4)
    bar.set_edgecolor('black')
ax2.set_ylabel("Count")
ax2.set_title("Survivability for different age groups")
```

Figure 7-26 shows the two bar charts overlapping each other.

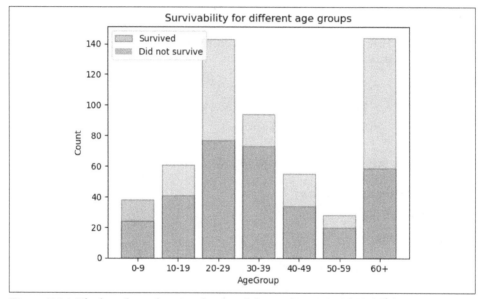

Figure 7-26. The bar chart showing the age of those who survived and did not survive

As you can gather from the updated chart, more than half of the children below the age of 9 survived, while more than half of the individuals in other age groups died. Also, the ratio of passengers older than 60 who died is greater than in any other age group.

So far all the examples that we have discussed are based on CSV files. However, in the real world a lot of data resides in databases—especially on database servers, such as MySQL server or PostgreSQL. In the next section, you will learn how to use JupySQL to work with a database server.

Integrating with MySQL

In this section, you'll learn how you can use JupySQL to load data from a database server. Specifically, we'll use MySQL in this section.

For JupySQL to connect to a database server, you need to install the driver for that specific database server. For example, to connect to a MySQL Server, you need to install the `mysqlclient` package:

```
!conda install mysqlclient -c conda-forge -y
```

 JupySQL can connect to other database servers as well, including PostgreSQL, Microsoft SQL Server, and Oracle. You can obtain more information about using JupySQL with different data sources and platforms from the JupySQL Quick Start guide (*https://oreil.ly/4bL9k*).

Here are links to the JupySQL documentation for some common database servers:

- PostgreSQL (*https://oreil.ly/iFePy*)
- Microsoft SQL Server (*https://oreil.ly/9wSXG*)
- Oracle (*https://oreil.ly/b37eZ*)

There are three main ways to connect to your database server in JupySQL:

- Using environment variables
- Using an *.ini* file
- Using keyring

You'll learn about each of these methods in the following sections.

Using Environment Variables

The first way to connect to your database server is using the `DATABASE_URL` environment variable. To do this, you first need to create a SQLAlchemy URL standard connection string to point to your database and assign it to the `DATABASE_URL` environment variable. Then, the `%sql` magic command will automatically connect to the specified database server.

Let's create the connection string to connect to a MySQL server:

```
from getpass import getpass

password = getpass()
username = 'user1'
host = 'localhost'
```

```
db = 'My_DB'

# connection strings are SQLAlchemy URL standard
connection_string = f"mysql://{username}:{password}@{host}/{db}"
```

For this example, assume that you have the following (as described in Chapter 2):

- An instance of MySQL server running on your computer.

- A database named *My_DB*, containing a single table named *airlines*.

- An account on the MySQL server named "user1," with a password of "password". This account has the necessary privileges to access the *My_DB* database and its tables.

Instead of hardcoding the password for the user account, this code uses the get pass() function to prompt the user (see Figure 7-27) for the password. Once the user has entered the password, you'll use it to create the connection string.

```
[*]:
from getpass import getpass
password = getpass()
username = 'user1'
host = 'localhost'
db = 'My_DB'
# connection strings are SQLAlchemy URL standard
connection_string = f"mysql://{username}:{password}@{host}/{db}"
........
```

Figure 7-27. Prompting the user to enter the password instead of hardcoding it

The connection string looks like this (assuming the password is "password"):

```
'mysql://user1:password@localhost/My_DB'
```

Next, assign the connection string to the DATABASE_URL environment variable:

```
from os import environ
environ["DATABASE_URL"] = connection_string
```

Once this is done, you can load the sql extension:

```
%load_ext sql
```

To load the connection to the database server, use the %sql magic command and JupySQL will automatically load the database connection:

```
%sql
```

To view the connections, use the connections option:

```
%sql --connections
```

You can see the connection, as shown in Figure 7-28.

Figure 7-28. The connections to the MySQL database

To view the tables in the connection, use the `%sqlcmd` magic command:

```
%sqlcmd tables
```

Figure 7-29 shows the *airlines* table in the *My_DB* database.

Figure 7-29. The table in the My_DB *database*

You can verify the content of the *airlines* table using the following query:

```
%%sql
SELECT * FROM airlines
```

Figure 7-30 shows the output of this query.

Running query in 'mysql://user1:***@localhost/My_DB'

14 rows affected.

[10]:

IATA_CODE	AIRLINES
AA	American Airlines Inc.
AS	Alaska Airlines Inc.
B6	JetBlue Airways
DL	Delta Air Lines Inc.
EV	Atlantic Southeast Airlines
F9	Frontier Airlines Inc.
HA	Hawaiian Airlines Inc.
MQ	American Eagle Airlines Inc.
NK	Spirit Air Lines
OO	Skywest Airlines Inc.

Truncated to displaylimit of 10.

Figure 7-30. The content of the airlines *table in the* My_DB *database*

Using an .ini File

The second way to connect to the database server is to store the database connection details in an *.ini* file. Storing database connection details in an *.ini* file is beneficial for separating configuration from code, enhancing flexibility and security. It allows different configurations for different environments (development, testing, and production) without altering the codebase, enabling easier maintenance and updates. Sensitive information such as usernames and passwords can be kept out of the source code, reducing the risk of exposure in version control systems.

Let's see how this is done. First, make sure you load the sql extension if you have not already done so:

```
%load_ext sql
```

Next, use the %config line magic command with the SqlMagic.dsn_filename option to view the file in which JupySQL will find the connection details:

```
%config SqlMagic.dsn_filename
```

This statement returns the following:

```
'/Users/weimenglee/.jupysql/connections.ini'
```

By default, JupySQL looks for the file named *connections.ini* located in the *.jupysql* folder (a hidden folder) of your home directory. You can change the location as well as the name of this file. For example, the following command sets the *connections.ini* file to be in the same folder as your Jupyter Notebook:

```
%config SqlMagic.dsn_filename = "connections.ini"
```

Once you have determined the location of the *connections.ini* file, the next step is to populate it with the details of the database connections:

```
[mysqldb]
drivername = mysql
username = user1
password = password
host = localhost
port = 3306
database = My_DB

[mysqldb2]
drivername = mysql
username = user1
password = password
host = localhost
port = 3306
database = Titanic
```

Our file has two sections—mysql and mysqldb2 enclosed in square brackets ([]; bolded for emphasis). The first section contains the details for connecting to the *My_DB* database while the second is the connection to the *Titanic* database (assuming you have a database on the MySQL server named *Titanic*).

To load the settings from the `mysqldb` section, use the `section` option followed by the section name:

```
%sql --section mysqldb
```

You'll see that JupySQL has now switched to the `mysqldb` connection:

```
Connecting and switching to connection 'mysqldb'
```

To view the current connections, use the `connections` option:

```
%sql --connections
```

Figure 7-31 shows that you now have two connections—one created in the previous section using an environment variable and the new one that you have just created.

Active connections:		
current	**url**	**alias**
	mysql://user1:***@localhost/My_DB	mysql://user1:***@localhost/My_DB
*	mysql://user1:***@localhost:3306/My_DB	mysqldb

Figure 7-31. The current database connections for JupySQL

The * in Figure 7-31 shows the currently active connection. To verify that the connection is working, view the content of the *airlines* table:

```
%%sql
SELECT * FROM airlines
```

You should see the same output as shown in Figure 7-29.

To load the `mysqldb2` section, use the following statement:

```
%sql --section mysqldb2
```

You'll see that the connection is switched to `mysqldb2`:

```
Connecting and switching to connection 'mysqldb2'
```

When you view the current connections, you'll now see three (see Figure 7-32):

```
%sql --connections
```

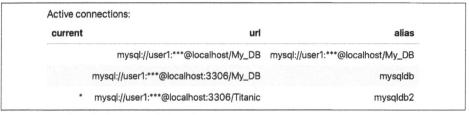

Active connections:		
current	**url**	**alias**
	mysql://user1:***@localhost/My_DB	mysql://user1:***@localhost/My_DB
	mysql://user1:***@localhost:3306/My_DB	mysqldb
*	mysql://user1:***@localhost:3306/Titanic	mysqldb2

Figure 7-32. JupySQL currently has three connections

To change to a different connection, use the `%sql` magic command and specify the connection that you want to change to:

```
%sql mysqldb
```

If you want to change to the first connection (created using the environment variable), use this command:

```
%sql mysql://user1:***@localhost/My_DB
```

Using keyring

So far you've used two methods to connect to MySQL databases:

- The environment variable approach, while secure, requires the user to enter the password every time you run the Jupyter Notebook. This poses a problem if you want to automate the running of your Jupyter Notebook.

- The *.ini* file approach, while not requiring you to hardcode the password in the Jupyter Notebook, still saves the password in plain text in the *connections.ini* file.

A much more secure approach is to see the operating system's credentials manager to securely store your password. To do so, you can use the *keyring* library. The keyring library provides an easy way to access the system keyring service from Python.

You can install the keyring library using the `pip` command:

```
!pip install keyring
```

Next, in Jupyter Notebook, define the constants of your database connection details:

```
username = 'user1'
host = 'localhost'
db = 'My_DB'
```

Use the `getpass()` function to prompt the user for the user account password and then save it to the operating system using the keyring library:

```
from getpass import getpass
import keyring

password = getpass()
keyring.set_password(db, username, password)
```

Once the password is saved, the previous code snippet is no longer needed, and you can delete it.

To retrieve the password, use the `get_password()` function from the keyring library and then use it to create the connection string:

```
import keyring

password = keyring.get_password(db, username)
db_url = f"mysql://{username}:{password}@{host}/{db}"
```

With the connection string, you can now use the `create_engine()` function from the SQLAlchemy library to create the database engine:

```
from sqlalchemy import create_engine
engine = create_engine(db_url)
```

You can now load the connection using the `%sql engine` command:

```
%load_ext sql
%sql engine
```

To verify that the connection is established correctly, use the `connections` option:

```
%sql --connections
```

Figure 7-33 shows the current connections in JupySQL. Note that the active connection is the same as the one that was loaded by the environment variable method.

Active connections:		
current	**url**	**alias**
*	mysql://user1:***@localhost/My_DB	mysql://user1:***@localhost/My_DB
	mysql://user1:***@localhost:3306/My_DB	mysqldb
	mysql://user1:***@localhost:3306/Titanic	mysqldb2

Figure 7-33. Viewing the database connections for JupySQL

Summary

This chapter introduced the simplicity and efficiency of querying data sources in Jupyter Notebooks using JupySQL. We explored JupySQL's integration with the DuckDB engine and gained insights into tips and tricks for optimizing your queries. Additionally, you acquired the skills to perform data visualization, creating various charts like histograms, pie charts, and bar plots. Towards the end, you delved into integrating JupySQL with a database server like MySQL. Of the three ways to connect to the database, the keyring method is the recommended method as it is the most secure of the lot, making use of the operating system credentials manager to securely store your password.

In the upcoming chapter, you will expand your knowledge by discovering how to use DuckDB for visualizing remotely stored data.

## CHAPTER 8

Accessing Remote Data Using DuckDB

So far, in all the previous chapters, you have used DuckDB to work with local data, whether the data is in MySQL databases or in CSV, JSON, and Parquet files. In practical scenarios, the data you work with typically resides on remote servers and is frequently sourced from multiple locations. Fortunately, DuckDB provides the `httpfs` extension to enable you to access remote datasets. What's more, DuckDB also provides support for accessing datasets hosted by Hugging Face, a platform where users can share pretrained models for machine learning. Hugging Face also hosts a large repository of datasets, which developers can download for training their own models.

In this chapter, you'll learn how to use the `httpfs` extension in DuckDB to work with remote datasets, as well as use DuckDB to access the vast datasets hosted by Hugging Face.

DuckDB's httpfs Extension

DuckDB's `httpfs` extension is an autoloadable extension that implements a file system that allows reading and writing remote files. This extension enables DuckDB to read and write files directly over the HTTP and HTTPS protocols, without needing to download them locally first. This is particularly helpful when handling large datasets that exceed local storage, accessing real-time or frequently updated data, querying distributed data from multiple remote sources, or integrating seamlessly with cloud storage. It enables efficient remote data analysis, making it ideal for scenarios involving cloud-based data lakes, web APIs, or distributed file systems.

The `httpfs` extension supports various file formats such as CSV, Parquet, and others that DuckDB natively supports.

The `httpfs` extension also supports reading and writing for object storage and file globbing using the Amazon S3 (Simple Storage Service) API.

To use the `httpfs` extension, you need to install and load it in your DuckDB session:

```
import duckdb

conn = duckdb.connect()
conn.execute('''
  INSTALL httpfs;
  LOAD httpfs;
''')
```

Note that you only need to install and load the `httpfs` extension once per DuckDB session.

In the next section, you'll learn how to use the `httpfs` extension to query CSV and Parquet files that are stored remotely.

Querying CSV and Parquet Files Remotely

With the `httpfs` extension, you can access files that are located remotely. If you have a file stored on a web server, simply use the URL that directly points to the file you want to read or write, and DuckDB will handle it without needing to download it locally first. But for files stored on sites such as GitHub, you need to obtain the URL that contains the raw file. In the next two sections, you'll:

- Learn how to access files stored on GitHub
- Learn how to access Parquet files and only download the columns that you need

Accessing CSV Files

To demonstrate how to download a file stored on GitHub using the `httpfs` extension, I will use a sample CSV file (*https://oreil.ly/ZKP1R*) that is hosted on GitHub. This CSV file contains the historical stock prices of Amazon.com.

To access this CSV file remotely on GitHub, you need to obtain the URL of the *raw* file (the original form of the data). To do so, load the sample CSV file URL in your web browser and then click on the Raw button as shown in Figure 8-1.

Figure 8-1. Obtaining the URL for a raw file on GitHub

You'll be directed to a page that loads the raw CSV file. Copy the URL of this page, which should be *https://raw.githubusercontent.com/weimenglee/DuckDB_Book/main/AMZN.csv*. DuckDB can use this URL to perform the query.

The following code snippet loads the CSV file remotely from GitHub and converts it into a pandas DataFrame (see Figure 8-2).

```
conn.execute('''
  SELECT
    *
  FROM
    'https://raw.githubusercontent.com/weimenglee/DuckDB_Book/main/AMZN.csv';
''').df()
```

	Date	Open	High	Low	Close	Adj Close	Volume
0	1997-05-15	2.437500	2.500000	1.927083	1.958333	1.958333	72156000
1	1997-05-16	1.968750	1.979167	1.708333	1.729167	1.729167	14700000
2	1997-05-19	1.760417	1.770833	1.625000	1.708333	1.708333	6106800
3	1997-05-20	1.729167	1.750000	1.635417	1.635417	1.635417	5467200
4	1997-05-21	1.635417	1.645833	1.375000	1.427083	1.427083	18853200
...	...	...	...	...	...	...	...
5660	2019-11-11	1778.000000	1780.000000	1767.130005	1771.650024	1771.650024	1946000
5661	2019-11-12	1774.660034	1786.219971	1771.910034	1778.000000	1778.000000	2037600
5662	2019-11-13	1773.390015	1775.000000	1747.319946	1753.109985	1753.109985	2989500
5663	2019-11-14	1751.430054	1766.589966	1749.560059	1754.599976	1754.599976	2264800
5664	2019-11-15	1760.050049	1761.680054	1732.859985	1739.489990	1739.489990	3927600

5665 rows × 7 columns

Figure 8-2. The remote CSV file downloaded and converted into a pandas DataFrame

You can also perform filtering on the remote data. The following code snippet shows how to retrieve all the rows for the year 2018:

```
conn.execute('''
  SELECT
    *
  FROM
    'https://raw.githubusercontent.com/weimenglee/DuckDB_Book/main/AMZN.csv'
  WHERE year(Date) = 2018;
''').df()
```

Figure 8-3 shows the query returning all the rows for the year 2018.

	Date	Open	High	Low	Close	Adj Close	Volume
0	2018-01-02	1172.000000	1190.000000	1170.510010	1189.010010	1189.010010	2694500
1	2018-01-03	1188.300049	1205.489990	1188.300049	1204.199951	1204.199951	3108800
2	2018-01-04	1205.000000	1215.869995	1204.660034	1209.589966	1209.589966	3022100
3	2018-01-05	1217.510010	1229.140015	1210.000000	1229.140015	1229.140015	3544700
4	2018-01-08	1236.000000	1253.079956	1232.030029	1246.869995	1246.869995	4279500
...	...	...	...	...	...	...	...
246	2018-12-24	1346.000000	1396.030029	1307.000000	1343.959961	1343.959961	7220000
247	2018-12-26	1368.890015	1473.160034	1363.010010	1470.900024	1470.900024	10411800
248	2018-12-27	1454.199951	1469.000000	1390.310059	1461.640015	1461.640015	9722000
249	2018-12-28	1473.349976	1513.469971	1449.000000	1478.020020	1478.020020	8829000
250	2018-12-31	1510.800049	1520.760010	1487.000000	1501.969971	1501.969971	6954500

251 rows × 7 columns

Figure 8-3. The query returning all the rows for the year 2018

If you want to read multiple CSV files at once, you can use the `read_csv()` function:

```
conn.execute('''
  SELECT
    *
  FROM read_csv([
    'https://raw.githubusercontent.com/weimenglee/DuckDB_Book/main/AMZN.csv',
    'https://raw.githubusercontent.com/weimenglee/DuckDB_Book/main/GOOG.csv'
  ]);
''').df()
```

This code snippet loads two CSV files from GitHub and concatenates the contents of the two files (see Figure 8-4). Note that if the two CSV files have different schemas, the contents will not be concatenated in row-wise fashion.

	Date	Open	High	Low	Close	Adj Close	Volume
0	1997-05-15	2.437500	2.500000	1.927083	1.958333	1.958333	72156000
1	1997-05-16	1.968750	1.979167	1.708333	1.729167	1.729167	14700000
2	1997-05-19	1.760417	1.770833	1.625000	1.708333	1.708333	6106800
3	1997-05-20	1.729167	1.750000	1.635417	1.635417	1.635417	5467200
4	1997-05-21	1.635417	1.645833	1.375000	1.427083	1.427083	18853200
...	...	...	...	...	...	...	...
5911	2020-07-13	1550.000000	1577.131958	1505.243042	1511.339966	1511.339966	1846400
5912	2020-07-14	1490.310059	1522.949951	1483.500000	1520.579956	1520.579956	1585000
5913	2020-07-15	1523.130005	1535.329956	1498.000000	1513.640015	1513.640015	1610700
5914	2020-07-16	1500.000000	1518.689941	1486.310059	1518.000000	1518.000000	1519300
5915	2020-07-17	1521.619995	1523.439941	1498.420044	1515.550049	1515.550049	1456700

5916 rows × 7 columns

Figure 8-4. The result of loading two CSV files

Note that the CSV files will be downloaded entirely to the local machine in most cases, because CSV stores the data in row-based format. This is time consuming, especially if you are dealing with large files. A much more efficient way to fetch remote data is to use Parquet format, which you'll learn about in the next section.

 You can refer to Chapter 2 for the basics of the Parquet file format.

Accessing Parquet Files

For Parquet files, DuckDB uses a combination of the Parquet metadata and HTTP range requests to partially download the parts of the file that are actually required by the query.

Consider the following example where you access a Parquet file (*https://oreil.ly/ xzOLV*) that is converted from a CSV file. This Parquet file is located on GitHub (*https://oreil.ly/uio_T*).

The following code snippet downloads the Parquet file using DuckDB:

```
conn.execute('''
  SELECT
    *
  FROM
  'https://github.com/weimenglee/DuckDB_Book/raw/main/travel%20insurance.parquet';
''').df()
```

This query downloads the entire Parquet file and converts it to a pandas DataFrame (see Figure 8-5).

	Agency	Agency Type	Distribution Channel	Product Name	Claim	Duration	Destination	Net Sales	Commision (in value)	Gender	Age
0	CBH	Travel Agency	Offline	Comprehensive Plan	No	186	MALAYSIA	-29.0	9.57	F	81
1	CBH	Travel Agency	Offline	Comprehensive Plan	No	186	MALAYSIA	-29.0	9.57	F	71
2	CWT	Travel Agency	Online	Rental Vehicle Excess Insurance	No	65	AUSTRALIA	-49.5	29.70	None	32
3	CWT	Travel Agency	Online	Rental Vehicle Excess Insurance	No	60	AUSTRALIA	-39.6	23.76	None	32
4	CWT	Travel Agency	Online	Rental Vehicle Excess Insurance	No	79	ITALY	-19.8	11.88	None	41
...	...	...	...	...	...	...	...	...	...	...	...
63321	JZI	Airlines	Online	Basic Plan	No	111	JAPAN	35.0	12.25	M	31
63322	JZI	Airlines	Online	Basic Plan	No	58	CHINA	40.0	14.00	F	40
63323	JZI	Airlines	Online	Basic Plan	No	2	MALAYSIA	18.0	6.30	M	57
63324	JZI	Airlines	Online	Basic Plan	No	3	VIET NAM	18.0	6.30	M	63
63325	JZI	Airlines	Online	Basic Plan	No	22	HONG KONG	26.0	9.10	F	35

63326 rows × 11 columns

Figure 8-5. The Parquet file downloaded and converted to a pandas DataFrame

However, you often do not need to use all the columns in a file. A better approach would first to get the schema of the remote file without downloading it and then decide which columns to download. The following code snippet downloads the schema of the remote file:

```
conn.execute('''
    DESCRIBE TABLE
  'https://github.com/weimenglee/DuckDB_Book/raw/main/travel%20insurance.parquet';
''').df()
```

Figure 8-6 shows the output.

	column_name	column_type	null	key	default	extra
0	Agency	VARCHAR	YES	None	None	None
1	Agency Type	VARCHAR	YES	None	None	None
2	Distribution Channel	VARCHAR	YES	None	None	None
3	Product Name	VARCHAR	YES	None	None	None
4	Claim	VARCHAR	YES	None	None	None
5	Duration	BIGINT	YES	None	None	None
6	Destination	VARCHAR	YES	None	None	None
7	Net Sales	DOUBLE	YES	None	None	None
8	Commision (in value)	DOUBLE	YES	None	None	None
9	Gender	VARCHAR	YES	None	None	None
10	Age	BIGINT	YES	None	None	None

Figure 8-6. The schema of the Parquet file

You can now decide which columns you want to download. The following code snippet only downloads the `Agency` and `Agency Type` columns from the Parquet file (recall from Chapter 2 that Parquet files store their data in column-wise format):

```
conn.execute('''
  SELECT
    Agency, "Agency Type"
  FROM
    'https://github.com/weimenglee/DuckDB_Book/raw/main/travel%20insurance.parquet';
''').df()
```

Figure 8-7 shows the DataFrame with two columns.

	Agency	Agency Type
0	CBH	Travel Agency
1	CBH	Travel Agency
2	CWT	Travel Agency
3	CWT	Travel Agency
4	CWT	Travel Agency
...	...	...
63321	JZI	Airlines
63322	JZI	Airlines
63323	JZI	Airlines
63324	JZI	Airlines
63325	JZI	Airlines

63326 rows × 2 columns

Figure 8-7. The result of the query contains two columns

The following code snippet only needs to download the age column and then it computes the mean of all the ages:

```
conn.execute('''
  SELECT
    avg(age)
  FROM
    'https://github.com/weimenglee/DuckDB_Book/raw/main/travel%20insurance.parquet';
''').df()
```

Figure 8-8 shows the result returned by the query.

avg(age)
0 39.969981

Figure 8-8. The result shows the mean of the age column

For the next query, DuckDB does not even need to download any data, as it can simply read the result from the metadata of the Parquet file:

```
conn.execute('''
  SELECT
    count(*)
  FROM
    'https://github.com/weimenglee/DuckDB_Book/raw/main/travel%20insurance.parquet';
''').df()
```

Figure 8-9 shows the result returned by the query.

	count_star()
0	63326

Figure 8-9. The result contains the number of rows in the Parquet file

Now that you have learned how to query CSV and Parquet files, in the next section you will learn how to query files from Hugging Face Datasets.

Querying Hugging Face Datasets

In addition to querying remote datasets over the HTTP(S) protocols using the `httpfs` extension, DuckDB also supports querying datasets hosted by Hugging Face. Hugging Face Datasets is a library that simplifies access to large-scale datasets for machine learning and natural language processing (NLP) tasks. It provides a vast collection of ready-to-use datasets for training, evaluation, and benchmarking models, eliminating the need for manual data collection and preprocessing. The platform also supports custom data handling with built-in functions for efficient loading, transforming, and splitting of datasets.

Additionally, Hugging Face Datasets is optimized for distributed and efficient data loading, making it ideal for large-scale projects. Its seamless integration with the Hugging Face Transformers library further streamlines workflows, making it a valuable tool for researchers and developers working on NLP and machine learning tasks.

Hugging Face is a company and open source community focused on NLP and machine learning. It hosts a wide variety of pretrained machine learning models and provides a wide array of tools, libraries, and resources to facilitate the development and deployment of machine learning projects.

In the following sections, you will learn how to use the various datasets in Hugging Face in DuckDB, as well as how to create private datasets in Hugging Face and access them remotely using DuckDB.

Using Hugging Face Datasets

To use the Hugging Face datasets (*https://oreil.ly/oE-4T*) in DuckDB, you need to first understand how they are structured. Let's consider an example. Figure 8-10 shows the Hugging Face datasets page. You can search and filter for the dataset that you want to use.

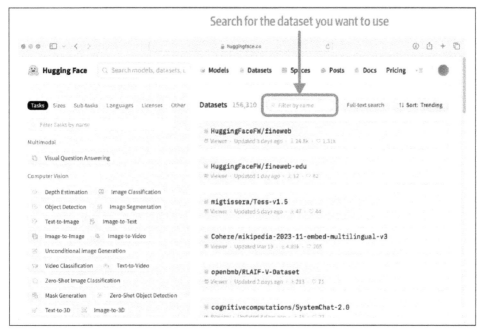

Figure 8-10. The Hugging Face datasets main page

Suppose you have located a particular dataset on Hugging Face that you want to use—in this case, the Tips dataset (*https://oreil.ly/7fL-6*) that ships with the scikit-learn (sklearn) library (see Figure 8-11).

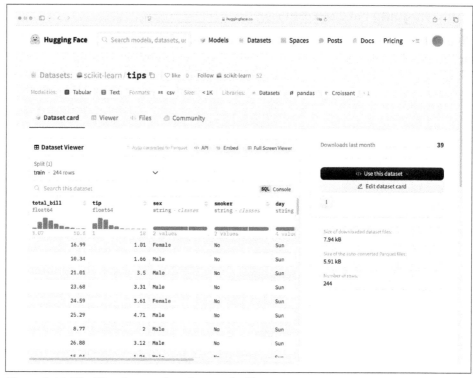

Figure 8-11. The Tips dataset that ships with sklearn

From the Tips dataset page, you can derive the user name and dataset name (see Figure 8-12).

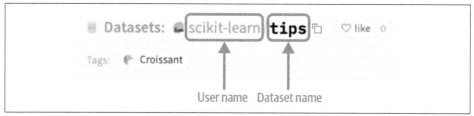

Figure 8-12. Getting the user name and dataset name

On the same page, click on the Files tab (1) to reveal the files available for this dataset. Specifically, look for the CSV, JSON, or Parquet files that you want to download (2). In this example, you want to download the *tips.csv* file (see Figure 8-13).

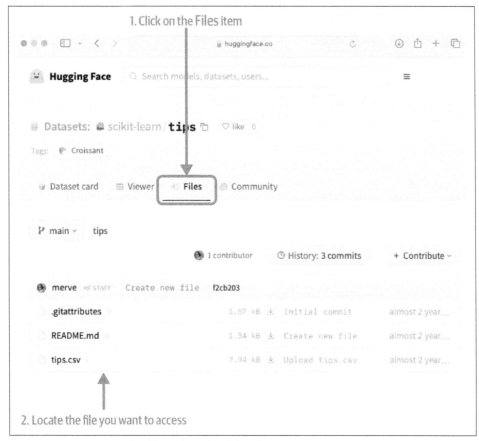

Figure 8-13. Locating the file to download for the dataset

You now have all the information needed to construct the URL that DuckDB needs to download the dataset from Hugging Face. Figure 8-14 shows how to put together the URL based on this information using the *hf://* path.

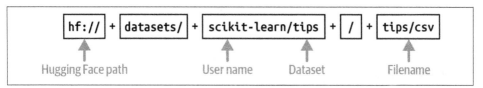

Figure 8-14. Forming the URL to download the file from Hugging Face

Reading the Dataset Using hf:// Paths

Using the URL format shown in Figure 8-13, you can now remotely access the file from Hugging Face:

```
import duckdb

conn = duckdb.connect()
conn.execute('''
  SELECT
    *
  FROM
    'hf://datasets/scikit-learn/tips/tips.csv';
''').df()
```

Figure 8-15 shows the Hugging Face dataset loaded and converted to a pandas DataFrame.

	total_bill	tip	sex	smoker	day	time	size
0	16.99	1.01	Female	False	Sun	Dinner	2
1	10.34	1.66	Male	False	Sun	Dinner	3
2	21.01	3.50	Male	False	Sun	Dinner	3
3	23.68	3.31	Male	False	Sun	Dinner	2
4	24.59	3.61	Female	False	Sun	Dinner	4
...	...	...	...	...	...	...	...
239	29.03	5.92	Male	False	Sat	Dinner	3
240	27.18	2.00	Female	True	Sat	Dinner	2
241	22.67	2.00	Male	True	Sat	Dinner	2
242	17.82	1.75	Male	False	Sat	Dinner	2
243	18.78	3.00	Female	False	Thur	Dinner	2

244 rows × 7 columns

Figure 8-15. The tips file downloaded from Hugging Face

I recommend that you save the data in a DuckDB table so that you don't have to access the remote endpoint for every subsequent query. To do this, modify the query as follows:

```
conn.execute('''
  CREATE TABLE Tips AS
  FROM
    'hf://datasets/scikit-learn/tips/tips.csv';
''')
```

When you run this query, the Tips dataset will be saved into the *Tips* table. To query the *Tips* table, you can now use the following:

```
conn.execute('''
  SELECT
    *
  FROM
    Tips
''').df()
```

Sometimes, files in a Hugging Face dataset are stored in specific folders. The next section shows you how to access them.

Accessing Files Within a Folder

Consider the example of the Adult Census Income dataset (*https://oreil.ly/uhHPu*) (see Figure 8-16).

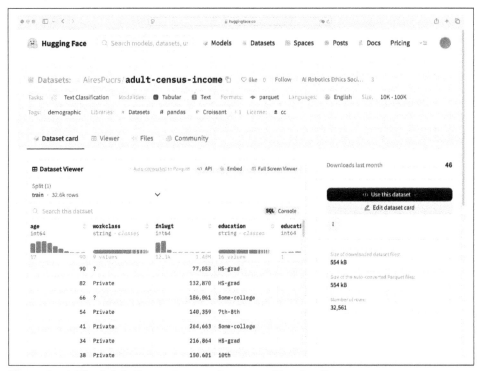

Figure 8-16. The Adult Census Income dataset on Hugging Face

When you click on the Files tab, you will see the *data* folder (see Figure 8-17).

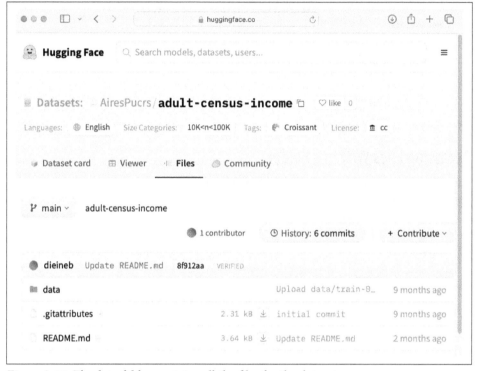

Figure 8-17. The data *folder contains all the files for the dataset*

The *data* folder contains the files that you want to download. To download a file, click on the icon displayed next to the file name (1) and then copy the file name (2), as shown in Figure 8-18.

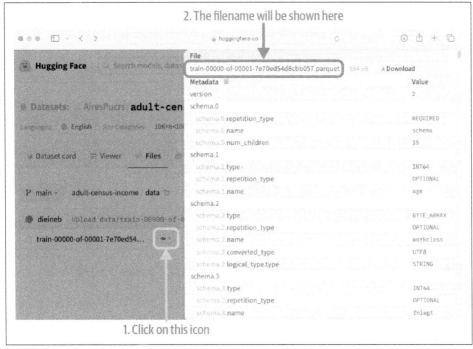

Figure 8-18. Viewing files in a folder and getting names of the files you want to download

For this example, the file we want to download is a Parquet file. The full URL will look like this (note the addition of the *data* folder name):

```
hf://datasets/AiresPucrs/adult-census-income/data/
train-00000-of-00001-7e70ed54d8cbb057.parquet
```

Using this URL, you can now download the file using the following code snippet:

```
conn.execute('''
  SELECT
    *
  FROM
    'hf://datasets/AiresPucrs/adult-census-income'
    '/data/train-00000-of-00001-7e70ed54d8cbb057.parquet'
''').df()
```

Figure 8-19 shows the output.

	age	workclass	fnlwgt	education	education.num	marital.status	occupation	relationship	race	sex	capital.gain	capital.loss	hours.per.week	native.cour
0	90	?	77053	HS-grad	9	Widowed	?	Not-in-family	White	Female	0	4356	40	United-St₂
1	82	Private	132870	HS-grad	9	Widowed	Exec-managerial	Not-in-family	White	Female	0	4356	18	United-St₂
2	66	?	186061	Some-college	10	Widowed	?	Unmarried	Black	Female	0	4356	40	United-St₂
3	54	Private	140359	7th-8th	4	Divorced	Machine-op-inspct	Unmarried	White	Female	0	3900	40	United-St₂
4	41	Private	264663	Some-college	10	Separated	Prof-specialty	Own-child	White	Female	0	3900	40	United-St₂
...	...	...	...	...	...	...	...	...	...	...	...	...	...	...
32556	22	Private	310152	Some-college	10	Never-married	Protective-serv	Not-in-family	White	Male	0	0	40	United-St₂
32557	27	Private	257302	Assoc-acdm	12	Married-civ-spouse	Tech-support	Wife	White	Female	0	0	38	United-St₂
32558	40	Private	154374	HS-grad	9	Married-civ-spouse	Machine-op-inspct	Husband	White	Male	0	0	40	United-St₂
32559	58	Private	151910	HS-grad	9	Widowed	Adm-clerical	Unmarried	White	Female	0	0	40	United-St₂
32560	22	Private	201490	HS-grad	9	Never-married	Adm-clerical	Own-child	White	Male	0	0	20	United-St₂

32561 rows × 15 columns

Figure 8-19. The Parquet file downloaded from Hugging Face and converted to a DataFrame

So far, you have only been querying single files. The next section shows you how to query multiple files using the glob syntax.

Querying Multiple Files Using the Glob Syntax

You can query multiple files using the glob syntax (as discussed in Chapter 6). As a reminder, here is the list of the glob patterns:

Wildcard symbol	What it does
*	Matches any number of any characters (including none)
**	Matches any number of subdirectories (including none)
?	Matches any single character
[abc]	Matches one character given in the brackets
[a-z]	Matches one character from the range given in the brackets

Consider the dataset on Hugging Face (*https://oreil.ly/NPnrZ*). Figure 8-20 shows the files available in this dataset: *geo_test.csv* and *geo_train.csv*.

Figure 8-20. Viewing the files available for download

To load all the CSV files, you can use the following code snippet:

```
conn.execute('''
  SELECT
    *
  FROM
    'hf://datasets/gabrielwu/city_country/*.csv';
''').df()
```

 All the files you are loading using the glob pattern must have the same schema. If they don't, an exception will occur.

Figure 8-21 shows the DataFrame containing the contents of both CSV files.

	question	answer0	answer1	answer2	answer3	label
0	The city of Quebec is in	Canada	Martinique	Uruguay	Uzbekistan	0
1	The city of Sao Paulo is in	Brazil	Grenada	Japan	Montenegro	0
2	The city of Klang is in	Malaysia	Denmark	Iran	Chile	0
3	The city of Sorong is in	Indonesia	Macedonia	Madagascar	Bahrain	0
4	The city of Zhengzhou is in	China	Swaziland	Mongolia	Djibouti	0
...	...	...	...	...	...	...
2474	The city of Karaj is in	Iran	Cyprus	Botswana	Tokelau	0
2475	The city of Yunfu is in	China	New Caledonia	Liberia	Brunei Darussalam	0
2476	The city of Huaibei is in	China	Ghana	Oman	Morocco	0
2477	The city of Luoyang is in	China	Niue	Brazil	New Caledonia	0
2478	The city of Hosur is in	India	Oman	Ethiopia	Indonesia	0

2479 rows × 6 columns

Figure 8-21. The DataFrame containing the contents of both CSV files

With the ability to access multiple files at once, it is now very easy for you to perform queries. The following code snippet looks for rows where the question contains the word "Huaibei":

```
conn.execute('''
  SELECT
    *
  FROM
    'hf://datasets/gabrielwu/city_country/*.csv'
  WHERE question LIKE '%Huaibei%';
  ''').df()
```

Figure 8-22 shows the result.

	question	answer0	answer1	answer2	answer3	label
0	The city of Huaibei is in	China	Ghana	Oman	Morocco	0

Figure 8-22. The result containing one row whose question contains the word "Huaibei"

The glob pattern is most useful when dealing with Parquet files because there is often no need to download the entire set of files. For example, consider this dataset (*https://oreil.ly/tLuLD*), which has two Parquet files. Using the following code snippet, you can download only the question column from the two Parquet files and display only the rows that contain the word "happened":

```
conn.execute('''
  SELECT
    question
  FROM
    'hf://datasets/Stanford/web_questions/data/*.parquet'
  WHERE question LIKE '%happened%';
''').df()
```

Figure 8-23 shows the DataFrame returned by the query.

	question
0	what happened after mr. sugihara died?
1	what happened in bosnia in the 90s?
2	what happened to jill valentine?
3	what happened at chernobyl?
4	what happened to dunkirk during ww2?
5	what happened at benghazi?
6	what happened to pope john paul ii?
7	what do they think happened to natalee holloway?
8	what happened to daddy yankee?
9	what would have happened if germany had won ww1?

Figure 8-23. The query returns all questions that contain the word "happened"

What happens if the dataset you are accessing is a private one? The next section shows you how to access private Hugging Face datasets.

Working with Private Hugging Face Datasets

So far, you have learned how to access public Hugging Face datasets. How about private datasets hosted on Hugging Face? The main difference between accessing public and private datasets is that for private datasets you need to provide the relevant credentials before you can access them. In the following sections, you will learn how to:

- Create a private dataset by uploading a CSV file to Hugging Face
- Create an access token to access the private dataset
- Provide the access token so that you can remotely access the private dataset using DuckDB

Before you can do all this, you need to create an account on Hugging Face. Go to *https://huggingface.co* and click on the Sign Up button. You'll see the page shown in Figure 8-24.

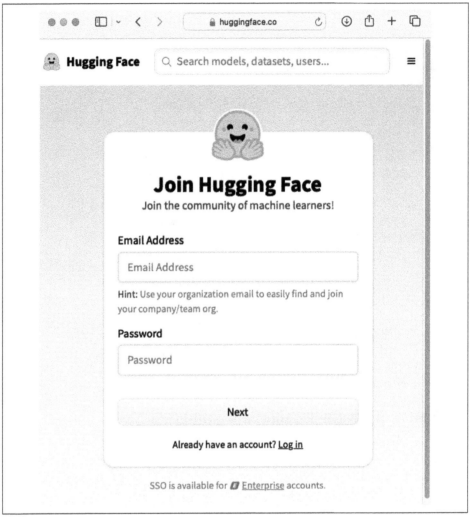

Figure 8-24. Creating an account on Hugging Face

Provide your email address and the password you would like to use and click Next.

Now we're ready to dig in! First, we'll create a private dataset.

Uploading a private dataset

Once you have set up your Hugging Face account, you can create a private dataset and upload some files to it.

Click on the user icon (1) and then click on New Dataset (2) as shown in Figure 8-25.

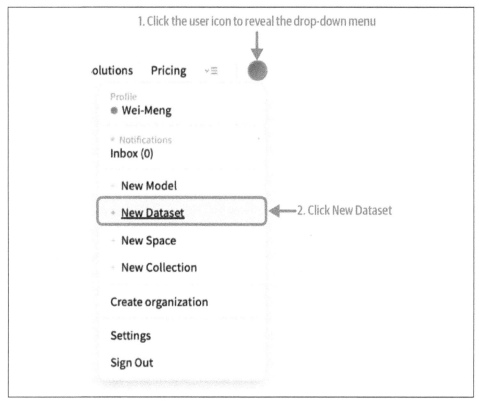

Figure 8-25. Creating a new dataset in Hugging Face

Fill in the details for your new dataset as shown in Figure 8-26. The Owner field should reflect your own user name. Also, make sure the dataset is set to Private. Once you've done that, click the Create dataset button.

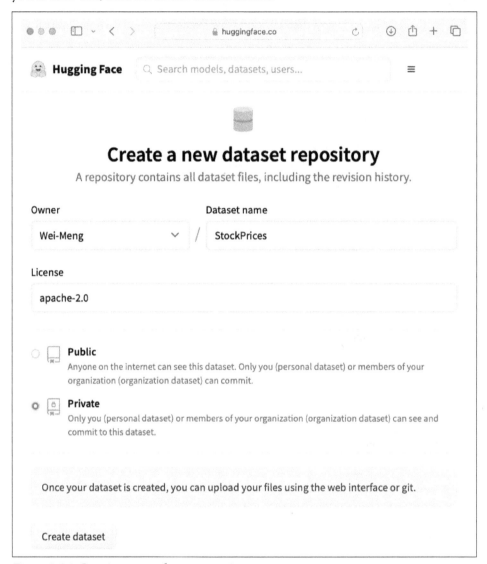

Figure 8-26. Creating a new dataset repository

On the next page, click the Files tab (1), then click the "Add file" button (2), and finally click the "Upload files" item (3), as shown in Figure 8-27.

Figure 8-27. Preparing to upload files to Hugging Face

Drag and drop the files you want to upload to the dataset. Once they are uploaded, the files will appear as shown in Figure 8-28. For this example, I have uploaded a CSV file containing the historical stock prices for Amazon.com.

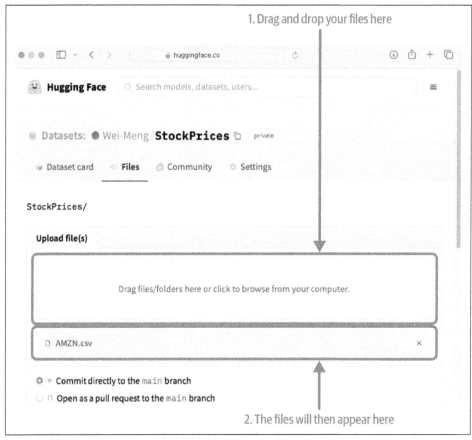

Figure 8-28. Uploading files to the dataset

At the bottom of the same page, select "Commit directly to the main branch." Once uploaded, your file will appear under the Files tab (see Figure 8-29).

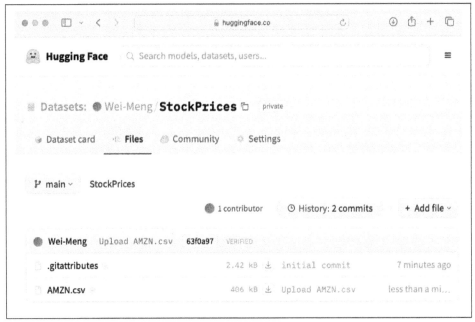

Figure 8-29. Verifying that files are uploaded to the dataset

With the file uploaded, you next need to create an access token so that you can use it to access your files. The next section shows you how.

Creating an access token

To access a private dataset, you need to create an access token in Hugging Face. To do that, click the user icon (1) and then click Settings (2) as shown in Figure 8-30.

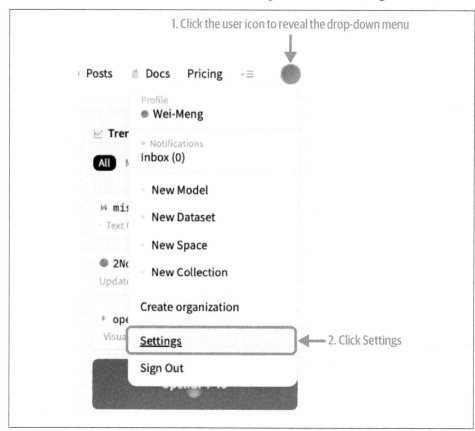

Figure 8-30. Going to the Settings page

Then, click on Access Tokens (see Figure 8-31).

Figure 8-31. Clicking on Access Tokens to create a new access token

To create a new access token, click the New Token button. Click the Read button and then enter a name to describe the use of this token (see Figure 8-32). Click the "Create token" button.

Figure 8-32. Creating a new access token

This will generate your access token (see Figure 8-33).

Uploading private dataset   READ   Manage ⌄

•••••••••••••••••••••••••••••••••••••   Show ⬚

New token

Figure 8-33. The generated access token

Click the copy icon to copy the access token and then paste it to a safe location. This token will not be shown again when you come back to it later. If you lose the access token, you'll need to invalidate and refresh it to generate a new token.

Performing authentication

Now that the access token is generated, you can use it to access your private dataset using DuckDB. There are two main providers that DuckDB supports:

CONFIG *provider method*
> This method requires you to specify your access token using a CREATE SECRET statement.

CREDENTIAL_CHAIN *provider method*
> This method automatically tries to fetch the access token from a directory on your local computer.

Let's see how to use the CONFIG provider method first. In this method, you manually provide authentication credentials, specifically the access token, when connecting to Hugging Face. This method is ideal when you need to authenticate using a specific, known token, such as when you're working in environments where tokens are rotated frequently or you need to set explicit credentials for each service.

You will use the CREATE SECRET statement to create an hf_token variable and set its value to the access token:

```
import duckdb

conn = duckdb.connect()
conn.execute('''
  CREATE SECRET hf_token (
    TYPE HUGGINGFACE,
    TOKEN '<HuggingFace_Token>'
  );
''')
```

You can now access the private dataset just like accessing a file from a public dataset:

```
conn.execute('''
  SELECT
    *
  FROM
    'hf://datasets/Wei-Meng/StockPrices/AMZN.csv';
''').df()
```

This code snippet displays the Amazon stock prices as a pandas DataFrame (see Figure 8-34).

	Date	Open	High	Low	Close	Adj Close	Volume
0	1997-05-15	2.437500	2.500000	1.927083	1.958333	1.958333	72156000
1	1997-05-16	1.968750	1.979167	1.708333	1.729167	1.729167	14700000
2	1997-05-19	1.760417	1.770833	1.625000	1.708333	1.708333	6106800
3	1997-05-20	1.729167	1.750000	1.635417	1.635417	1.635417	5467200
4	1997-05-21	1.635417	1.645833	1.375000	1.427083	1.427083	18853200
...	...	...	...	...	...	...	...
5660	2019-11-11	1778.000000	1780.000000	1767.130005	1771.650024	1771.650024	1946000
5661	2019-11-12	1774.660034	1786.219971	1771.910034	1778.000000	1778.000000	2037600
5662	2019-11-13	1773.390015	1775.000000	1747.319946	1753.109985	1753.109985	2989500
5663	2019-11-14	1751.430054	1766.589966	1749.560059	1754.599976	1754.599976	2264800
5664	2019-11-15	1760.050049	1761.680054	1732.859985	1739.489990	1739.489990	3927600

5665 rows × 7 columns

Figure 8-34. Retrieving the private dataset and converting it to a pandas DataFrame

The CONFIG provider method of accessing private datasets exposes the access token in your code. The CREDENTIAL_CHAIN method, where you store your access token in a file, is much more secure. This method relies on DuckDB automatically fetching credentials from a default location, such as your local machine, an environment variable, or a credentials file. The system follows a *credential chain* process, which means that it checks multiple predefined locations for credentials, stopping when it finds valid authentication information. This method is beneficial for scenarios where you want seamless authentication, particularly in environments like cloud-based virtual machines or local development where credentials are stored and managed automatically.

Let's explore how to use the CREDENTIAL_CHAIN method now.

First, install the Hugging Face Hub Python package using the pip command:

```
$ pip install huggingface_hub
```

Once the package is installed, run the huggingface_cli utility with the login option:

```
$ huggingface-cli login
Token: <HuggingFace_Token>
```

You'll be prompted for your access token. Paste your access token (note that there will be no feedback on screen) and then press Enter. Next, you'll be asked if you want to add the access token as a git credential. Type **n** and press Enter:

```
Add token as git credential? (Y/n) n
Token is valid (permission: read).
Your token has been saved to /Users/weimenglee/.cache/huggingface/token
Login successful
```

The access token will now be saved in a file named *token* in the *~/.cache/huggingface/* directory. You can now use the CREATE SECRET statement to create an hf_token variable and set its value to the access token using the CREDENTIAL_CHAIN provider method:

```
import duckdb

conn = duckdb.connect()
conn.execute('''
  CREATE SECRET hf_token (
    TYPE HUGGINGFACE,
    PROVIDER CREDENTIAL_CHAIN
  );
''')
conn.execute('''
  SELECT
    *
  FROM
    'hf://datasets/Wei-Meng/StockPrices/AMZN.csv';
''').df()
```

You should now see the same output as shown in Figure 8-34.

If the token becomes invalid (for example, if you have deleted it on Hugging Face), you can simply delete the *token* file in the *~/.cache/huggingface/* directory. If the token changes, you can update it in the *token* file.

Summary

In this chapter, you saw how DuckDB can easily help you to fetch remote files (CSV, Parquet, JSON, etc.) using the httpfs extension. Due to the way Parquet stores its content, fetching remote Parquet files is particularly efficient because only the required columns need to be downloaded to the local machine.

In addition, DuckDB supports accessing datasets from Hugging Face, an online repository of pretrained machine learning models and training sets. Using the *hf://* path, you can access files from Hugging Face datasets, both public and private.

Finally, you learned the two methods of accessing private datasets in Hugging Face—the CONFIG provider method as well as the CREDENTIAL_CHAIN provider method.

In the next chapter, you'll learn how to use MotherDuck, a cloud native data platform that leverages the capabilities of DuckDB. Using MotherDuck, you can perform advanced data analytics with ease, seamlessly integrate with various data sources, collaborate in real time with your team, create interactive visualizations, scale your data processing tasks efficiently, simplify data management, ensure robust security and compliance, and optimize costs with a user-friendly platform.

## CHAPTER 9

Using DuckDB in the Cloud with MotherDuck

So far, we've learned how to use DuckDB installed on your machine to manipulate your data, whether that data is stored locally or on a remote server. Using DuckDB on your machine involves installing DuckDB and setting up the development environment, such as with Anaconda. But what if you want a fast way to analyze your data without the hassle of setting up your machine? Enter MotherDuck.

MotherDuck is a serverless cloud analytics platform built on DuckDB. It enhances DuckDB by providing cloud-based manageability, scalability, and advanced analytics capabilities. In essence, you can perform all the operations you've learned in this book using MotherDuck, without needing to set up your own machine. Exciting, isn't it?

In this chapter, I'll guide you through getting started with MotherDuck and using it for analytical tasks. Specifically, you'll learn how to:

- Upload and create databases
- Share databases with others
- Attach shared databases
- Query databases
- Use AI to help write your SDL statements
- Connect your local DuckDB databases with MotherDuck
- Perform hybrid queries to work with local and remote DuckDB databases

We'll start with some basics about MotherDuck.

Introduction to MotherDuck

For many data analytics users, complex data infrastructure isn't always necessary. What they often need is a serverless data warehouse that can easily host and share their data. This is where MotherDuck comes in. With MotherDuck, you can effortlessly upload your data to the cloud and begin querying it. MotherDuck supports various data formats such as Parquet, CSV, JSON, Iceberg, and Delta Lake. Moreover, through a feature called *Dual Execution*, you can run parts of your queries locally and other parts in the cloud.

Additionally, MotherDuck assigns separate, isolated compute instances to each user, streamlining administration and reducing costs for organizations. These compute instances can scale individually to manage workloads spanning several terabytes.

In the upcoming sections, I'll demonstrate how to get started with MotherDuck and create databases in the cloud.

Signing Up for MotherDuck

To start using MotherDuck, begin with the free 30-day trial. After the trial period, you can opt to continue with a free account or upgrade to a paid plan. Here's how to get started:

1. Visit *https://motherduck.com*.
2. Click on the 30-DAY TRIAL button (see Figure 9-1).

MotherDuck's production infrastructure is hosted on Amazon Web Services and its services run primarily as Kubernetes-controlled containers.

This trial period lets you explore MotherDuck's features before deciding on your account preference.

Figure 9-1. The MotherDuck home page

Choose your method of signing in; you can use a Google account, a GitHub account, or simply use your email and create a password (see Figure 9-2).

Figure 9-2. The various ways to sign in to MotherDuck

After signing in, you'll access MotherDuck's web UI (refer to Figure 9-3). On the left side, you'll find panels with sections such as Notebooks and Attached databases. On the right side, there's a notebook where you can write SQL queries. The interface resembles Jupyter Notebooks, providing a familiar environment for seamless navigation and query writing.

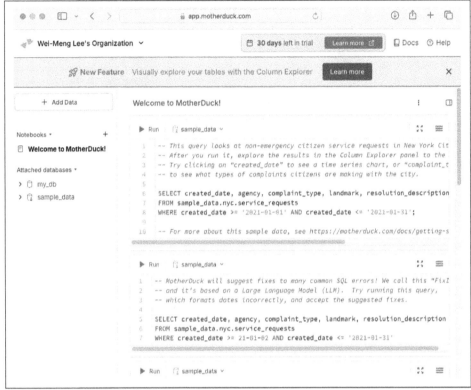

Figure 9-3. The web UI of MotherDuck resembles Jupyter Notebook

MotherDuck Plans

If you click on the "Learn more" button at the top of the screen, you'll be able to view the two plans (*https://oreil.ly/Ub7Lw*) that MotherDuck offers (see Figure 9-4).

Once your 30-day trial ends, you can switch to the free plan by clicking the "Switch to Free" button. If you need more resources than it offers, you can upgrade immediately to the standard plan. The primary distinction between these plans lies in the compute units (CUs) and storage options available. The standard plan allows you to purchase additional CUs and storage, while the free plan does not offer these options.

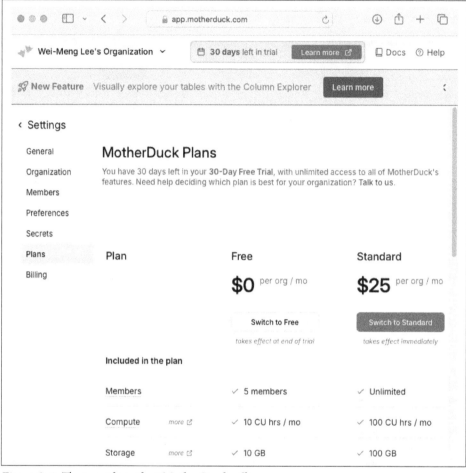

Figure 9-4. The two plans that MotherDuck offers

Getting Started with MotherDuck

Once signed in, you'll notice two main sections on the left side of the window:

- Notebooks
- Attached databases

I'll cover Notebooks in the next section, but for now, let's focus on the Attached databases section.

Figure 9-5 shows that you have the following databases attached to your account by default:

my_db
A database where you can upload and manage your own data

sample_data
A sample database containing several tables for experimentation and practice

Within each database, you can organize your tables into one or more schemas. *Schemas* serve as a logical grouping for related tables, helping to structure and manage your data effectively. Figure 9-5 shows the various items in the attached databases.

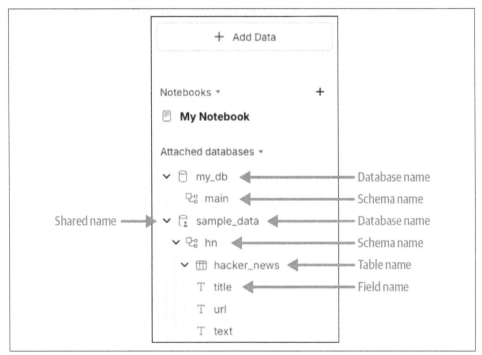

Figure 9-5. The organization of the attached databases

Notice that the *sample_data* database icon features an image of a person, indicating that it is a shared database accessible to multiple users. Hovering your mouse over the database name will display its type and permissions. For instance, you have read and write access to the *my_db* database (refer to Figure 9-6), whereas you only have read access to the shared *sample_data* database, as it is shared among multiple users.

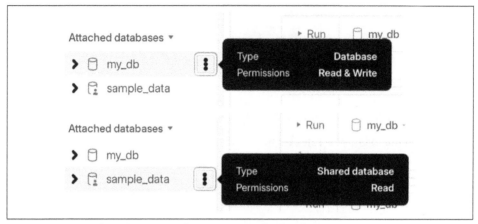

Figure 9-6. Revealing the type and permissions of a database

In the next couple of sections, I'll demonstrate how to add your own tables to the databases, share them with others, and remove them once they are no longer needed.

Adding Tables

To upload your own data to MotherDuck, click the Add Data button (see Figure 9-7) located at the top of the left panel in MotherDuck.

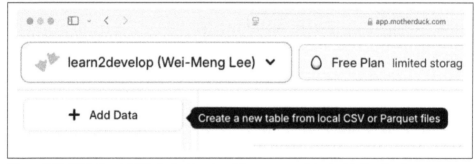

Figure 9-7. Click the Add Data button to add your own data to MotherDuck

You will be prompted to select the file you want to upload to MotherDuck. Choose a CSV file for this example. Once the CSV file is selected, a new cell is created, displaying its content (refer to Figure 9-8). In this example, I am using the *airlines.csv* file.

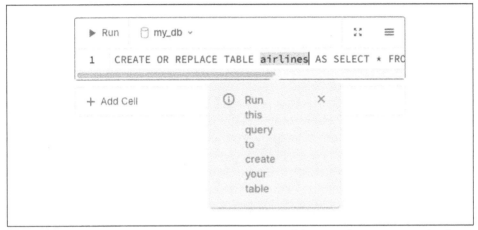

Figure 9-8. The statement that is automatically created for you when you are uploading a file to MotherDuck

The statement in the cell looks like this:

```
CREATE OR REPLACE TABLE airlines AS SELECT *
FROM read_csv_auto(['airlines.csv']);
```

Before running the code, you need to specify the destination where the data will be stored—specifically, the database and schema. Given that the *my_db* database has a schema named "main," you can simply insert the content of the *airlines.csv* file into the main schema:

```
CREATE OR REPLACE TABLE my_db.main.airlines AS SELECT *
FROM read_csv_auto(['airlines.csv']);
```

Figure 9-9 shows the modified SQL statement.

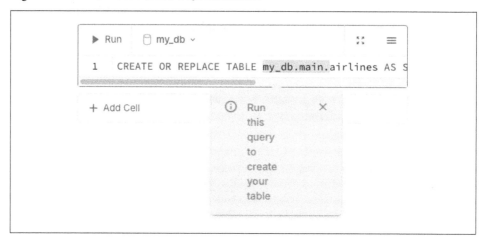

Figure 9-9. Modifying the SQL statement to indicate the destination of the data to upload

To execute this query, click the Run button. Once the data has been uploaded to MotherDuck, you should be able to see the *airlines* table listed under the main schema (see Figure 9-10).

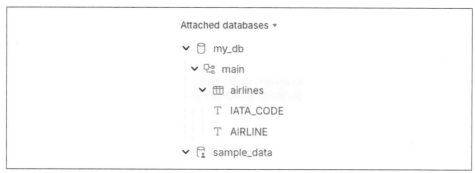

Figure 9-10. Verifying that the data has been successfully uploaded to MotherDuck

 If you don't see the newly created *airlines* table, refresh the page.

If you wish to remove the *airlines* table once you no longer need it, you can use the DROP TABLE statement:

```
DROP TABLE my_db.main.airlines;
```

Doing so will remove the *airlines* table from the main schema of the *my_db* database.

Next, let's learn how to create schemas in MotherDuck.

Creating Schemas

While you can upload your data and organize it under the default main schema, you may want to create your own schema for grouping related tables together. You can do this with the CREATE SCHEMA statement.

First, click on the Add Cell button below the current cell (see Figure 9-11) to add a new cell.

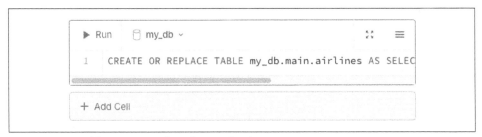

Figure 9-11. Adding a new cell to the notebook

Then, type the CREATE SCHEMA statement in the cell, together with the name of the database followed by the schema name (see Figure 9-12):

```
CREATE SCHEMA my_db.Titanic
```

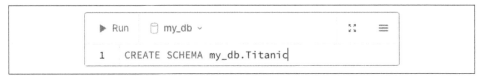

Figure 9-12. Creating a new schema called Titanic under my_db

After you run the statement, a new schema named Titanic will be created under the *my_db* database (see Figure 9-13).

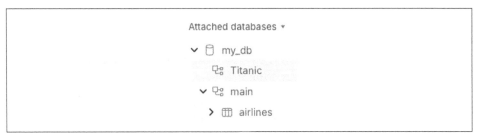

Figure 9-13. The newly created Titanic schema

To upload a new dataset under this new schema, click the Add Data button, select the CSV file, and then specify the database name, schema, and the proposed table name in your SQL statement:

```
CREATE OR REPLACE TABLE my_db.Titanic.Titanic_train AS
SELECT * FROM read_csv_auto(['Titanic_train.csv']);
```

This loads the *Titanic_train.csv* file as a table named *Titanic_train* under the Titanic schema (see Figure 9-14). You can upload your own CSV file for this example if you prefer.

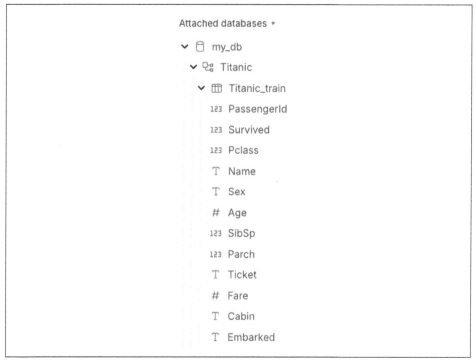

Figure 9-14. The Titanic_train *table under the Titanic schema*

If you need to remove the schema that you have created, you can use the DROP SCHEMA statement:

```
DROP SCHEMA Titanic;
```

However, do take note that you won't be able to delete the schema if there's a database under it. You can either delete the table first before deleting the schema, or use the DROP ... CASCADE statement:

```
-- delete the schema, along with databases contained within it
DROP SCHEMA Titanic CASCADE
```

In the next section, you'll learn how to share your databases with other MotherDuck users.

Sharing Databases

One of the standout features of MotherDuck is its capability to share databases with users, both within your organization and publicly. For instance, if you have a large dataset with millions of rows, rather than having each team member load the dataset into their account, you can upload it once and share access. When you share a database, users create a link to it—no duplicate copies are made, ensuring efficient data management and collaboration.

To share a database, click on the three vertical dots shown next to the database name and select Share (see Figure 9-15).

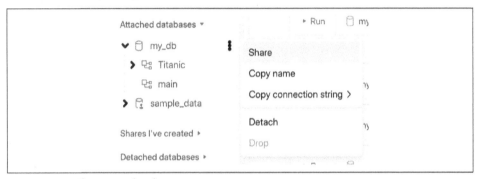

Figure 9-15. Sharing a database

You can specify a share name and choose whether to share with people in your organization or with any MotherDuck user (see Figure 9-16). For this example, let's name the share "my_db_WeiMengLee" and share it with everyone (using the "Anyone with the share link" option). Click the "Create share" button to proceed.

 The first access option—"Anyone in my organization"—allows you to share data with all members of your organization (*https:// oreil.ly/q_4Z4*). This is a common use case for small, highly collaborative data teams.

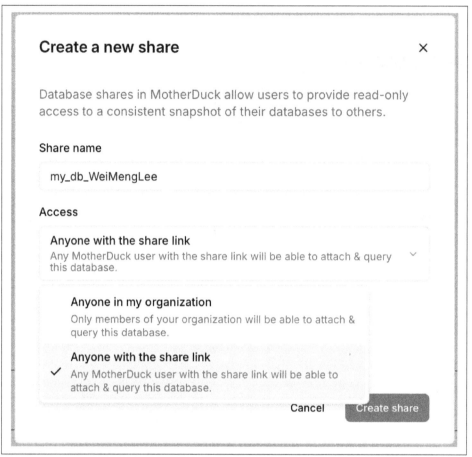

Figure 9-16. Creating a share and specifying the level of access

Once the share is created, you'll see the SQL statement as shown in Figure 9-17. Note that shared databases are read-only—users will not be able to modify them.

Figure 9-17. The share link for connecting to the shared database

At the same time, you'll see the newly created share in the "Shares I've created" section (see Figure 9-18).

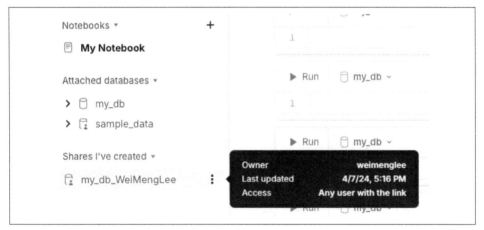

Figure 9-18. Viewing the shares you created

To connect to the shared database, users simply run the generated SQL statement provided, which adds the database to their MotherDuck account:

```
-- Run this snippet to attach database
ATTACH 'md:_share/my_db_WeiMengLee/79ec5e33-a605-4ee2-a350-78b0378976c7';
```

This statement loads the shared database into the user's current attached databases. Because the user might already have a database named *my_db*, it is advisable to rename the shared database to something more distinctive. Let's modify the database name to *my_db_WML*:

```
-- Run this snippet to attach database
ATTACH 'md:_share/my_db_WML/79ec5e33-a605-4ee2-a350-78b0378976c7';
```

When you run this statement in another MotherDuck account (see Figure 9-19), the shared database will be loaded as *my_db_WML* (see Figure 9-20).

Figure 9-19. Loading a shared database

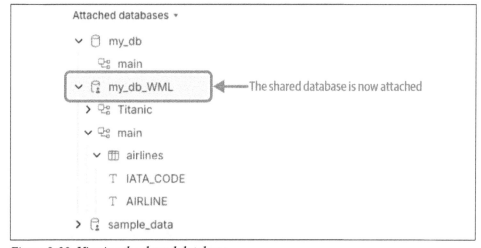

Figure 9-20. Viewing the shared database

If changes have been made to the original shared database, you can propagate those changes to other users who have access to your shared database by using the UPDATE SHARE statement:

```
UPDATE SHARE my_db_WeiMengLee;
```

If you want to view the databases you are sharing, use the `LIST SHARES` statement (see Figure 9-21):

```
LIST SHARES
```

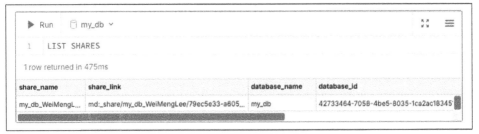

Figure 9-21. Listing the databases you are currently sharing

If you decide to revoke access to the shared database from specific users, click on the three vertical dots and select Alter (refer to Figure 9-22).

Figure 9-22. Altering the share access of a database

You can now change the access of the database (see Figure 9-23).

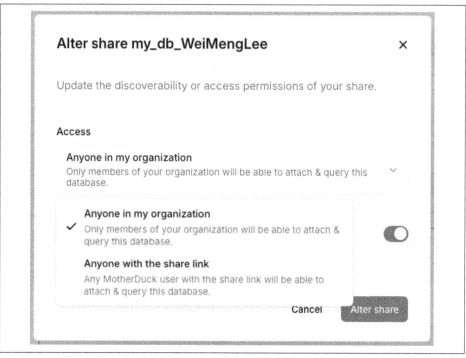

Figure 9-23. Changing the access control of the shared database

To stop the sharing, simply click on the three vertical dots next to the share and select Drop (see Figure 9-24).

Figure 9-24. Stopping the share

Once you drop the shared database, it is no longer accessible to or shared with other users.

Creating a Database

Besides the *my_db* that comes by default with your MotherDuck account, you can create your own database using the CREATE DATABASE statement:

```
CREATE DATABASE flights_db;
```

This statement creates a new database named *flights_db*. Upon creation, it automatically includes a schema named "main" (refer to Figure 9-25).

Figure 9-25. Creating a new database

When you have multiple databases in your MotherDuck account, use the USE statement to set the currently active database:

```
USE flights_db;
```

This statement sets *flights_db* as the active database and all future queries will be directed to it.

Currently, you can only create a new database using an SQL statement; creating a database through the web UI is not supported at this time.

Detaching a Database

Sometimes, when working with multiple databases, it's beneficial to detach databases that are not currently in use. This helps focus on the active database while freeing up memory and other resources allocated to attached databases.

To detach a database (whether it is local or a shared remote database) from your account, click on the three vertical dots next to the database you wish to detach, and select Detach (see Figure 9-26).

Figure 9-26. Detaching a database

Alternatively, you can use the DETACH statement:

```
DETACH flights_db;
```

Once a database is detached, it will be listed in the "Detached databases" section (refer to Figure 9-27) on the left side of the window.

Figure 9-27. The detached database will be listed in the "Detached databases" section

To reattach it to the account, click the three vertical dots next to the detached database and select Attach.

Now that you have a good understanding of how to manipulate databases in Mother-Duck, it's time to focus on the core feature of MotherDuck: performing analytics in the cloud.

Using the Databases in MotherDuck

Now let's explore how MotherDuck makes querying your databases easy and efficient. In the following sections, you will learn how to examine the results returned by a query and how to leverage AI to automatically generate SQL statements for your queries. How cool is that?

Querying Your Database

Remember when you first logged in to MotherDuck and saw the cell with the query as seen in Figure 9-28? Running this query extracts the URLs and their respective counts from the *service_requests* table (within the nyc schema) in the *sample_data* database.

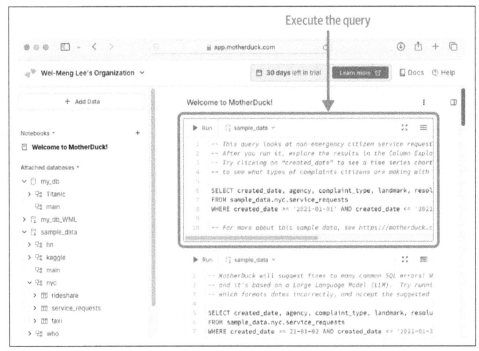

Figure 9-28. Running the query that is created by default

On the right of the window, you will also see statistics for the four fields in the result: `agency`, `complaint_type`, `landmark`, and `resolution_description` (see Figure 9-29).

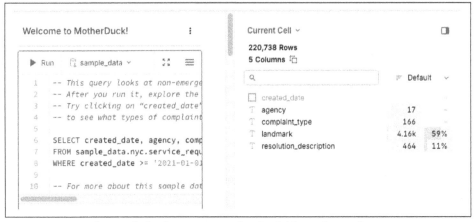

Figure 9-29. MotherDuck displays statistics for the fields in the result

Clicking on the fields will display detailed statistics (see Figure 9-30). For example, since `agency` is a string field, it shows the distribution of counts for unique agency names. If the field is a numeric field, it will display summary statistics such as the maximum count, minimum count, and other relevant metrics.

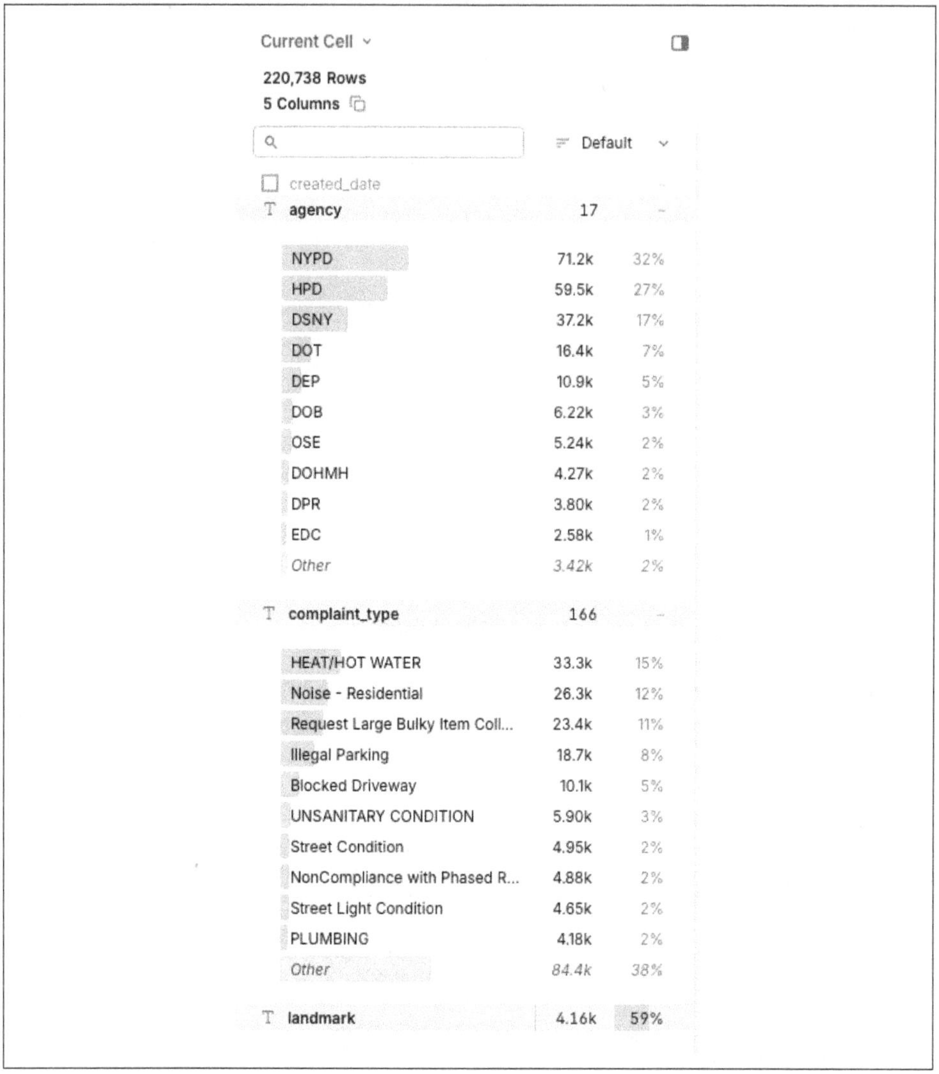

Figure 9-30. Displaying the statistics for the result fields

Let's try some queries using the *Titanic_train* table that we uploaded earlier. The following query retrieves all passengers whose age and embarked fields are not null:

```
SELECT
    Survived, PClass, Sex, Age
FROM my_db.Titanic.titanic_train
WHERE age NOT NULL AND embarked NOT NULL
```

You will see the result as shown in Figure 9-31.

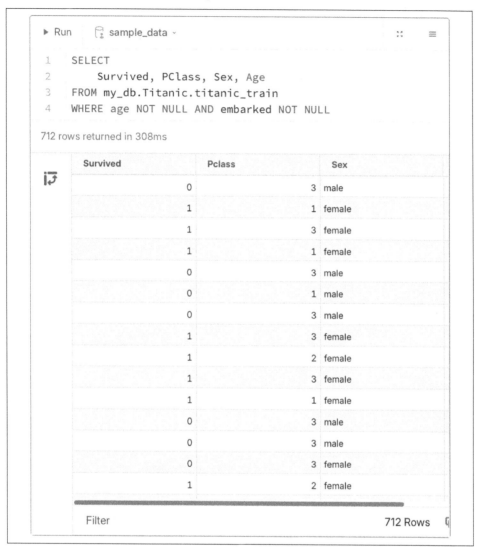

Figure 9-31. The result for the Titanic query

On the right side of the result, there is a list of fields that were returned with the query results. For example, clicking on the Survived field will display a histogram showing the number of people who survived and those who did not (refer to Figure 9-32).

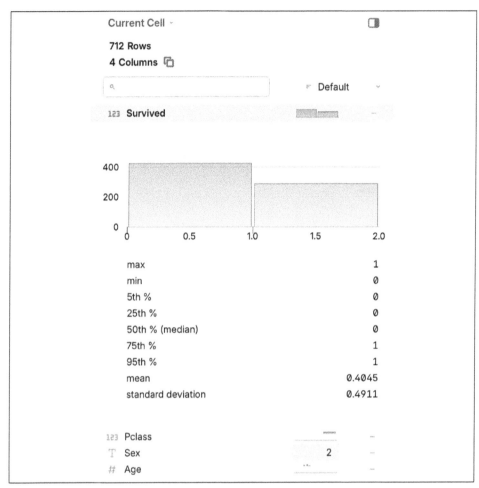

Figure 9-32. Histogram showing the number of passengers who survived and those who did not

If you click on the Pclass field, it similarly shows a histogram depicting the number of passengers in each class (see Figure 9-33).

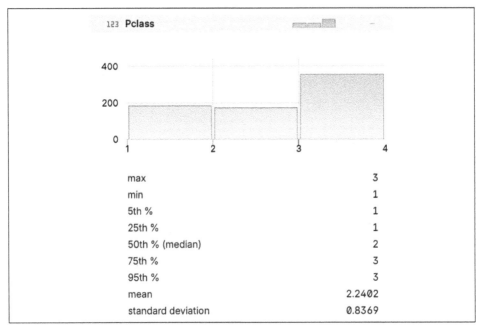

max	3
min	1
5th %	1
25th %	1
50th % (median)	2
75th %	3
95th %	3
mean	2.2402
standard deviation	0.8369

Figure 9-33. Histogram showing the number of passengers in each class

The same applies to the Sex field, which displays a bar chart showing the number of male and female passengers (see Figure 9-34).

T Sex	2	–
male	453	64%
female	259	36%

Figure 9-34. Bar chart showing the number of male and female passengers

For the Age field, it displays both the distribution of ages as well as the summary statistics of the field (see Figure 9-35).

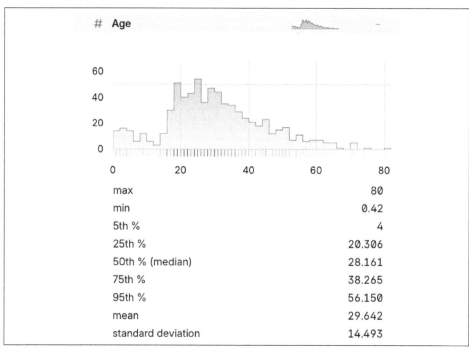

Figure 9-35. Displaying a histogram and summary statistics of the Age field

Writing SQL Using AI

One exciting feature of MotherDuck is its AI capabilities, which enhance the platform's functionality and usability. These AI functions and pragmas provide advanced tools for performing automated tasks and optimizing analytical workflows. They enable users to streamline query generation, automate data analysis tasks, and leverage machine learning algorithms directly within the database environment. This integration of AI empowers users to extract deeper insights, make data-driven decisions faster, and efficiently manage large datasets with enhanced precision and efficiency.

Functions in MotherDuck execute specific tasks or computations within SQL queries, while pragmas provide directives to control database behavior and optimizations without executing tasks directly.

Here are some AI functions/pragmas you can use:

Function/pragma	What it does
prompt_sql()	A function to generate a SQL statement for your query
prompt_query	A pragma to answer questions about your data
prompt_fixup()	A function to correct and fix your SQL query
prompt_fix_line()	A function to correct and fix your SQL query line-by-line
prompt_schema()	A function to help you understand the contents of a database
prompt_explain()	A function to help you understand a SQL query

Let's use the prompt_sql() function as an example. Imagine you're interested in discovering how many solo passengers on the Titanic survived. You can call the prompt_sql() function using the CALL statement. Before you ask the question, be sure to set the active database with the USE statement:

```
USE my_db;
CALL prompt_sql("How many people who were alone survived");
```

The result is a generated SQL statement, as shown in Figure 9-36.

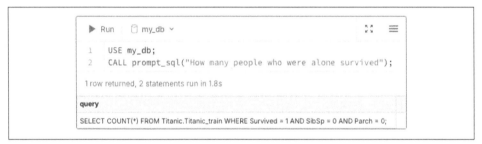

Figure 9-36. The SQL statement generated by the prompt_sql() function

You can now execute the SQL statement:

```
SELECT COUNT(*) FROM Titanic.Titanic_train WHERE Survived = 1 AND SibSp = 0 AND Parch = 0;
```

And the result is 163. Pretty impressive!

As another example, let's calculate the survival chance for each age group to determine which age group had the highest survival rate. To do this, let's call the function with the following question:

```
CALL prompt_sql("Calculate the survival chance for each age group")
```

And the function returns the following SQL statements:

```
SELECT
    CASE
        WHEN Age < 10 THEN '0-9'
        WHEN Age BETWEEN 10 AND 19 THEN '10-19'
        WHEN Age BETWEEN 20 AND 29 THEN '20-29'
        WHEN Age BETWEEN 30 AND 39 THEN '30-39'
        WHEN Age BETWEEN 40 AND 49 THEN '40-49'
        WHEN Age BETWEEN 50 AND 59 THEN '50-59'
        WHEN Age BETWEEN 60 AND 69 THEN '60-69'
        WHEN Age >= 70 THEN '70+'
        ELSE 'Unknown'
    END AS age_group,
    AVG(Survived) * 100 AS survival_chance
FROM Titanic.Titanic_train
GROUP BY age_group
ORDER BY age_group;
```

Executing this query returns the results shown in Figure 9-37, demonstrating that children had the best chance of survival when the Titanic sank.

age_group	survival_chance
0-9	61.29
10-19	40.20
20-29	35.00
30-39	43.71
40-49	38.20
50-59	41.67
60-69	31.58
70+	14.29
Unknown	29.38

Figure 9-37. The survival chances for different age groups

What if you just want the result but not the SQL statement? Use the `prompt_query` pragma! For example, if you want to know how many airlines are in the *airlines* table, you could use the following statement:

```
PRAGMA prompt_query('How many airlines are there?')
```

It returns a result of 14 (see Figure 9-38). Isn't it cool?

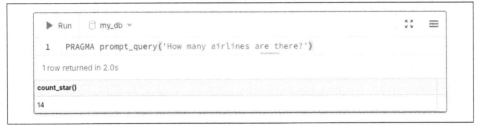

```
▶ Run    my_db ⌄                                                    ⤢  ≡

1    PRAGMA prompt_query('How many airlines are there?')

1 row returned in 2.0s

count_star()

14
```

Figure 9-38. The `prompt_query` *pragma returns the result directly*

One more example. Let's say I want to know what the SQL query about age and survival on the Titanic is doing. I can use the `prompt_explain()` function to help me understand (see Figure 9-39).

```
▶ Run    my_db ⌄                                                    ⤢  ≡

1    CALL prompt_explain("""
2      SELECT
3        CASE
4            WHEN Age < 10 THEN '0-9'
5            WHEN Age BETWEEN 10 AND 19 THEN '10-19'
6            WHEN Age BETWEEN 20 AND 29 THEN '20-29'
7            WHEN Age BETWEEN 30 AND 39 THEN '30-39'
8            WHEN Age BETWEEN 40 AND 49 THEN '40-49'
9            WHEN Age BETWEEN 50 AND 59 THEN '50-59'
10           WHEN Age BETWEEN 60 AND 69 THEN '60-69'
11           WHEN Age >= 70 THEN '70+'
12           ELSE 'Unknown'
13        END AS age_group,
14        AVG(Survived) * 100 AS survival_chance
15    FROM Titanic.Titanic_train
16    GROUP BY age_group
17    ORDER BY age_group;
18    """)
19

1 row returned in 2.7s

explanation

This SQL query categorizes passengers from the Titanic based on their age into groups (such as '0-9', '10-19', '20-29', etc.) and calculates the ...
```

Figure 9-39. Calling the `prompt_explain()` *function to explain what the SQL statement is doing*

The function returns the following explanation:

This SQL query categorizes passengers from the Titanic based on their age into groups (such as '0-9', '10-19', '20-29', etc.) and calculates the average survival rate for each age group, presenting it as a percentage. It creates an `age_group` for the passengers' age ranges and calculates the `survival_chance` by averaging the `Survived` column for each age group. The results are then grouped by `age_group` and ordered by `age_group`.

In the next section, I'll demonstrate how to use MotherDuck via the DuckDB CLI, which is especially useful for working in environments like Terminal or SSH.

Using MotherDuck Through the DuckDB CLI

With all the databases uploaded to MotherDuck, you might sometimes prefer to execute queries directly from the command line instead of using the web UI. In the following sections, I will show you how to:

- Connect to MotherDuck through the DuckDB CLI
- Query the databases on MotherDuck
- Create new databases on MotherDuck
- Perform hybrid queries using local data as well as data hosted on MotherDuck

Before you continue, make sure to update DuckDB to the latest version (*https://oreil.ly/b51BJ*). You should use the stable release of DuckDB 1.0.0 or higher.

Connecting to MotherDuck

To connect to MotherDuck using the command line, first launch the DuckDB CLI (discussed in Chapter 3):

```
$ duckdb
v1.0.0 1f98600c2c
Enter ".help" for usage hints.
Connected to a transient in-memory database.
Use ".open FILENAME" to reopen on a persistent database.
D
```

Then, type the ATTACH command to connect to MotherDuck:

```
D ATTACH 'md:';
Attempting to automatically open the SSO authorization page in your default browser.
1. Please open this link to login into your account: https://auth.motherduck.com/activate
2. Enter the following code: CQMP-DQHV
```

This will generate a code (CQMP-DQHV in the preceding example). Your web browser should now display a confirmation message (see Figure 9-40). Ensure that the code displayed on this page matches that displayed by the DuckDB CLI. Click the Confirm button.

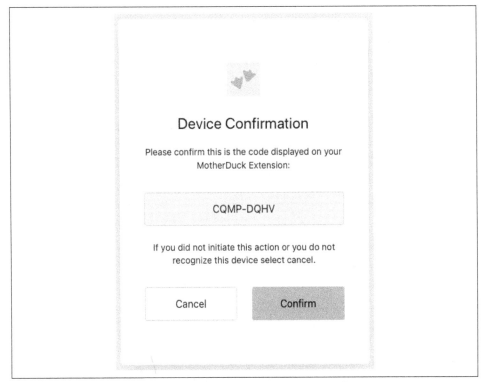

Figure 9-40. Confirming the code generated on the MotherDuck Extension

If you're not already logged in to MotherDuck, you'll be prompted to log in (see Figure 9-41).

Figure 9-41. Logging in to MotherDuck

Once you've logged in, you should see a message indicating that the MotherDuck Extension is requesting access to your MotherDuck account. Click Accept (see Figure 9-42).

Figure 9-42. The MotherDuck Extension requests access to your MotherDuck account

On the DuckDB CLI, you'll see the following:

```
Token successfully retrieved ✓

You can display the token and store it as an environment variable to avoid
having to log in again:
  PRAGMA PRINT_MD_TOKEN;
100% ████████████████████████████████████████
D
```

You are now ready to query your databases stored on DuckDB. The next section will show you some examples.

Querying Databases on MotherDuck

With MotherDuck connected, we'll begin by checking what databases are available:

```
D SHOW databases;
┌───────────────┐
│ database_name │
│    varchar    │
├───────────────┤
│ memory        │
│ my_db         │
│ sample_data   │
└───────────────┘
```

It's also useful to view the current database:

```
D SELECT current_database();
┌────────────────────┐
│ current_database() │
│      varchar       │
├────────────────────┤
│ memory             │
└────────────────────┘
```

In addition, you can see the current schema:

```
D SELECT current_schema();
┌──────────────────┐
│ current_schema() │
│     varchar      │
├──────────────────┤
│ main             │
└──────────────────┘
```

Let's query the *titanic_train* table by specifying its full database name, schema, and table name:

```
D SELECT
      Survived, PClass, Sex, Age
   FROM my_db.Titanic.titanic_train
   WHERE age NOT NULL AND embarked NOT NULL;

┌──────────┬─────────┬─────────┬─────────┐
│ Survived │ Pclass  │   Sex   │   Age   │
│  int64   │  int64  │ varchar │ double  │
├──────────┼─────────┼─────────┼─────────┤
│       0  │      3  │ male    │   22.0  │
│       1  │      1  │ female  │   38.0  │
│       1  │      3  │ female  │   26.0  │
│       ·  │      ·  │  ·      │    ·    │
│       ·  │      ·  │  ·      │    ·    │
│       ·  │      ·  │  ·      │    ·    │
│       1  │      1  │ female  │   19.0  │
│       1  │      1  │ male    │   26.0  │
│       0  │      3  │ male    │   32.0  │
├──────────┴─────────┴─────────┴─────────┤
│ 712 rows (40 shown)         4 columns  │
└────────────────────────────────────────┘

D
```

To make querying easier, you can set the database name and schema with the USE statement:

```
D USE my_db.Titanic;
```

This statement sets the current database to *my_db* and the current schema to Titanic.

To verify this use the current_database() and current_schema() functions again:

```
D SELECT current_database();
```

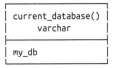

```
┌──────────────────┐
│ current_database() │
│      varchar      │
├──────────────────┤
│ my_db            │
└──────────────────┘
```

```
D SELECT current_schema();
```

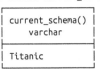

```
┌──────────────────┐
│ current_schema() │
│      varchar     │
├──────────────────┤
│ Titanic          │
└──────────────────┘
```

You can now access the *titanic_train* table using the table name directly:

```
D SELECT count(*) FROM titanic_train;
```

```
┌──────────────┐
│ count_star() │
│     int64    │
├──────────────┤
│          891 │
└──────────────┘
```

Besides accessing databases on MotherDuck, you can also create new ones. The next section shows you how.

Creating Databases on MotherDuck

Using the DuckDB CLI, you can upload data directly into MotherDuck just like you did in the web UI, as well as create new databases.

First, let's upload the *airports.csv* file to MotherDuck and place it under the *my_db* database within the main schema:

```
D CREATE OR REPLACE TABLE my_db.main.airports AS SELECT *
    FROM read_csv_auto(['airports.csv']);
```

Please ensure that the *airports.csv* file is in the same directory from which you launched the DuckDB CLI.

If you go to the MotherDuck web UI, you should see that the *airports* table has been created (see Figure 9-43).

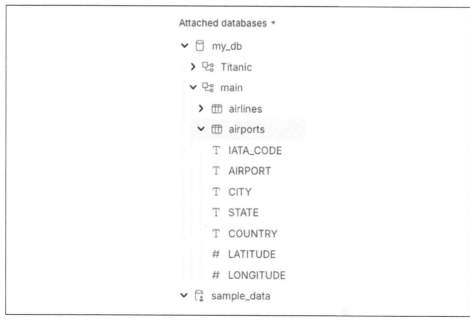

Figure 9-43. The airports *table created in the* my_db *database*

Now let's create a new database, schema, and table on MotherDuck:

```
D CREATE DATABASE new_db;
D USE new_db;
D CREATE SCHEMA new_schema;
D USE new_schema;
D CREATE TABLE new_schema.example_table (
        id INTEGER,
        name TEXT
    );
D INSERT INTO new_schema.example_table (id, name) VALUES (1, 'Sample Data');
D SELECT * FROM new_schema.example_table;
```

```
┌───────┬─────────────┐
│  id   │    name     │
│ int32 │   varchar   │
├───────┼─────────────┤
│     1 │ Sample Data │
└───────┴─────────────┘
```

This example first connects to the MotherDuck service using the token you obtained earlier. Once connected, you create a new database named *new_db* and set it as the current database. Next, you create a new schema and then create a table named *example_table* within that schema. Finally, you insert a record into the table and verify that the record was successfully inserted. You can verify that the new database was indeed created in MotherDuck by refreshing the page (see Figure 9-44).

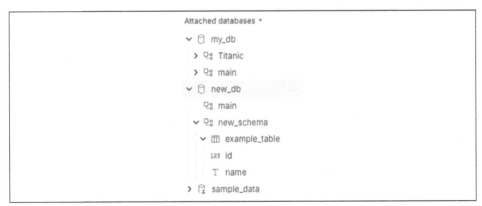

Figure 9-44. The new_db *database created on MotherDuck using the DuckDB CLI*

In the next section, I'll demonstrate how to perform hybrid queries. You'll learn to seamlessly combine tables from local databases with those hosted on MotherDuck.

Performing Hybrid Queries

One very cool feature of MotherDuck is its ability to perform hybrid queries, allowing you to query your local DuckDB databases alongside the databases in MotherDuck.

Remember earlier we had the *airlines* table in MotherDuck? Let's view its content:

```
D SELECT * from my_db.main.airlines;
```

| IATA_CODE | AIRLINE |
varchar	varchar
UA	United Air Lines Inc.
AA	American Airlines Inc.
US	US Airways Inc.
F9	Frontier Airlines Inc.
B6	JetBlue Airways
OO	Skywest Airlines Inc.
AS	Alaska Airlines Inc.
NK	Spirit Air Lines
WN	Southwest Airlines Co.
DL	Delta Air Lines Inc.
EV	Atlantic Southeast Airlines
HA	Hawaiian Airlines Inc.
MQ	American Eagle Airlines Inc.
VX	Virgin America

| 14 rows | 2 columns |

I have another file, *flights.csv* (first used in Chapter 2), which I want to load locally as a DuckDB database. The following statement loads the first 10 rows (and two columns) into the local database:

```
D SELECT AIRLINE, FLIGHT_NUMBER FROM './flights.csv' LIMIT 10;
```

```
┌─────────┬───────────────┐
│ AIRLINE │ FLIGHT_NUMBER │
│ varchar │     int64     │
├─────────┼───────────────┤
│ AS      │            98 │
│ AA      │          2336 │
│ US      │           840 │
│ AA      │           258 │
│ AS      │           135 │
│ DL      │           806 │
│ NK      │           612 │
│ US      │          2013 │
│ AA      │          1112 │
│ DL      │          1173 │
├─────────┴───────────────┤
│ 10 rows      2 columns  │
└─────────────────────────┘
```

For this table, I want to display the airline name for each row. Since each airline is represented by its airline code, I need to perform a join with the *airlines* table (which is hosted on MotherDuck) to display the full airline name. To do this, I can execute the following hybrid query:

```
D SELECT f.AIRLINE, f.FLIGHT_NUMBER, a.AIRLINE
    FROM (SELECT AIRLINE, FLIGHT_NUMBER FROM './flights.csv' LIMIT 10) AS f
    JOIN my_db.main.airlines AS a
    ON f.AIRLINE = a.IATA_CODE;
```

```
┌─────────┬───────────────┬───────────────────────┐
│ AIRLINE │ FLIGHT_NUMBER │        AIRLINE        │
│ varchar │     int64     │        varchar        │
├─────────┼───────────────┼───────────────────────┤
│ AS      │            98 │ Alaska Airlines Inc.  │
│ AA      │          2336 │ American Airlines Inc.│
│ US      │           840 │ US Airways Inc.       │
│ AA      │           258 │ American Airlines Inc.│
│ AS      │           135 │ Alaska Airlines Inc.  │
│ DL      │           806 │ Delta Air Lines Inc.  │
│ NK      │           612 │ Spirit Air Lines      │
│ US      │          2013 │ US Airways Inc.       │
│ AA      │          1112 │ American Airlines Inc.│
│ DL      │          1173 │ Delta Air Lines Inc.  │
├─────────┴───────────────┴───────────────────────┤
│ 10 rows                             3 columns    │
└──────────────────────────────────────────────────┘
```

The result of the hybrid query combines data from both the local DuckDB database and the table hosted on MotherDuck, providing a comprehensive view that includes the airline codes and the corresponding full airline names. This approach leverages the hybrid query capability of MotherDuck to seamlessly integrate and analyze data from different sources in a single query execution.

Summary

This chapter has provided you with a comprehensive understanding of how to manage and manipulate databases using MotherDuck. You've learned how to add new data, perform complex queries, and leverage AI functionalities to simplify and enhance your data analysis processes.

Additionally, we covered how to execute queries both in the web UI and via the command line, enabling you to work seamlessly across different environments. With these skills, you are now well-equipped to use MotherDuck's powerful features for efficient and effective data analytics in the cloud.

So, is MotherDuck the solution for you? If you're looking for a powerful, cloud-based analytics platform that simplifies data management, enhances query performance, and integrates seamlessly with local and remote databases, then MotherDuck could be the ideal choice. Its combination of serverless architecture, AI capabilities, and user-friendly interface makes it a robust tool for modern data analysis. Whether you're working independently or as part of a team, MotherDuck provides the scalability, efficiency, and flexibility to handle complex data tasks with ease.

In conclusion, DuckDB represents a significant advancement in the realm of analytical database systems, offering a unique combination of high performance, flexibility, and ease of use. Throughout this book, we explored how DuckDB's efficient design—rooted in its columnar storage, vectorized execution, and in-process architecture—empowers it to handle complex queries with remarkable speed. We also delved into its seamless integration with various data frameworks such as pandas and Polars, support for a wide range of data formats, and straightforward deployment within existing workflows.

As you move forward, I hope this book has equipped you with the knowledge and confidence to fully leverage DuckDB's capabilities in your projects, opening new possibilities for efficient data processing and analysis.

Index

About the Author

Wei-Meng Lee is a technologist and founder of Developer Learning Solutions, a company that provides hands-on training on the latest technologies. He is an established developer and trainer, specializing in data science, blockchain, and mobile technologies. Wei-Meng speaks regularly at international conferences and has authored and co-authored numerous books on topics ranging from blockchain to machine learning. He currently writes a regular column for *Medium* and *CODE Magazine*, with a focus on making complex technologies easy for beginners to understand.

Colophon

The animal on the cover of *DuckDB: Up and Running* is a tufted duck (*Aythya fuligula*). The name comes from the tassel at the back of their heads, while the Latin "fuligula" from their scientific name means "sooty throat."

The male duck is depicted on the front of this book, while the female is a little more brown and less sharply contrasted in coloring. Tufted ducks are native to northern Eurasia, although they have been seen in coastal regions of the United States and Canada—and as far south as Australia. Their habitat is near water with vegetation for nesting purposes.

During mating season, male and female choose a location for the nest, which the female then builds out of grass and other materials in a process that can last about a week. She then lays 8 to 11 eggs, although her nest can house more eggs (sometimes up to 22) due to a practice called "egg dumping." The timing of the egg-laying is often chosen based on insect patterns and availability. For example, in Scotland, tufted ducks tend to lay their eggs such that the adult midges are most plentiful when the ducklings hatch.

Many of the animals on O'Reilly covers are endangered; all of them are important to the world.

The cover illustration is by Karen Montgomery, based on an antique engraving from *British Birds*. The series design is by Edie Freedman, Ellie Volckhausen, and Karen Montgomery. The cover fonts are Gilroy Semibold and Guardian Sans. The text font is Adobe Minion Pro; the heading font is Adobe Myriad Condensed; and the code font is Dalton Maag's Ubuntu Mono.

O'REILLY®

Learn from experts.
Become one yourself.

60,000+ titles | Live events with experts | Role-based courses
Interactive learning | Certification preparation

Try the O'Reilly learning platform free for 10 days.